ADVA...

Educing Ivan Illich: Reform, Contingency and Disestablishment

"In this magnificent book, John Baldacchino has imaginatively returned Ivan Illich to the intellectual ground of his life and ideas. Not only does Baldacchino present a rich philosophical reading of Illich, that goes beyond the decontextualized or anecdotal treatments that plague Illich's legacy, Baldacchino also manages to theorize a constructive relation to tradition in a sympathetic and radical way."
—Samuel D. Rocha, Associate Professor, Department of Educational Studies, University of British Columbia

"In this scholarly reading of Ivan Illich, John Baldacchino conducts an astonishing feat; namely, to find ignored and minimized connections in Illich's contribution to education. *Educing Ivan Illich* creates a new educational 'language,' with original viewpoints and perspectives, which expands our repertoire of thinking and our competence of acting—that we so desperately need when faced with educational situations. This volume should be read by anyone who has an interest not only in education but also in that which is good for humanity."
—Herner Saeverot, Professor of Education, Western Norway University

"Reading Illich's work by relating the disestablishment of institutions to re-form and contingency, thereby implying radical freedom, this book situates Illich's thought in a 'Golgotha' that is found outside the polis, the church and the market. It wonderfully shows the relevance of Illich's topicality of conviviality and the relevance of the attention he pays to the quality of hiddenness and of the way Illich contests widespread concepts like 'life' and 'responsibility'. In this way *Educing Ivan Illich* offers a really refreshing and fascinating entry into Illich's thinking."
—Jan Masschelein, Professor, Katholieke Universiteit Leuven

"Another outstanding monograph by John Baldacchino. A fresh, thorough and truly comprehensive work on Ivan Illich, an interdisciplinary theorist who is particularly relevant to our age given the massive problems we face with politicians and institutions. Baldacchino insightfully explains and justifies the theological foundation of Illich's work, a foundation that strongly defines Illich's crucial understanding of dissent and conviviality."
—John P. Portelli, Professor, OISE, University of Toronto

Educing Ivan Illich

TEACHING
CONTEMPORARY
SCHOLARS

Shirley R. Steinberg
General Editor

Vol. 12

The Teaching Contemporary Scholars series is part of the Peter Lang Education list.
Every volume is peer reviewed and meets
the highest quality standards for content and production.

PETER LANG
New York • Bern • Berlin
Brussels • Vienna • Oxford • Warsaw

John Baldacchino

Educing Ivan Illich

Reform, Contingency and Disestablishment

PETER LANG
New York • Bern • Berlin
Brussels • Vienna • Oxford • Warsaw

Library of Congress Cataloging-in-Publication Data
Names: Baldacchino, John, author.
Title: Educing Ivan Illich: reform, contingency and disestablishment /
John Baldacchino.
Description: New York: Peter Lang, 2020.
Series: Teaching contemporary scholars; vol. 12 | ISSN 1533-4082
Includes bibliographical references and index.
Identifiers: LCCN 2019058459 | ISBN 978-1-4331-7643-2 (hardback: alk. paper)
ISBN 978-1-4331-7642-5 (paperback: alk. paper) | ISBN 978-1-4331-7644-9 (ebook pdf)
ISBN 978-1-4331-7645-6 (epub) | ISBN 978-1-4331-7646-3 (mobi)
Subjects: LCSH: Education—Philosophy. | Sociology—Philosophy. | Social
problems—Philosophy. | Illich, Ivan, 1926–2002.
Classification: LCC LB885.I442 B35 2020 | DDC 370.1—dc23
LC record available at https://lccn.loc.gov/2019058459
DOI 10.3726/b16394

Bibliographic information published by **Die Deutsche Nationalbibliothek**.
Die Deutsche Nationalbibliothek lists this publication in the "Deutsche
Nationalbibliografie"; detailed bibliographic data are available
on the Internet at http://dnb.d-nb.de/.

The paper in this book meets the guidelines for permanence and durability
of the Committee on Production Guidelines for Book Longevity
of the Council of Library Resources.

© 2020 Peter Lang Publishing, Inc., New York
29 Broadway, 18th floor, New York, NY 10006
www.peterlang.com

All rights reserved.

Reprint or reproduction, even partially, in all forms such as microfilm,
xerography, microfiche, microcard, and offset strictly prohibited.

Printed in the United States of America

In memory of Charles Miceli
public intellectual, comrade and friend

CONTENTS

Introduction — 1

1. Books — 9
   Las Meninas — 10
   Reading as Stranger — 12
   A Boat that Sailed? — 14
   The Tyranny of Empirie — 16
   Tables of Friendship — 17

2. Immanence — 23
   Conversos — 23
   Humanistic Peripheries — 26
   Hiddenness — 28
   Educing Illich — 31

3. Utopia — 37
   As "It" Perpetuates — 37
   Freedom and Intelligence — 39
   Milking the Family Goat — 41

Dreamers	43
A Promise	45
Quandaries	48
4. Tradition	**53**
Epoché	53
After Deschooling …	55
… What?	59
The Laic and the Ecclesial	61
Processed Emancipation(s)	65
Beneath God's Nose	67
"Progressive conservative"	70
Philosophia Perennis	71
The Convivial Challenge	74
5. Learning	**81**
Equality, Liberty and Meaning	82
Theory, Choice and Common Sense	85
Damned Assumptions	85
Opinionated Evidence	86
The Three-Legged Stool	88
Kant's Futuring	89
Lewis and Marx	92
Within the Spheres	96
6. Reform	**103**
Idolatrous Hypotheses	104
Colored Circles	106
Returning (to) Form	109
Shadow-Less Affairs	112
Abolished Worlds	115
7. Contingency	**121**
Golgotha's khôra	121
Kenotic Tools	124
After Contingency's Sunset	128
Metaphor and Agency	132
Watersheds	136

    Synchronically Possible   136
    Franciscan Hope?   138

8. Disestablishment   143
    A Journey's Ends   143
        Tools of Possibility   143
        A Changed Nemesis   145
    Myth and Transparency   147
        Constructed Equity   148
        Fabled Worlds   150
    A Tomorrow without a Future   153
        Responsibility   153
        Algorithms   155
        Neighbors and Foreigners   157
    Maritain's Beautiful Face   160
    Beyond Sinful Planning   164

    Bibliography   169
    Index   175

- Canonical author
- Never claimed to be in any ideological position
- page 2 assume "a position of ignorance"
    ↳ read the work with "openness"
                        disappear p. 3

- mistook as someone engaged in critical pedagogy 4
- the role of tradition as important as the role of dissent
- ONTOLOGY OF DISSENT p. 5
- Eight distinct essays
- NOT a primer but a conversation 11, 12
- Critical with superficial readings that have reduced Illich to the de-schooling concept, and of biased readings of what de-schooling means. 14
- EMPIRIE - reification of factual experience

INTRODUCTION

A few months ago, I met a colleague who asked me what I was up to. Without hesitation I mentioned Ivan Illich and "this book which I have been writing for a few years and for which I finally made some time to complete."

Knowing this colleague's progressive credentials, his response at first startled me. He said that, as it happens, he was recently re-reading *Deschooling Society* and was surprised to find how much Illich's words now resonate with current conservative thinking in education. I am paraphrasing, but that was the gist of his comments, which were not intended to be negative but came from a very well meant and objective set of informed observations.

I don't think I am wrong in saying that, not unlike me and many others, this colleague comes from a generation of teachers and academics who grew up reading Gramsci, Illich, Freire, Greene and others whose works have gained a degree of canonical value. Knowing these texts, most of us return to them with a degree of expectation, though often one finds that what they signified and appeared to tell us when we were younger seems to have taken a very different meaning.

While for a few seconds my colleague's words stopped me in my tracks, I realized that I shouldn't be at all surprised by his assessment. Two reasons come to mind. In the first place, Illich never claimed to belong to any specific ideological, let alone political, designation. Even when many would place his work in one pigeonhole or another, far from progressive or conservative, radical or liberal, he purposefully kept out of those expected spheres within which, as he always claims, our thinking remains trapped. Secondly, even when his words might appear to have resonance with what some on the right have appropriated by way of critiquing and dismantling public schooling, one must bear in mind that Illich was not addressing what current conservatives have managed to misrepresent as being an educational system that to them embodies the epitome of progressive and liberal forms of thinking. Actually, Illich's critique renders irrelevant any objectification of education in its schooled forms. This is because immaterial whether it is institutionalized along progressive or conservative arrangements, in Illich's ultimate concern a schooled context remains the main source of his objection. This is also the basis on which he approached other sectors, especially healthcare, with which he engaged with the same degree of enthusiasm and dedication.

Working on this project, I came to understand this very gradually—for which, in a sense, I am grateful that this book took several years to complete. As I kept reading through Illich's expansive work, and as I took the opportunity to read a number of books that influenced him directly—especially those by Ladner, Luckmann and Blumenberg, which I have now appropriated for myself as an enthusiastic follower—I now appreciate why my understanding of Illich has been challenged and took a number of unexpected turns.

I say this with a sense of humility, which I do not intend to flaunt as some moral virtue. After all, upon reading Illich one nurtures a degree of disdain for cheap righteousness. By "a sense of humility" I mean the need to assume a position of ignorance—to use the term in a Rancièrian manner—where, while wading through a slurry of books, papers and other materials, all preconceptions that I might have had before I started this project, found themselves challenged. Altering my approach to Illich's work I realized how this has changed my own outlook on matters related to education and healthcare, but more so on matters related to notions of social change and political reform. Going through this experience I couldn't but feel humbled by how much I did not know about Illich, and how, on attempting to travel the horizons from where he drew much insight, I had to ditch the presuppositions that originally prompted my decision to embark on writing this book.

To read Illich is to nurture a sense of discipline that will stop one from remaining closed into predetermined concepts. The point of discipline is also made by a peculiar sense of openness by which Illich invites one to read his work, as he takes a number of strict assumptions to task by means of his rigor as a theorist and historian. This might explain how, while Illich comes across as being radical in his dedication to the causes that he embraces, he still adheres to the idea of tradition and universal values, and just as he never urges anyone to militancy, he never hesitates to warn young clerics against the mindset of a missionary zeal that would summarily dismiss and change someone else's habits and customs.

When I embarked on writing this book, I never realized that this process will take me into fields that, though I was aware and somewhat appreciative of, I never intended to engage with in detail. Foremost would be Illich's theological foundations, which initially I only appreciated as a biographical element belonging to Illich the Catholic priest. However, the more I tried to steer away from Illich's theological background, the quicker I got lured by its historical and philosophical implications to a point where everything that I initially brought to my conversation with Illich's work was profoundly altered.

The initial suggestion to write this book came from Shirley Steinberg who, after supporting me to write and publish my book on Maxine Greene, *Education Beyond Education* (Peter Lang 2009), she then *dared* me to write a book about Illich's theory of education. I say "dared" because inasmuch as Illich was always on my mind in terms of my interests and engagement with education, it never occurred to me that I could possibly present and even support what, more often than not, was somehow considered to be Illich's utopian approach to schooling. When I accepted Shirley's invitation, I decided to do so because I sincerely (and hastily) assumed that Illich should be read from his engagement with social theory and not with history and theology. I also went in with the assumption that his challenge would bring a new approach to critical pedagogy—a claim that I dismissed as soon as I started to read Illich with a newly gained focus on what influenced and informed his *oeuvre*. Just as I had to radically challenge the initial approach by which I decided to write a book about Greene (where I soon realized that I had to forego and move beyond the liberal mischaracterization of her work by which many would still claim to "know" her), my engagement with Illich went even further from what I had originally set out to do. Once I found myself beyond the fallacy of Illich's "critical pedagogy," I was challenged with the choppy waters which Illich navigated as, amongst other, a historian whose work was firmly underpinned by a unique (and often dissenting) theological trajectory.

Though choppy, the waters which Illich navigated were not unfamiliar to me. My *old* Catholic formation gave me sensitive antennae to claim to know where he was coming from. However, this was not enough. As in the case of Illich the educator, I was way off beam when it came to his Catholicism. In the same way I mistook Illich for someone broadly engaged in critical pedagogy, I wrongly thought that Illich was one of those Catholic dissident priests whom I greatly admired in my youth.

Given his connection with Central and Latin America it was all too easy to presume how Illich's work would be mostly informed by a theology of liberation and some derivation of critical pedagogy, by which I thought that in my book on him I would find the means to explain why he embarked on elaborating the anti-institutional theories found in his *Deschooling Society* and *Medical Nemesis*. Again, this turned out to be deeply flawed.

Reading around, behind and *with* Illich, I realized that the manner by which I have previously read him as a student and how I subsequently presented him to my own students, were pretty off the mark. As I progressed in following his works' theoretical "ancestry," far from leaving behind Illich's theological groundwork, I needed to move closer. Increasingly I wanted to understand the nature of his critique which, inasmuch as it could be characterized as being radical, it remained steadily embedded in what Illich cherished to be a tradition to which he owed everything. More significantly, I concluded that to fully engage with his work, I had to figure out how his notion of disestablishment operated through that of reform and contingency.

While I could understand the tension that characterized his ministry within the Roman Church, I began to appreciate that just like all of us who shared this religious and cultural formation, for Illich the role of tradition was as important as that of dissent. This is because the tradition that he claims comes from a narrative rooted in the dissent for which Jesus the Rabbi from Nazareth was condemned to his crucifixion on Golgotha. One quickly realizes that for Illich, more than just a place and an occurrence that characterize his faith, Golgotha and the crucifixion represent a space and an event which radically changed the course of history, and with it our own self-understanding as *historical* beings rather than beings who are not of this world. While Golgotha becomes that place which moves outside the closed walls of the polis's order as shared by state and church, for Illich the event of the crucifixion embodies a significant shift in how humanity relates to its own contingent existence, which in itself widens the possibilities that this relationship could, freely and willingly, open or suppress in equal measure.

INTRODUCTION

While the narrative is clearly Christian, what drives the Illichian idea of history cannot be limited to a faith or denomination. Dissent is core in that it becomes a manner of defying what is established; which somehow is paradoxically prescient in how this idea found itself corrupted by the institutionalized forms of religion that followed suit. Illich bases the possibility of both dissent and how it got perverted on the freedom of choice, which he articulates in revisiting the story of the Samaritan. This is a story that becomes central to a radical change in the ethical order of friendship, love and human living, and so, in how we *are* with each other (as in being *beings* together). I regard this as an ontology of dissent which, as I read it through Illich, cannot be based, let alone limited to (or conditioned by) the obligation to help each other, but by the freedom to choose to do so, and thereby the ability to elect who is one's neighbor in the most radical way and against all imaginable customs, prejudices and expectations.

Illich knew that it is never easy to take back one's choice freely. It gets even more difficult when one realizes that this takes the idea of free choice away from the obliging philanthropy by which our individualist liberal-democratic societies always comfort their citizens' moral imaginary by structures of "giving" through institutionalized state, church and corporate systems of welfare, charity and aid. Contrary to the expectations by which we claim to have built a society rooted in a social contract, the freedom to choose to recognize the other is demanding and disturbing. Choice cannot be rooted in palliative charity; nor is it a result of a manufactured scarcity that is conveniently played on an excuse to sustain a hierarchy of needs. Illich reminds us that beyond the distorted image that it got through centuries of institutionalization, the Samaritan's choice is rooted in a sense of willed conviviality whose radical freedom defies the fallacy of a transactional, and thereby rewarding, construct of love and mutual respect.

When Illich excavates his way back into history to salvage the significance of what loving one's neighbor actually entails without it becoming self-defeating, he also shows how the acts of giving and living through education, healthcare and other forms of provision that we have long assumed to conform with our Judeo-Christian democracies, amount to disembodied and estranged semblances that have nothing to do with the radical way by which the convivial world outlook that emerged from the crucifixion changed history on the Golgotha. While this continued reference to the Christian narrative might raise apprehension from those who prefer to move beyond faith, this concern fades into the background upon taking a closer look at how the dynamics of the Illichian idea of history is focused on the relationship between reform, contingency and disestablishment.

From the sources that Illich brings to us, reform stands for the plurality of a continuous reiteration of what comes down to desired forms of *accordance*. This accordance could be based on an aspiration to a coming together with a sense of the divine, though it would also signify a point in our historical existence where intelligently and freely we realize the need to reclaim the realm of the possible. Although Illich clearly stakes this on his faith in the Incarnation, the claim to plural possibilities do not have to assume the existence of a divinity or an ensuing order.

This makes more sense with the realization where to state that reform (qua re-form) is to be gained from a reiteration of an aspiration towards a form of accord—as such, whatever the accord is or is *with*—it cannot be taken out of the possibilities that are brought to us by contingency. It is important to note that far from a rejection of necessity, Illich presents contingency as an awareness that is neither felicitous nor catastrophic. Contingency becomes central to our understanding through a collective realization that at some point in history humans decided to take the fate of their universe away from the hands of God and back to their own. I would qualify this as being both a turn which was marked by the choice to eliminate the sense of a divinity or a personal God in the human imaginary, but also in a context where the sense of the human relationship with the divine has matured to a point that believers came to recognize their own freedom as a form of responsibility towards their work with God. Whichever way one looks at it, this human investment in contingency remains ominous to believers and non-believers alike, *unless*— and this is a challenging point in our understanding of history—we regard contingency as an advent of synchronous possibilities. Not without surprise, this notion comes from Scholastic theology; more specifically from the philosophy of John Duns Scotus, where, as Illich reminds us, we freely claim that even as we might recognize the presence of universality in how everything appears on a shared horizon, we are not denied the existence and dynamic reality of plural possibilities in their inherent contradictions.

Without throwing possibility into this bargain of synchronicity, we cannot disestablish the reified universe by which we have, for so long, traded, staked and even lost our freedom and intelligence to the immediacies by which we have now yielded ourselves to systems in whose universe we even forfeited the critical power of dialectical logic. The aspiration to disestablish our most cherished certainties (as they have emerged from the institutionalization of our existence) must be read as the desire to reclaim conviviality in all its utopian possibilities. By this we must bear the courage to move our attention to a "non-place"—an οὐ τόπος (*où tópos*)—where we would seek the freedom to engage together with what has been (and continues to be) taken away from us as persons. Better put, what we have forfeited in the bargain that we played with our own institutional conventions must be reclaimed and fought for.

How all this turns out to retain central relevance to Illich's work is what I am presenting in this project; a project which apart from being intellectually stimulating, also took me back into the depths of which a theologian with a similar surname, Paul Tillich, whose work has intensely challenged many assumptions that I formed in my youth, regards as the source of what we seek in Truth itself. This book is the result, which I consider as being just a start on what could be a massive project of a lifetime that would bring together other works which chime in and follow similar paths to both Illich's and Tillich's.

As is customary and right to do, I would add that just as I am indebted to all of those who wrote about Illich and whom I cite, and just as I am equally full of admiration and love towards the figure and work of the late Ivan Illich himself, the shortcomings found in this book remain mine and only mine. Yet I also hope that with all its faults and enthusiasm this work serves as a way of revealing aspects of Illich's work which are often ignored or minimized.

More so, I do hope that while one remains freely provoked and surprised by Illich's resonance with what, in one's eyes, might look like current thinking—be it of the right, left or center—one must also heed to his insistent invitation to move out of these ideological spheres and start looking at the universe in a radically different way. As someone said somewhere, notwithstanding Albert Einstein and Stephen Hawking, our thinking often remains trapped in a pre-Galilean space. This has always intrigued me, and in Illich I found ways of explaining why. More importantly, reading and writing *with* Illich I hope that I began to find a way out of this widely shared predicament, which would in turn offer a similar form of exiting for my readers.

* * *

The discerning reader will sense a certain tension in how this book was written. Its chapters often feel like essays that want to assert a degree of autonomy from each other while retaining their claim to form part of a coherent whole. I am here confessing to this from the very start, not because I want to anticipate any possible criticism from the odd reviewer, but because this has characterized my toing and froing between writing a book with chapters leading from one to the other and presenting a collection of eight distinctly written essays where readers are left to their own approach in terms of making sense of this offering.

The exigencies of current publishing (which I often find rather uncomfortable) now require that authors consider each chapter separately by referencing and even writing individual abstracts for them. Whether this happens after one writes the blessed thing as a book and then goes on to fulfil the publisher's request, or whether one is constantly thinking of how to make one's project work both ways, is indeed a challenge that should be taken into consideration from the start. From the publisher's point of view there is a practical reason for this dual way of disseminating books (even monographs like this one), which seems to be tied to the way books are now distributed and ultimately *sold*.

Writing a book about Illich, one cannot avoid the irony of this state of affairs. It seems that the nature of the academic tome is changing and we might need to understand what this entails if we ever want to ascribe to this form of distribution. Many books are now published as books but also sold on line both as volumes and as individual chapter-essays. This methodology is slowly changing the way by which one engages with the dual reality of writing and reading. It is further compounded by the manner by which many would approach scholarship—on line, in hard copies, as a whole or piecemeal, virtually or while literally smelling the paper as one buries one's face in a book. I do hope that whatever that may be for the reader, it somehow remains rewarding.

· 1 ·

BOOKS

How is writing a book about other books ever justified? Instead of trying to *explain* a book, why shouldn't one just pass it on as originally written by its author? Do we feel compelled to somehow *teach* or *convey* how to read another author's work instead of trusting in the power of different interpretations of texts, as we often do for images? Wouldn't writing a book about other books always amount to a distancing—a removal by *mimetic* means—away from the original text?

The art of writing books about books is well established and forms the backbone of scholarship and tradition. The justification for such an art is vast and almost tautological. A great many books have been written to justify the writing of books about books. Why go to the extents of *priming* books by other books? Some say that to prime is to prepare a ground, just as one would prime a canvas; though in the case of books and their authors, to present a primer is to present an author once more; authors brought back to readers by other authors. However, as one speaks of priming and layering, authoring and re-authoring, presenting and re-presenting, there is a further flavor to this process: we cannot forget that the body of work that is being presented is itself a representation of other influences and other works. To write books about books is to partake of a tradition where what is played between the various iterations that build it retains an element of contingency within it, carried through the open-ended process of interpretation.

Be they written, played, painted, performed, or represented in any way, works belong to chains of ideas, iterations and a myriad of other forms of representation whose hermeneutic existence engages in processes of re-form, through a contingent set of events by which the book itself is never ossified, but continuously disestablished. In this way, works belong to genealogies that would need to be presented and represented by way of reference and explanation, consolidation and transformation. This takes us back to how the task of writing a book about someone's work would still require us to own up to a number of responsibilities which will invariably explain why one decides to embark on such a project—that is, to write a book about other books.

Las Meninas

How does one begin to justify the need for yet another book about Ivan Illich? First off, this is neither a biography nor a guide to Illich's work. In this volume, specific themes emerge from a conversation with a body of work which speaks to the author in certain ways.

As I accentuate the first person to make it a *personal* matter, I am very much aware that writing another book about someone else's books is always risky. However, I also regard this risk as carrying a degree of hope that emerges from a personal and not just an academic interest. While all forms of authorship remain personal, this aspect comes in degrees of importance and relevance. Normally, in academic works, to make one's study personal is to open it to ambiguity. There was a time when such an approach used to be harshly contested by those who maintained that such studies must uphold a measurable degree of objectivity. In reply to this valid objection, I would argue that the first person plays a *methodological* role. In other words, the claim for a personal approach has to do with how I went about *doing* (rather than just *writing*) this project. In a manner of speaking, in writing (and doing) this book I am hoping that what I "hear" from my "conversation" with Illich's work, will also interest my readers. The aim is to prompt *them* to have further conversations with others and more so "with" Illich, because I regard this as a way of *generating* further *layers* to the act of *reading* as a way of *making* in the sense of *poíesis*.

I cannot deny that in using words like priming, generating, layering, doing and making, I am speaking as someone whose trade is art. As an academic (that is, as someone who works in higher education) I see myself as an educator and visual artist—or an "arts practitioner," as we are often called by the so-called knowledge and creative "industries" whose work is deeply engaged with ideas as they emerge from the fields of philosophy and education. While institutionally speaking, doing this work might be regarded as being rather schizoid, if not entirely contradictory (because some would try to measure it against benchmarks that only suit the "industry"), at the personal level of engagement, I regard reading and writing as forms of making and therefore as extensions to what I do in the studio as a painter. However, even as I make use of terms that come from art-speak, I do not regard this book as a *primer*, and less so as a form of *portraiture*. My approach comes closer to the process by which a visual artist engages with another artist's work. To do so, my aim is to represent a number of elements from this other artist's work on a new canvas with the specific intent of creating a new work in all its autonomy.

To represent another artist's work as a new work has nothing to do with copying or interpreting. This process is an engagement with a work through which artists and their audiences add further layers of significance to what was initiated by and within the canonical work which other artists elect and select. Some call these "studies." Yet here we are not even talking of a study which an artist might have done of another artist's work, but a process which, perhaps is best exemplified by what Picasso does when painting Velázquez's *Las Meninas*. Picasso does not simply *study* but *takes to task* the master's canonical work. This involves a new *manner*, offered on Picasso's behalf, through which a line of artistic continuity brings about an intended break with the canonicity that it represents. More than originality or some myth of amelioration or engendering, in this method of bringing another work *to manner* (that is, to its ways of being made, but also to its inherent *demeanor*) one begins to openly recognize the centrality of influence in the process of *re-forming*—that is, giving form *once more*—as we find with Illich vis-à-vis those whom he regarded as his teachers, influencers and peers.

Bodies of work become larger bodies of ideas that are engaged with each other in being read and discussed; in being absorbed into several reiterations; and where the mastery of this bringing *to manner* requires (very rigorously) that the idea of copying is superseded, if not made obsolete, by how others continue to take forward new works to their own specificity and autonomy as an act of *re-forming*.

In philosophy, a good written example of this process of re-forming comes to mind with Adorno's (1993) *Hegel: Three Studies*. Although normally, the expectancy would have been for Adorno to identify and explain several themes in Hegel's work and then problematize, elaborate and write about them, instead, Adorno selected themes from Hegel and took them further into his own rendition of how he reads them with Hegel "on his side," as it were. On this note, and while I would never dare suggest that I am presuming to reach, let alone emulate, Adorno's remarkable book, I do hope that the themes discussed in this present volume will help me reach a point where Illich's and my own authorship come together in conversation. I do so with the aim of giving context to (and to some extent *retain*) a clear recognition of an identifiable body of work, an *oeuvre*, as it emerges from an engagement with Illich's unique outlook. Often exegetic, often interpretive; at times close, at times free-floating; in manners analytical but almost aphoristic, the aim is to provide points of continuity through a method of reading and presentation by which I would in turn move beyond an explanatory repositioning of what Illich "says" to me.

Reading as Stranger

This is my third monograph that is focused on a thinker and doer, an intellectual and activist, who is fearless in crossing boundaries and whose approach to scholarship radically defies what, in our institutionalized knowledge of the world, is hailed as an era of specialization. My first such study was *Education Beyond Education: Self and the Imaginary in Maxine Greene's Philosophy* (Baldacchino 2009), where I took the approach of reading "with" Greene as if I were sitting beside her while trying to look at the world from her vantage point. A shorter book, *John Dewey: Liberty and the Pedagogy of Disposition* (Baldacchino 2014), emerged from a similar method where I sought to understand the questions that prompted Dewey's versatile engagement with the array of philosophers, artists, activists and educators who inform his work. Put another way, in both books I tried to look *with*—rather than *at*—Dewey's and Greene's oeuvre while attending to what they read, by reading what they wrote.

When it comes to Ivan Illich there is one marked difference. Engaging with Greene's work was particularly challenging in that while I knew her as a friend and colleague at Teachers College Columbia University, my initial approach to her work was somewhat *estranging* in that I found myself grappling with a complexity of ideas and contradictions as they emerged (mostly around her students and admirers) beyond the expectations by which Greene was then enthusiastically "known" by her followers (often against her own instincts, if not to her consternation) while attempting to converse with the mind of this brilliant woman from New York who encouraged her eager adulators to become and teach *as strangers* in a world which they presumed to know. That world was anywhere to be found—in the classroom, studio, theatre, museum, the square or where anyone finds herself engaged in an established yet ever-changing agôn without necessarily knowing so.

Being then a new migrant in New York City, I had to overcome not only the fear of the place which volunteered me to be a total stranger, but where, true to Greene's word, the need for *strangeness* (qua *foreignness*) was never a choice but a call to which the existentialist within Greene's literary and philosophical imaginary was wedded throughout her life with what often struck me as being rather diffident of what by then made her an academic superstar in her adulators' eyes. I now realize that working with Maxine helped me ride a steep learning curve. It turned out to be a fast trajectory to track, though Maxine also taught me how to survive the cosmopolitan village by being a stranger, just as she, the quintessential New Yorker, had grown up to be an existentialist *virtuosa*.

With Illich, I have neither presence nor enough direct references with which I can relate on the same plane I did with Greene. I never met him nor even seen him from a distance giving a lecture "in the flesh" as many of us had the opportunity to listen and be in the distant presence of a Jacques Derrida or an Ernesto Laclau, Chantal Mouffe, Jacques Rancière, Slavoj Zizek or Susan Butler. Nor is Illich a John Dewey whose discursive legacy and presence gained a perennial force in anyone's own academic upbringing within the field of education. Writing *about* or *with* Dewey, one is bound to build a conversation with those who see themselves as "Deweyans," whatever that would entail (see Baldacchino 2014, pp. 2–6). When it comes to "Illichians," one is confronted with an aporia.

If to define a "Deweyan" is impossibly difficult, it is virtually impossible to define an "Illichian." These days, one would be lucky to get polite silence when attempting to broach on the notion of deschooling—which has become Illich's burden, just as critical pedagogy has become Freire's, especially when both of them are not here to defend their legacy. As Umberto Eco once said somewhere, the irritating mania of citing book titles and overused terms has become a dastardly habit for those who, being too lazy to read deeply and widely, are inclined to bluff their way out of engaging with the complexity of concepts in the work in question. Apart from the wider purview of Illich's dynamic and original work, assumptions about his work that have relied on an uninformed rejection of deschooling are confused with loaded misconceptions. At best, the name Illich is often attributed to the absurd notion that deschooling means a world without schools. In countries like the United States, some would even go as far as mistaking deschooling for an inward notion of home schooling—even when clearly the two concepts could never relate to each other because home schooling tends to domesticate, and thereby reinforce, what creates and sustains a schooled society. At the very worst, many have bandied the term "deschooling" to summarily dismiss it (and with it, all of Illich's work) as one of those radical and utopian arguments that have no cat in hell's chance of any political traction with both the left and right of educationalist opinion.

A Boat That Sailed?

Inasmuch as one will always write a book with Illich's work on one's side with all the risks involved, the themes that Illich raised belong to a horizon of challenges that have never been settled. It is with this in mind that I chose to write this volume, which here I am presenting in eight chapters that together would cluster around the relationship between immanence, utopia, tradition and learning as the book gains more focus on reform, contingency, and disestablishment. As this was first prompted by Illich's deep analysis of education, following the remit by which this volume was originally conceived, one must emphasize how even when the notion of a schooled society has become so internalized that many educationalists would consider it as the proverbial "boat that has sailed," the wider case for reform, and more so for disestablishment, continues to underpin the way by which these themes are gathered around the institutionalization of what we often condense within the area of "human knowing."

This comes with a caveat. Those who have cared to read Illich, should, at the very least, take note of the shortcomings by which words and terms that are often expected to flag some all-embracing meaning, fall short of that objective and instead come to mean the opposite of what was intended. In this book, this phenomenon will be considered when touching upon Illich's discussion of what he calls "amoeba words" (IC, p. 254) with reference to Uwe Poerksen's concept of "plastic words." (see Poerksen 1995, p. 7) Invariably, the ways by which plastic words operate shed light on how the triangulation of learning, schooling and education remains elusive, even when we know that such tenets are temporary and do not necessarily imply possible solutions for what has become a complex state of affairs that continuously confirms the need for an idea of reform as embedded in the disestablishment of what reform itself might stand for in its various political iterations bandied by the left, right and center. Put another way, it is because many remain reluctant to identify themselves with deschooling (especially when the concept itself has been misrepresented and turned into a plastic word by friends and foes alike) that most criticism levelled at Illich is characterized by a second and third hand approach to what his critique of education essentially stands for.

To heed to Illich's challenge, by moving outside the formalist assumption of an ideological sphere, is to stand for the urgency by which we must recognize a tessellated history in whose immanence we take courage in embracing a myriad possibility. Ultimately, Illich's sense of creative risk is the bedrock of his legacy; a legacy that prompts us to take stock of a history which we do not *own* in that we have no right to streamline, rationalize or manage it; which is what ideologies have done, even when they attest to the inherent historicity of human existence. Rather than *own*, we *belong* to history, which far from indicating a passive sense of being within it, we are encouraged by Illich to embrace it as a perennial point of departure. By its immanent nature, history's departure is never fixed; thereby implying that by belonging to its iterative potentiality, history is an indicator of where we *are*.

I do not think I am alone in saying that Illich's methods uphold a perennially expanding value. This might be partly explained by his reference and engagement with the work of scholars like his teacher Jacques Maritain, the historian Gerhard Ladner, the philosopher Hans Blumenberg, sociologist Thomas Luckmann, and his interlocutors Uwe Poerksen and Barbara Duden, to mention a few whose contribution to social, philosophical and theological history are key to Illich's reading of Christianity as being central to his approach to modernity. This should be read as a sign of rigor in how Illich the historian, theologian and philosopher, who as an educator moves from priest to public intellectual in bringing together a constellation of ideas that do not simply apply or repeat expected paradigms and procedures in scholarly methods. On the contrary, Illich's endeavor emerges from a singular persistence in revealing what our sense of belonging to a time and place essentially means, without being bound by those parameters by which we have suppressed the same sense of space and being. Found at the root of his approach to it this is marked by a discomfort that pushes us to make sense of our present from beyond the immediate and short-term "solutions" that are often peddled by our elected representatives, not to mention our religious leaders and opinion makers, managers and priests, bankers and advisers, teachers and social workers ... therapists and doctors.

The Tyranny of Empirie

Ivan Illich was fearless in transcending the limitations by which contemporary scholarship has been, and remains, suppressed by the tyranny of *empirie*. This refers to that *empeiría* (ἐμπειρία) by which knowledge is fossilized on the presumption of testing, and where factual experience itself is expediently reified and detached from a complex reality which warrants more than a battery of metrics to make sense of itself. At a time when truth has been reduced to a banality that is bandied between the nonsensical poles of "real" and "alternative" facts, a concoction of deviant conjectures has clearly become *another* empirie; this time characterized by the polity's brand of cruel clownery that would have come as no surprise to Illich. In many ways, Illich anticipated and warned against the epistemological hierarchies of the *empeiría*. He clearly explained how such a twist on knowledge has stultified education from kindergarten through to academia, and he offered more than one way out, as he does with healthcare, employment, travel, bureaucracy, or the very water we drink.

Against this backdrop, I would characterize Illich's approach as an *exiting-into* a wider world of possibilities—a concept which elsewhere I have called *pentecostal* (not to be confused with a denomination; See Baldacchino 2012) in terms of how Christ's disciples lost all their fear and from within their relative hiding they exited into the world after being visited by the Holy Spirit as they celebrated Shavuot, which occurs fifty days after the second day of Passover and which in the Christian context coincides with fifty days after the Resurrection. A good example of this *exiting* is found in Illich's methods of inquiry, where he defies time as he reads the present from the lines of medieval texts and narratives that afford him ample analytical distance from the immediate. By exiting into these other worlds, he seeks insights that cannot be achieved if one were to simply begin from the here and now, and from what appears to be the immediate safety of an elusive belonging to a closed and settled world. This method is particularly effective in his books *Shadow Work* (SW), *Medical Nemesis* (MN), *Tools for Conviviality* (TFC) and *In the Vineyard of the Text* (VT), together with *The Alphabetization of the Popular Mind* (ABC) which he wrote with Barry Sanders. Aided by his brilliant linguistic skills, exegetical tools and inventive synthesizing, Illich transports himself and his readers across a world where nothing feels alien or anachronistic, and where, looking back into the present, he seeks to reveal knowledge in its comprehensive gnoseological splendor. Remarkably, he does this without ever falling into a false pre-modern nostalgia (see Tijmes 2002, pp. 205ff), and more so by keeping a clear distance from pandering to leftist romantics or appearing to offer comfort to conservative pundits.

Tables of Friendship

The choices made in this book partly relate to Illich's own choices in his calling, beginning from that of his priesthood to that of his roles in education and wider engagement with society as a public intellectual. This relates to the nature of his work, which some sought to displace from an inherently theological approach whose underlying philosophical anthropology grows out of his formation; a formation that gains its full sense of specificity in how it relates to sociological and historical fields which, from a secular point of view, risk being removed beyond their immanent point of origin. The formative specificity that captures Illich's work cannot be estranged from the pluralistic choices that characterized and moved his métier. As a Monsignor he publicly pulled out of major ecclesiastical roles, including that of a high-ranking advisor in the Second Vatican Council, that of Vice-President of Puerto Rico's Catholic University, and ultimately by voluntarily resigning from his role in the priesthood. Apart from walking away from a university vice-presidency, his academic pursuits remained true to their disestablished nature where he would consciously refuse to partake of what academics customarily seek in consolidating their career through tenured tracks that lead to one's being ensconced in an identifiable discipline. As he tells David Cayley,

> I have to point out first of all that changes in the nature of the university, particularly during the last hundred years, have made this institution almost an enemy to the collegial procedure which I've tried to cultivate. Yes, I have made my living out of the university, soberly milked that sacred cow and making my nest with the hand-outs I've received. I've never accepted a regular university job, but only a semester at a time at different institutions or at one institution—I've now been teaching at the University of Bremen for seven or eight years, and at Penn State for twelve. This has provided my friends and me with the wherewithal for a hospitable table. (RNF, p. 147)

In the spaces provided by academic hospitality, Illich managed against all odds to find a table whose wherewithal gave him a system of support that was non-intrusive enough for him to freely articulate his own objections to the institutionalization of knowledge. This search for hospitable tables marked and sustained a unique critique where he took uncomfortable positions to major institutional campaigns such as those launched by the Catholic International American Cooperation Program in the 1960s, which, in his essay "The Seamy Side of Charity" he describes as "men and money sent with missionary motivation [to] carry a foreign Christian image, a foreign pastoral approach, and a foreign political message." (CoA, p. 58)

Addressing this issue, Illich chooses to set up a center in Cuernavaca, which becomes a sort of permanent symposium and from where he primarily seeks *friendship*: "With two friends, Miss Feodara Stancioff and Brother Gerry Morris, I set up a center in Cuernavaca." Their intent ran on two objectives. First, they wanted to try to soften the damage caused by the Papal order and approach to the missionary program. "Through our educational program for missionaries we intended to challenge them to face reality and themselves, and either refuse their assignments or—if they accepted—to be a little bit less unprepared." Their second objective was to exert influence on mission-sponsoring agencies and institutions "to dissuade them from implementing the plan." (CoA, p. 54)

One would be forgiven for asking why I am here directing the reader to recognize two levels of friendship—the one that brought Illich and his friends to found the *Centro Intercultural de Documentación* (CIDOC) in Cuernavaca, and a second moment where friendship emerges from a table, indeed a symposium, that seeks to confront and dissuade an institutionalized program of charity from pursuing its original route. I would argue that the two senses of friendship—that of a collaborative founding and that of a clear disagreement—emerges from the consensus of dialogue. Here friendship does not rescind or refuse the duty to argue, both in the sense of making an argument in conversation as *well as* confronting with argument a state of affairs to which one finds objection by force of civic duty and the civility that friendship brings. This requires us to follow Illich's discussion of Plato's idea of *philia*, or love, as it emerges from the friendship that is signified by the conversation that springs out from the symposium as a meal and drinking party that occasions serious debate and lively conversation.

Qualifying his approach towards the university's "hospitable table" Illich argues that while being inspired by Plato's *Symposium*, especially "Plato's idea of *philia*, of love, as the way into knowledge," he also realized that to him friendship meant something different from what Plato had in mind (RNF, p. 147). Taking his approach from the perspective of the polis in its original sense of the Greek city state, Illich contends that virtue is linked to a juncture that crosses ethics (which he relates to *ethos*) with the people (as *ethnos*). He articulates the "foundation of friendship" as "the flowering of civic virtue and its crown," as he explains his idea of friendship as a catalyst of forms of agonistic contestation that are carried forth by civic virtue.

> [T]he ethics that developed around the circle of my friends arose as a result of our search for friendship, and our practice of it. This is a radical inversion in the meaning of *philia*. For me friendship has been the source, condition, and context for the possible coming about of commitment and like-mindedness. For Plato it could only be the result of practices befitting a citizen. (RNF, p. 147)

Cayley qualifies this as an inversion where "ethics are founded on friendship rather than friendship on ethics," which he in turn attributes to Illich's thoroughly Christian view (TCC, p. 45). I find this qualification as being crucial to how we engage with Illich's work. The backdrop to this is found in how, unless we recognize this relationship between ethics and friendship, it would be difficult to understand why no manner of streamlined expectations, as they stand rationalized and institutionalized, would ever rectify the ills of the world. The rectification itself is flawed *a priori*. Without first assuming this simple, yet radical, shift in relating friendship with ethics, the claims made by those who seek to address world problems through charity, overseas aid, or missionary zeal remain unchallenged. This makes it difficult to identify the problems that inherently lie within a structure of charity on whose institutional establishment of needs we perpetuate an erroneous investment in managerially presumed "solutions" to world "problems."

Illich's take is not easy because the reader is never afforded with any consolation derived from expectations of social cohesion that would somehow emerge from the structures which he ultimately shows to be the very enforcers of the same ills. Tracing the benign to its own fallacies, Illich puts the conventional view of philanthropy out of joint. This invariably produces difficult conversations, especially when all the conventional safety nets identified with institutions such as the church, the state or the university, are removed, if not exposed as being nothing but part of the same problem.

Illich could never expect, let alone pretend, to be anyone's guru. He is more of a scrutinizer who, in his hopeful Epimethean ways, consistently remarks that nothing is what it seems. In this he is not trying to play the game of spotting the "false consciousness" by which we all become the object of the critical theorist's or the semiotician's gaze. Nor does he claim to reveal the truth behind a blindfold. Rather, Illich claims that now we stand at a point in history where because of the freedom that God gave the world through the Incarnation, the world has no choice but to own up to its own contingency in a way that would leave it with no moral safety net of good or evil, as this would simply resort back to a world outlook whose comfort with contingency was allayed by its reassurance in God's will. As he argues in his testament *The Rivers North of the Future* (See RNF and TCC), and as will be discussed in the chapter on contingency, this reassurance is now historically impossible.

As we become aware of the *historical* impossibility of reassurance, we cannot but conclude that to emulate Illich would spell disaster both for the aspiring idealistic cleric who dreams of changing the world, and more so for the budding scholar seeking institutional recognition. These two examples are crucial to the trajectories by which Illich resorts back to the monastic origins (as he does in *In the Vineyard of the Text*) from where cleric and scholar alike would be scandalized by his proclamations on modernity while never encouraged to take refuge in the false nostalgia of pre-modernity. It is also through the bifurcated paths of cleric and scholar, as they recognize their mutual monastic origins of contemplative reading, that we are invited to wander off in Illich's own historical accounts; accounts which uncannily reflect his life trajectory, and which he openly embodies, as he describes himself as both wandering Jew and Christian pilgrim (RNF, p. 147).

In this wandering pilgrimage one finds an important clue to Illich the man, the author and the intellectual. If one could speak of a major obstacle in trying to make sense of his work it would not be found in its presumed "unorthodoxy," but in how his approach subverts the structures by which knowledge has been institutionalized, and where society has been schooled and health has become proprietary. As will be repeatedly argued throughout this volume, while Illich often perplexes readers (even those who may be familiar with aspects of his work) with the unexpected leaps that he takes in theory, history, theology as well as philosophy, and more so in how he remains a harsh critic of institutions like the church while retaining his fidelity to the essence of what makes a church, it remains difficult to try to categorize him. Categories like "orthodox" or "unorthodox" become irrelevant due to ansive nature of his enterprise, which demands a space where one (that is, all of us) could breathe away from established disciplinary "clarity." In its energetic ways, Illich is crystal clear in how he gives one cause to walk out and denounce the schooling of knowledge and its proprietary practices. And yet this entails a great deal of hard work. Often, what appears to be a call for activism he would quickly denounce as a rain dance, not because a cause is unworthy but because without care, the same cause could easily result in the reinforcement of what it is meant to oppose.

Confronted with this, Eric Fromm grapples with describing Illich's work without putting it in a pigeon hole. He resorts to call it a form of "radical humanism" whose central tenet would be "*de omnibus dubitandum*." This is because "everything must be doubted, particularly the ideological concepts which are virtually shared by everybody and have consequently assumed the role of indubitable commonsensical axioms." (see Fromm, in CoA pp. 7–8) He goes on to say how the importance of Illich's thoughts "lies in the fact that they have a liberating effect on the mind by showing entirely new possibilities; they make the reader more alive because they open the door that leads out of the prison of routinized, sterile, preconceived notions." (CoA, p. 10) To me, this means that Illich's work leaves us with an urgent necessity to unlearn our reading habits, just as the trajectory of his ideas tasks us with challenging the dispositions by which we have hitherto read history. Taking account of Illich's challenge we cannot be satisfied with a sense of history that attends to what happened in the past. Rather, Illich's presentation of history comes to us as an avenue that is travelled with what we are able to retain and partake of that which remains eternally *now* by dint of its inherently contingent, and thus reformist and disestablished, character.

Abbreviations: Works by Illich

ABC   *The Alphabetization of the Popular Mind*
CoA   *Celebration of Awareness*
IC   *Ivan Illich In Conversation*
MN   *Medical Nemesis*
RNF   *The Rivers North of the Future*
SW   *Shadow Work*
TCC   *The Corruption of Christianity*
TFC   *Tools for Conviviality*
VT   *In the Vineyard of the Text*

References

Adorno, T. W. (1993). *Hegel: Three Studies*. Cambridge, MA: The MIT Press.
Baldacchino, J. (2009). *Education Beyond Education: Self and the Imaginary in Maxine Greene's Philosophy*. New York: Peter Lang.
Baldacchino, J. (2012). *Art's Way Out. Exit Pedagogy and the Cultural Condition*. Dordrecht: Sense.
Baldacchino, J. (2014). *John Dewey: Liberty and the Pedagogy of Disposition*. Dordrecht: Springer.
Illich, I. (1981). *Shadow Work*. New York: M. Boyars. (SW)
Illich, I. (1993). *In the Vineyard of the Text: A Commentary to Hugh's Didascalicon*. Chicago, IL: University of Chicago Press. (VT)
Illich, I. (2001). *Tools for Conviviality*. New York: Marion Boyars. (TFC)
Illich, I. (2010). *Limits to Medicine. Medical Nemesis: The Expropriation of Health*. New York: Marion Boyars. (MN)
Illich, I. (2012). *Celebration of Awareness: A Call for Institutional Revolution*. New York: Marion Boyars. (CoA)
Illich, I. & Cayley, D. (1992). *Ivan Illich in Conversation*. Toronto: House of Anansi Press. (IC)
Illich, I. & Cayley, D. (2000). *The Corruption of Christianity*. CBC Ideas transcript. Toronto: Canadian Broadcasting Corporation. Accessed: May 4, 2019, http://www.davidcayley.com/transcripts (TCC)
Illich, I. & Cayley, D. (2005). *The Rivers North of the Future: The Testament of Ivan Illich*. Toronto: House of Anansi Press. (RNF)
Illich, I. & Sanders, B. (1988). *The Alphabetization of the Popular Mind*. San Francisco, CA: North Point Press. (ABC)
Poerksen, U. (1995). *Plastic Words. The Tyranny of Modular Language*. Mason, J. & Cayley, D. (trans.). University Park: Penn State University Press.
Tijmes, P. (2002). Ivan Illich's Break with the Past. In Hoinacki, L. & Mitcham, C. (eds.) *The Challenges of Ivan Illich: A Collective Reflection*. Albany: State University of New York Press.

· 2 ·
IMMANENCE

As one converses with Illich's writings, one becomes increasingly aware of a single important connection which many of his commentators, especially those who only focused on his theories of education, seem to have chosen to ignore: his cultural and formative foundations. By "formative" I mean his upbringing by Jewish and Catholic parentage, and more so the character of his formation, which is not just his education but also a disposition towards the forms that determined the choices made by his parents to bring him up in the Catholic faith; a faith in which he sought a home as a student of philosophy and theology, and ultimately as an ordained priest.

Conversos

To highlight Illich's parental genealogies might appear distracting if not inclined to take a personalist approach. However, I would argue that to forfeit this aspect of Illich's work would present a major obstacle in engaging with what it stands for. By way of backing my choice of approach I refer to Rebecca Goldstein's *Betraying Spinoza* (2006) where she highlights the formative element which sheds a different light on the work of Baruch Spinoza.

Goldstein's book is bound to catch the attention of any admirer of Spinoza's philosophy. However, she presents more than just a personal take on this excommunicated Jewish philosopher who, deemed a heretic by both Synagogue and Church, could not escape Goldstein's unique attention. In her account of Spinoza's philosophy, Goldstein takes a different route from mainstream scholarship. She digs deep and closely follows the genealogical trails of those Sephardic Jewish *conversos* who betrayed their *marrano* existence by how they perceived the world. But she does not stop there. Claiming that one of the most inspiring Christian theologians—Teresa de Jesus, better known as St. Teresa of Avila—had Jewish ancestry, Goldstein presents the reader with a feeling that as in Teresa's case, there is a probable kinship that one could trace in the Mediterranean and Semitic ways by which Catholicism seems to have been cultivated; which is where Ivan Illich comes to mind.

While *natality* may be valorized in the wider context by which Hannah Arendt (1998) brings our thoughts to bear on that of one's *being born* into specific circumstances of human living and action (see Kristeva 2001), the accident of birth itself must be kept at considerable distance from the reactionary fetish of distorted narratives of identity which come with nativism. As one remains mindful of the dangers of the latter, at the same time, to value that into which one is born gives Goldstein a plausible vehicle through which she travels on a series of genealogical tracks that could only be characterized as a latent *converso* existence. It is by the same methodological legitimation that she would ultimately have to "betray" Spinoza insofar as he would have been reluctant to explain, let alone justify, his philosophical argument along genealogical lines.

In this sense, history is read from layers of hybridity where claims to nativism are made redundant by segmented realities that construct a sense of self beyond a fixed myth of origin. Yet it would be fair to question how this could have any weight in terms of what Illich or St. Teresa would stand for outside a genealogy such as Goldstein's reading of Spinoza. Countering such objections, I would argue that the opposite is equally valid, especially when one begins to challenge the notion of a unified sense of identity and how in Illich's work this remains fair game especially in his parallel travels betwixt time, place, text and meaning.

This should by now help readers appreciate how, taking this approach from within a Catholic narrative, hybridity is often carried into a secular sphere—in the very same way by which Illich would presume Modernity to be Christian in its *perverted* sense (see Charles Taylor's Foreword and David Cayley's Introduction in RNF p. xiii and p. 42; and TCC, pp. 1–2; 30ff). Of this relationship there are several examples, the most common being socialism, where the notion of redemption is all too close for any comfort for the reluctant conservative who wants to hold onto a deep-seated fear of the left within the church. Though Paul Tillich also reminds us of his own Protestant brand of "religious socialism" (Tillich 1965, pp. 30–37) he would be the first to agree that the Catholic sphere carries a *heavier* approach in terms of its centralized view. This comes from the hierarchical framework which Tillich identifies with the Roman Church, even when he appreciates its ability to self-reform—the best example being Pope John XXIII's Second Vatican Council—in contrast with which Tillich cites the fragility of the Protestant and liberal humanist individual's personal decision (Tillich 1965, p. 62).

This is where the secular is built from the rubble walls of *laïcité* in its full sense of the word, moving from the *laikós* (that which is the people's) of the Greek *ecclesía* (a gathering qua assembly) to the church's own laity, where the secular is denounced from the pulpits by presbyter and prelate alike, though it remains intrinsic to what makes Christian immanence fold onto itself as it seeks to denounce what it regards as its perverted opposite. In this tautology one finds Illich's agôn as that space of dispute-turned-playground found at the threshold of the city, which by its very definition is a liminal non-space that grasps sameness and otherness in one go as *khôra* (see Chapter 7, below). While the Catholic immanence of Rome's hierarchical approach presents us with a logocentric event that remains in line with that of the Son of Man entering history to redeem it, in the case of socialism's own immanent approach, the sons and daughters of humanity become a laic embodiment of the working class. I would not say Illich was a socialist or even anything identifiable with lateral forms of liberation theology or critical pedagogy, as many would have it. Yet he would not be that alien to the convivial narrative by which Elio Petri's film *La Classe Operaia va in Paradiso* (1971/2002) reminds us that the working class is destined to its salvific end—by going to Heaven—not because it is by any way Lutheran or Calvinist, justified or predestined, but because without a paradisaical destiny, its own inherent existence as a class would hold no claim to the terrestrial heaven that socialism was meant to be.

Humanistic Peripheries

Many accounts present Ivan Illich as an impatient fast talker who comes across as a monomaniacal and sometimes arrogant interlocutor. But beyond this polyglot genius who almost entirely sustained his life *exousía* (ἐξουσία)— that is, supporting an approach to the world by dint of one's own authority— one must also look for Illich's sense of unease with all that is quickly affirmed or espoused as being good and benign.

One thing is sure: Illich could never be taken for a *buonista*. He could never be a "do-gooder" not because he nurtured a disdain for a pluralistic and inclusive world—as we often find in the reactionary politics of an American Republican or an Italian Leghista—but because, in direct opposition to the racist Leghista or the misogynist Republican, Illich could never reduce human action to absolute and simplistic solutions to the world's problems. This is especially the case when in his passionate and radical view of the world, Illich appears to have a sense of certainty, even when behind his passion there is disdain for the institutionalized certainties of the church and the state by whose policy asserts its inordinate power and arrogance over all of us.

In the traditions of a Nicolas Cusano or a John of the Cross, Illich drew his thought from his theological foundations, mostly arrived at by way of negation (See Hartch 2015; Hoinacki & Mitcham 2002; IC and RNF). Illich's *via negativa* is often greeted by the same frustration by which positivists and constructivists alike deem non-identitarian and apophatic thinking as being obscure or deliberately difficult. Yet the apophatic method takes the form of diverse iterations within several theological and philosophical traditions that feed into each other, such as the continuous process of questioning, often couched in doubt and negation in Talmudic argument, which finds distinct echoes in philosophers like Adorno (1990), Buber (1948 and 1970), Levinas (1998 and 1990) and Rose (1992).

To frame this, I want to draw the reader's attention to the late Gillian Rose's philosophical journey which, not unlike that of other philosophers—amongst whom I would prominently include Edith Stein and Hannah Arendt—took several iterations that travelled between Jewish and Catholic traditions. It is not surprising that this journey is best accessed in shorter texts which, in their bold and beautiful directness, stand oddly within Rose's body of work. Not unlike Adorno, on whose work she wrote her doctoral dissertation that was subsequently published as *The Melancholy Science* (1978), Rose was never shy of tasking her readers with a taxing read, drawing full attention to the lacunae of non-identitarian and apophatic thinking in all its obscure splendor. However, three books come to mind, which anyone who wants to introduce Rose's work to non-philosophy majors, would probably start with. These are *Love's Work* (1995), *Mourning Becomes the Law* (1996) and *Paradiso* (1999), all of which convey and speak of significant biographical experiences in this remarkable philosopher's life which ended prematurely on the 9th December 1995 when she was just 48.

In *Paradiso* we are led by an engagement with Rose's own religious interlocutor, this time an Anglo-Catholic nun, Sister Edna. Remarkably, these two women travelled together through their work—an echo of which I could sense in my journey with Illich's work, though with Illich as *my* interlocutor, the journey goes in the other direction, as it travels "back" from the modernist to the humanistic. This distinction occurred to me when I read this beautiful, albeit fragmentary book, which, like *Mourning Becomes the Law*, was published posthumously after Rose's untimely passing.

> I have nothing to clutch, nothing to point to as my burden, nothing from which to beg alleviation. My soul is naked: it has lost its scaffolding of regret and remorse or even repentance: it is turned: and the unexpected result is the sensation and the envelope of invisible and visible beauty. This does not make me ecstatic, unreal, unworldly: it returns me to the vocation of the everyday—to [Agatha Christie's] Miss Marple's sense of quotidian justice—but it needed some response, some way of singing its mystery so that I can concentrate as ever on any fellowship or fickleness which presents itself. (Rose 1999, pp. 20–21)

Rose's is a deliberate meditation brought upon her after reading a paper on the *Song of Songs* which Sister Edna shared with her. From Rose's reading, one could appreciate how and why Edna grapples with "the intellectual and spiritual reasons why the modern world cannot hear this mystery of the soul." In Edna's eyes, the modern world seems to be resorting to a mechanistic approach to the appetites of the soul (Rose 1999, p. 19). Yet Rose remarks that Edna, somehow, is missing the heteronomous character of the modern world.

> I search for the way to say that this is an inadequate understanding of modern thought: that modernity is Protestant, not humanistic; it is founded on Luther's 'bondage of the Will' not on Erasmus's 'freedom of the Will', on heteronomy not on autonomy. Kant not Descartes, Kant in all his Pietism, is the source for both the modern world's destruction of the traditional metaphysical and spiritual nature of the soul (*die Seele*) and the reinsinuation of the 'soul' (*das Gemüt*) in all its divine precipitation and aspiration. After Kant, it is Hegel and Nietzsche who seek to reinvent the classical preoccupation with the soul, the city and the sacred for the modern

> world. In short, Edna's intellectual history is thin. I think I can bring her into the modern perspective by introducing her to Kant as the invention of the modern, critical spirit in philosophy, the philosophy of freedom, and as a Pietist, a reformer of the Reformation. (Rose 1999, p. 20)

This seems to offer a key to how Illich himself is often misunderstood. But this time he is not misunderstood by the Roman or Anglo-Catholic's misreading of modernity, but by the modernist reading of his humanism. There is, however, a caveat to this comparison. Unlike Edna, Illich comes to the modern world well-equipped with his intellectual history. In this case, it is the modern reader—that is, most of us—who comes to Illich's work, thin, as it were, in the same intellectual history that delimits and defines what we *are* or *want* to know.

Hiddenness

The distinction that Rose elicits from her reading of Sister Edna's paper is highly significant for any reading of authors and theorists like Illich who hail from a strong humanistic tradition. This is best illustrated by Hannah Arendt's approach to the mind, as she brings it into the realm of the soul. In *Life of the Mind* (1978, p. 72) Arendt argues how in this respect "the mind is decisively different from the soul, its chief competitor for the rank of ruler over our inner, non-visible life." If we were to regard this consideration of the mind alongside the soul as being somewhat anachronistic, this is not because of the juxtaposition of a modern sensibility on what was more customary to humanistic consideration, but because, as Rose puts it, there is a seemingly ironic twist to this appearance of anachronism.

Rose asks whether to invoke irony would seem anachronistic, especially when irony is regarded as "the vehicle of modern romanticism or post-modern skepticism: a way of advancing a view without risking any commitment to it, a play of signifiers without any theory of being, knowledge or love." But Rose reminds us that irony has deeper roots, indeed "an older pedigree: I mean to refer to Socratic irony, to biblical irony and to their fusing in Kierkegaardian irony—that is, respectively, to philosophical irony, to narrative irony and to the irony of hiddenness and erotic self-revelation." (Rose 1999, p. 24)

It is in this hiddenness that the humanistic narrative finds itself reclaimed. Arendt reminds her readers that, "seen from the perspective of the world of appearances and the activities conditioned by it, the main characteristic of mental activities is their *invisibility*." (Arendt 1978, p. 71) The play between mind and soul in the corollary of appearances as that which is revisited along the question of the visible and the invisible does not sound as pertinent to the strictly modern assumption of a heteronomous sense of freedom.

To begin to weigh and gauge the nature of an awareness by which the humanistic sense of immanent autonomy is embodied in a matter such as the soul, one can only resort to the language of the invisible, that which the body cannot manifest. To this argument of the manifest, Arendt adds the weight of the invisible soul. She elucidates the soul's locating capacity as "where our passions, our feelings and emotions arise." While the soul is "a more or less chaotic welter of happenings which we do not enact but suffer (*pathein*)"; and while the effect of pain and pleasure are overwhelming, in the matter of the soul they could only manifest themselves by the soul's unique attribute of invisibility: "its invisibility resembles that of our inner bodily organs of whose functioning or non-functioning we are also aware without being able to control them." (Arendt 1978, p. 72) The value of resemblance is the only way of explanation, which is to say that the soul's freedom is principally found in the unique capacity of its remaining outside the realms of the visible and the tangible. Such discourse can only make sense on a humanistic horizon, which is why Arendt could then qualify how "[t]he life of the mind, on the contrary, is sheer activity, and this activity, like other activities, can be started and stopped at will." (Arendt 1978, p. 72)

As discussed later in Chapter 6, Illich engages in a longstanding discussion of the visible and the hidden which bears some resonance with Arendt's. He does this not only in his discussion of the evolution of the iconic and the scopic in their ethical concern (see RNF, pp. 114ff and Illich 1998) but especially in his discussion of the idolatry of "life" as an object of visibility and scopic disembodiment. Following his extensive discussions with Barbara Duden, he often refers to the pink and blue lights that have become iconic of the fertilized human egg and the blue planet, and which in their respective representation became strong referents of a scopic order where not only is life deprived from its quality of hiddenness, but where a systemic process of disembodiment turns life into an object of manipulation (see IC, pp. 263–268; and Duden 1993). One cannot avoid noticing the cruel irony by which an iconography that is frequently loaded with quick phrases-turned-slogans like "the sanctity of life," effectively becomes life's visible perversion.

Back to Rose's invocation of irony's deeper roots, the invisible is also a means by which one could lay claims that are not restricted by the conditions of modernity:

> St Augustine appears in his disappearance: this is the meaning of the *Confessions*. St Teresa's *Autobiography* somehow goes further: her mystical experiences, her charismas of levitation and tears, are juxtaposed with her institution-building, her organisational and managerial skills, her tremendous worldly power, in a way that enlarges our rational powers as it approaches the actuality of eternal life, keeping her soul hidden. (Rose 1999, p. 24)

In this ironic location by which the invisible sustains its perennial claims, one begins to get closer to what has already been described as Illich's shared sense of pain, partaken from the crucifixion as if it were an event that one has just experienced upon witnessing Christ's death just outside one's own city. None of this makes any sense in the context of modernity. Yet it holds full sense when, to reuse Rose's words, we set aside Kant's invention of the modern—which I would regard as a process of unlearning. A good example of how Illich's humanistic claims encounter a modern context is found in the opening pages of his book *The Vineyard of the Text* (VT);

> I want to tell the story of reading during a distant past century of transition. (...) I dream that outside the educational system which has assumed entirely different functions there might be something like houses of reading, not unlike the Jewish *shul*, the Islamic *medersa*, or the monastery, where the few who discover their passion for a life centered on reading would find the necessary guidance, silence, and complicity of disciplined companionship needed for the long initiation into one or the other of several "spiritualities" or styles of celebrating the book. In order that a new asceticism of reading may come to flower, we must first recognize that the bookish "classical" reading of the last 450 years is only one among several ways of using alphabetic techniques. (VT, p. 3)

Where is the irony? Partly in its invisibility. Perhaps in its utopian ways by which the disestablished learning that Illich dreams of can only come from a modern reading of medieval sources. The irony seems to come from the agonizing awareness that one's sense of journey—what Antonio Machado calls the *caminar*—retains the hallmark of an agonizing faith. This has less to do with a rectification of divine existence and more in common with a sense of fidelity to a humanistic universe that could have never come by accident even when the truth of contingency is what marks one's existence. Illich asserts this paradox almost everywhere and all the time.

> As you know, I have written a book called *In the Vineyard of the Text* in which I argued that the development of conscience is linked to the new prevalence of writing around this same time [the 12th Century]. Conscience was conceived as an inner writing, or record, and this idea was reinforced by the appearance in churches of statues of writing devils who note people's sins, and by the image of the Last Judgement as the reading of a book in which all sins are recorded. (RNF, p. 90)

Insofar as Catholicism is not limited to a religion but is also perceived from its deep-seated cultural formations of a historical sense of community; and given that Illich's work cannot be read outside the premises of the desideratum of truth borne out of a *philosophia perennis*, to read his work one needs to immerse oneself in a conversation which is often too close to untangle from the way by which culture, faith, philosophy and representation deliver an awareness of immanence. By such a continuous sense of interiority one is meant to live the world and care for all of it in the most direct manner. This is why his engagement with education that is found "outside the educational system which has assumed entirely different functions," (VT, p. 3) warrants special attention to the hidden and invisible attributes by which Arendt and Rose present the soul and irony. This is demanding of a particular approach which cannot but revisit a space that is often regarded as being found within the periphery of a humanistic narrative that is all too often ignored.

Educing Illich

In *Shadow Work* (SW, pp. 31–51) and *The Alphabetization of the Popular Mind* (ABC, pp. 65–70), Illich describes at some length how in the service of Queen Isabella I, Elio Antonio de Nebrija was instrumental in imposing the Castilian language over the nations of the Iberian Peninsula, thereby overriding the vernacular values and the plurality that they upheld.

Nebrija's case for Castilian was a moment which Illich describes as the state adopting the role of the Mother which was hitherto only attributable to the church. "Nebrija addresses this new secular balance between *armas y letras*. He argues with the queen for a new pact between sword and book and proposes a covenant between two spheres—both within the secular realm of the Crown a covenant distinct from the medieval pact between Emperor and Pope, which had been a covenant bridging the secular and the sacred." (ABC, p. 66)

This had profound implications on those notions of education which appear to have been lost in their original meaning. Illich explains how *educatio* was originally adopted and located within "the bosom of Mother Church" and how in Nebrija's political and linguistic use it has become extended, that is secularized, by the modern state. In a rich discussion of education and language as domains where the pluralism of the vernacular finds itself suppressed by a shared matriarchal assumption of state and church symbolized by the figures of the Queen and the Mother, Illich takes everyone to task. He reminds his readers that "*[e]ducatio prolis* is a term that in Latin grammar calls for a female subject" and being designated to feeding and nurturing applied to animal and human alike. He insists that "[t]o educate has etymologically nothing to do with 'drawing out' as pedagogical folklore would have it." (SW, p. 46) Taking some exception to Johann Heinrich Pestalozzi, Illich argues that:

> Pestalozzi should have heeded Cicero: *educit obstetrix — educat nutrix*: the midwife draws — the nurse nurtures, because men do neither in Latin. They engage in *docentia* (teaching) and *instructio* (instruction). The first men who attributed to themselves educational functions were early bishops who led their flocks to the *alma ubera* (milk-brimming breasts) of the Mother Church from which they were never to be weaned. This is why they, like their secular successors, call the faithful alumni — which means sucklings or suckers, and nothing else. (SW, p. 46)

In keeping his work on my side, and in what would seem to be an act that defies Illich's own admonitions, I am here inviting readers to consider a number of themes by holding onto my intention of *drawing* Illich, not *nursing* him. Apart from appearing to betray him (as Goldstein admits to *Betraying Spinoza*) I want to imagine what his dream of houses of reading would look like by what he refuses to *educe* from education. One could imagine how the scripting of reading itself is *drawn out* with the same hope by which Illich's work propounds a world that is reviewed (in the sense of it being viewed *once more*) from the Epimethean perspective by which he concludes *Deschooling Society* (DS).

The concurrent acts of reading, scripting, *drawing out*, not to mention simply *drawing* as an act of imaging (*dibujar, disegnare, dessiner*) would imply processes that begin with marking what is visually impacted, aurally heard and orally read (On the complex notion of *drawing out*, see Pistola 2017). On close proximity, this drawing back comes closer to Epimetheus than Rabbi Nicodemus. The distinction is pertinent in that while Jesus drew Nicodemus's attention to the need to be born again through kenotic love and faith, Epimetheus was burdened with the duty to save the world with what was left in Pandora's box: hope. This was a peculiar kind of hope; one which is immanent inasmuch as it remains hidden in the box that should have never been opened. Invariably this hope is deemed in its absolute state, by which is meant that while in its hiddenness it conceals the fullness of its image, in its manifestation it is perceived in its own kind of fullness. It is a manner of hope which, unlike any promise announced on the platform of politics or religion, education or the economy, its possibilities remain all-embracing; meaning that inasmuch as happiness is an ultimate desire, it must not deny those acts of suffering and fear that it seeks to heal and allay.

Illich qualifies this approach to hope as being Epimethean for a very clear reason. He insists on rediscovering the "distinction between hope and expectation." While hope is in all its fullness "trusting faith in the goodness of nature," Illich poses expectation as a "reliance on results which are planned and controlled by man." (DS, p. 104) This reliance is exemplified in how Illich explains the child in New York City, at a time which predates the gentrification of Harlem and the Upper West Side.

> Life today in New York produces a very peculiar vision of what is and what can be, and without this vision life in New York is impossible. A child on the streets of New York never touches anything which has not been scientifically developed, engineered, planned, and sold to someone. Even the trees are there because the Parks Department decided to put them there. (…) Power and violence are organized and managed: the gangs versus the police. (DS, p. 108)

We must bear in mind that historically, Illich's remarks predate the subtler ways by which the child everywhere is now chained to his smartphone, and by how expectations have become further reified under the guise of algorithmic forms of communication which anticipate and in turn manipulate one's needs. As he puts it, "[l]earning itself is defined as the consumption of subject matter, which is the result of researched, planned, and promoted programs. Whatever good there is, is the product of some specialized institution. It would be foolish to demand something which some institution cannot produce." (DS, p. 108) This exudes a sense of prescience, especially when Illich remarks on how no one could "expect anything which lies outside the possible development of institutional process." This is because "[e]ven [the child's] fantasy is prompted to produce science fiction. He can experience the poetic surprise of the unplanned only through his encounter with 'dirt,' blunder, or failure: the orange peel in the gutter, the puddle in the street, the breakdown of order, program, or machine are the only take-offs for creative fancy." (DS, p. 108)

Due to the precision and accountability of planned expectations, the Promethean powers of technology have clearly taken over the spaces that have become devoid of hope. Illich argues that the only viable approach to push back this advance is to take on the fullness of Epimethean hope. This might sound clear enough, though in effect to reclaim an Epimethean approach is to engage oneself with the same dilemmas that faced Sister Edna's reading of modernity. Be that as it may, one cannot ignore the fact that as children "phantasize flying their spacecrafts away from a crepuscular earth" (DS, p. 115) in their fulfilment of the school's Promethean standards, the benchmarks for their generation have been solidly committed to an "unlimited quantitative increase" which Illich adds, "vitiates the possibility of organic development." (DS, p. 43)

This explains why Illich goes back to his 12th century sources to figure out how an Epimethean hope would reclaim the spaces occupied by Promethean expectations. To do this, he claims a tradition that—not unlike other philosophers like Maritain, Gilson, Levinas, Derrida, Nancy or Caputo, who in their different ways reclaimed and often deconstructed their own Christian and Jewish traditions—Illich's radical earnestness excavates the foundational grounds of a tradition that supersedes its own institutionalized boundaries. He figures out how to challenge both the tradition by taking it to the logic of its radical conclusions to a point that appears to deconstruct it; and the world, which invariably fails to respond to one tradition, even when he states that Modernity cannot escape from the church that made it. As Charles Taylor succinctly puts it in his Preface to Illich's *The Rivers North of the Future*, "Illich argues that Western modernity finds its original impetus in a mutation of Latin Christendom, a mutation in which the Church began to take with ultimate seriousness its power to shape and form people to the demands of the Gospel." (RNF, p. x)

This informed synoptic statement sustains the argument that unless the junction where Illich the Catholic priest meets Illich the provocative historian is clearly recognized, the core point of Illich's philosophical work will be severely deformed. This argument is frontloaded, as it were, from the start, as it reflects on what Illich finally articulates at the very end of his life and his work. To that effect, as we try to *educe* Illich (and risk betraying him), we are not intent on drawing him out, or give him some rebirth, but perhaps wean ourselves—indeed *educed* as in *being delivered*—out of the *alma ubera* of an education that never really pushed us beyond itself. It is, after all, Epimethean to nurture hope, knowing very well that it was always taken away from us by monarch and prelate alike, as it is still done by their contemporary offspring, and more so in this age of cataclysmic absurdity.

Abbreviations: Works by Illich

ABC   *The Alphabetization of the Popular Mind.*
DS   *Deschooling Society.*
IC   *Ivan Illich In Conversation.*
RNF   *The Rivers North of the Future.*
SW   *Shadow Work.*
VT   *In the Vineyard of the Text.*

References

Adorno, T. W. (1990). *Negative Dialectics*. London: Routledge.
Arendt, H. (1978). *The Life of the Mind*. New York: Harcourt Brace Jovanovich.
Arendt, H. (1998). *The Human Condition*. Chicago, IL: University of Chicago Press.
Buber, M. (1948). *Tales of the Hasidim*. New York: Schocken Books.
Buber, M. (1970). *I and Thou*. New York: Scribner.
Duden, B. (1993). *Disembodying Women. Perspectives on Pregnancy and the Unborn*. Hoinacki, L. (trans.). Cambridge, MA: Harvard University Press.
Goldstein, R. (2006). *Betraying Spinoza. The Renegade Jew Who Gave Us Modernity*. New York: Nextbook, Schocken.
Hartch, T. (2015). *The Prophet of Cuernavaca: Ivan Illich and the Crisis of the West*. New York, NY: Oxford University Press.
Hoinacki, L. & Mitcham, C. (2002). *The Challenges of Ivan Illich: A Collective Reflection*. Albany: State University of New York Press.
Illich, I. (1981). *Shadow Work*. New York: M. Boyars. (SW)
Illich, I. (1993). *In the Vineyard of the Text: A Commentary to Hugh's Didascalicon*. Chicago, IL: University of Chicago Press. (VT)
Illich, I. (1998). The scopic past and the ethics of the gaze. Ivan Illich, Kleftingstr. 16, D-28203 Bremen. Accessed: April 4, 2019, http://www.davidtinapple.com/illich/1998_scopic_past. PDF
Illich, I. (2012). *Deschooling Society*. New York: Marion Boyars. (DS)
Illich, I. & Cayley, D. (1992). *Ivan Illich in Conversation*. Toronto: House of Anansi Press. (IC)
Illich, I. & Cayley, D. (2005). *The Rivers North of the Future: The Testament of Ivan Illich*. Toronto: House of Anansi Press. (RNF)

Illich, I. & Sanders, B. (1988). *The Alphabetization of the Popular Mind*. San Francisco, CA: North Point Press. (ABC)

Kristeva, J. (2001). *Hannah Arendt*. New York: Columbia University Press.

Lévinas, E. (1990). *Nine Talmudic Readings*. Bloomington: Indiana University Press.

Lévinas, E. (1998). *Otherwise than Being, or, Beyond Essence*. Pittsburgh, PA: Duquesne University Press.

Petri, E. et al. (2002). *La classe operaia va in paradiso*. DVD. Roma: Minerva Pictures Group.

Pistola, R. (2017). *DwA: Draw with(out) Authority*. Unpublished doctoral dissertation. Faculty of Fine Arts, University of Porto.

Rose, G. (1978). *The Melancholy Science: An Introduction to the Thought of Theodor W. Adorno*. New York: Columbia University Press.

Rose, G. (1992). *The Broken Middle: Out of our Ancient Society*. Oxford, UK; Cambridge, MA: Blackwell.

Rose, G. (1995). *Love's Work: A Reckoning with Life*. New York: Schocken Books.

Rose, G. (1996). *Mourning Becomes the Law: Philosophy and Representation*. Cambridge; New York: Cambridge University Press.

Rose, G. (1999). *Paradiso*. London: Menard Press.

Tillich, P. (1965). *Ultimate Concern: Tillich in Dialogue*. London: SCM Press.

· 3 ·
UTOPIA

To make a case for *utopia* is to recognize the possibility of a *no place* that is twice removed from, firstly, the unquestioned immediacy by which we continue to approach the world, and secondly, those localized states of affairs where liberty is posed by the condition of a heteronomy devoid of autonomy. To ignore the need for utopian thinking is to overlook the fact that in attempting to reverse the condition of heteronomous immediacy would amount to the same: where a case for freedom becomes a negation of obstacles that props its opposite in forms of liberty that posits what it denies (see Berlin 1998). While this binary might appear to nurture a dialectical value in terms of how we approach place and liberty, all it does is flood freedom with a stream of tautologies.

As "It" Perpetuates

Democracy is being constantly manipulated into legitimizing an illiberal state of affairs. This is witnessed by the emergence of a reactionary politics whose distortion of history constructs a desire to "return" to a time that never was. Examples of the latter are found in Vladimir Putin's claim to have restored Russia's perceived glory; Donald Trump "making America great again"; and the Brexiteer's dream of restoring an empire on which the sun was never meant to set. In all these narratives, autonomy is regarded as a distraction from systems of control that sustain a heteronomy devoid of otherness.

One must not forget that current reactionary politics is not just a consequence but an extension of the imperialist legacy of a Cold War that supposedly ended thirty years ago. This extended period, which alternated between tacit and overt conflicts sustained by proxy and away from its epicenters, was nurtured by a mutual rejection of freedom, played on a binary track of positive and negative forms of liberty. In this dyadic game, a horizon of sustained conflict systematically curtailed freedom under the pretexts of liberty and democracy on one hand, and socialism and equality on the other, respectively, purporting negative and positive liberty while equally suppressing the possibility of a politics of autonomy and conviviality. Epitomized by show trials, pogroms, conspiracies and assassinations across the globe, the cruelty that the Cold War institutionalized by its claim for peace and detente deemed it fit to control millions of innocent people through systematic oppression, overt forms of slavery, hidden networks of torture, institutionalized forms of political murder, and a culture schooled in a perpetual fear of nuclear holocaust.

At the receiving end of this legacy we now mischaracterize our age as an historical period where truth is no more. Yet there is nothing new in what we are now reaping from a century of cruelty, whose proclaimed "end" is now denied by the same Francis Fukuyama (2006) who touted it back in 1992 in the most publicly proclaimed misreading of Hegel's philosophy of history. Far from "post-truth"—a hackneyed term that would never assuage the assumption of truth per se—we are now expected to live through a construct of fiction that exudes the feeling of a Groundhog Day perpetuated to eternity, leaving most of us grappling to find historical parallels while desperately trying to make sense of "what is yet to come."

What is to come has always been there, because contrary to what we have learnt in schools, history is not a sequential montage, but a lived immanence that is expressed as a human construct. While the trap of sequential essentialism must always be eschewed, those forms of historical parallelism by which we seek to make sense of the present cannot be dismissed as a simple cliché, particularly when history permeates through every aspect of our daily living.

Now that this affair is being brought home by the habits of social media, we might be better poised to figure out how heteronomy keeps being distorted by the realization that humanity has never been so atomized into self-centered individuals as it currently is. This is happening at an age when even the young have, at the touch of a smart phone, all the possible means to live a solipsist's dystopia in its full glory of self-adulation and performativity. While emancipation is increasingly hollowed out of any of the significance it might have had, the way its politics have been twisted on both the right and the left has not ceased to consume us with the addiction of the words-made-putrefied-flesh of trivial information and stylistic mimicry.

Though one would be keen to argue that more than ever before, any approach to historical parallels (whether critical or affirmative) should pay closer attention to the relationship between freedom and intelligence, this is turned into a cliché by the dystopic sociology of "free" knowledge from which nothing and no one appears to be immune—be it at an individual or institutional level, at home or at school, whether in hospital or homeless in the street. What has become more of a cruel sobriety is that we might have to face the fact that the vantage point we could claim through autonomy's prism cannot be taken for granted because the urgency of rediscovering utopia has become a matter of savage desperation, and by implication it is itself swallowed by immediacy.

Freedom and Intelligence

To speak of autonomy does not simply aim at excluding or denouncing a short-lived assumption of liberty perceived as that which is qualified by a human prerogative for intelligence—understood in its classic sense of *intelligere*, as a way of realizing and discerning what it is to know and understand by dint of being. The utopian condition for freedom means that being's immanence prompts us to mediate what we *do* and where we *are* as we place our understanding within a historical context that is not simply received but actively understood by being *lived*.

As John Dewey has repeatedly shown, liberty, in and of itself, means nothing without conceptualizing how human intelligence is directly associated with a notion of freedom that is socially expressed. In *Liberalism and Social Action* (which he wrote in the 1930s) Dewey argues that liberalism went into crisis when it failed to "develop and lay hold of an adequate conception of intelligence integrated with social movements and a factor in giving them direction." (Dewey 2000, p. 51) While this might appear to condition intelligence on a social dynamic, without its social qualification, liberty remains (as it has invariably become) a heteronomous state of affairs, especially when it asserts itself as a negation of perceived obstacles which in turn posits itself as a tautology. By critiquing an approach to liberty as being positively or negatively heteronomous, it does not imply that freedom must be understood outside the social realm. When left detached from adequate conceptions of intelligence, a concept of liberty that is conveniently distanced from autonomy reduces history to a mere *record* that would in turn reject the immanence of living.

Dewey's qualification of his critique of liberalism's conceptions of intelligence does not hone in on the distinction between heteronomy and autonomy. At first glance, it appears to take an opposite view. It seems to argue that in its social iterations, intelligence assumes a heteronomous approach. This is a misreading of Dewey's position and a common misconception found in the positivistic reading of pragmatism. Not without irony, this also reduces pragmatic thinking to the same predicament that the concept of intelligence had in the liberal thinking of the 1930s. It does not come as a surprise that the following might sound familiar to us as it was then: "Social and historical inquiry is in fact a part of the social process itself, not something outside of it. The consequence of not perceiving this fact was that the conclusions of the social sciences were not made (and still are not made in any large measure) integral members of a program of social action." (Dewey 2000, p. 51)

The distance between freedom and autonomy intentionally brings about an implicit omission of social association, tacitly impairing the possibility of democracy. This is not down to autonomy. Rather, this concept of intelligence impedes autonomy from being articulated beyond an individualistic assumption that is mistaken for a form of autonomous living. Dewey's critique of individualism brings this to mind when he argues how liberalism missed the opportunity to engage in social action: "just at the time when the problem of social organization was most urgent, liberals could bring to its solution nothing but the conception that intelligence is an individual possession." (Dewey 2000, p. 52) If "individual possession" is misread as an autonomous approach, then one is bound to assume that social action, as often understood by empiricists (of the right and the left), is a heteronomous assumption that *reacts* (rather than *acts*) to reality without recognizing the need for a social understanding of intelligence. This positivistic method is strongest when it concerns notions of learning, and particularly in how it distorted the idea of autonomy as a form of freedom, resulting in a heteronomous affair that sustains an instrumentalized view of society. Dewey's verdict in the 1930s is frightfully relevant to the state of education today:

> When "learning" is treated not as an expansion of the understanding and judgment of meanings but as an acquisition of information, the method of cooperative

experimental intelligence finds its way into the working structure of the individual only incidentally and by devious paths. (Dewey 2000, p. 53)

Milking the Family Goat

Dewey's critique of liberalism's inadequate concept of intelligence begins to give some context to Ivan Illich's critique of history. Illich's qualm is with a historical narrative that presents a line of production where even the best of intentions is expected to yield a series of desired effects. This desire is found in a heteronomous assumption of power that is reinforced without any hope for freedom to come anywhere near a sense of autonomy. Illich's critique of this state of affairs takes an unusual route. He draws parallels with models which are customarily assumed to represent specific forms of associated living, and where democracy is presumed to become their core existence. The model is that of a church as originally understood to be an iteration of the ancient *assembly*, the *ecclesia*. In this assembly democracy is expected to carry the very meaning of associated living, where those who operate it (in this case the clergy) are chosen by being elected (by God and his people), to sustain this presumption of freedom. Illich turns this upside down, and he presents us with a critique of clericalism, implicit in his evaluation of the narrative of best intention as it hides the very opposite.

> In each of the seven United Nations-defined world regions a new clergy is being trained to preach the appropriate style of austerity drafted by the new need-designers. Consciousness raisers roam through local communities inciting people to meet the decentralized production goals that have been assigned to them. *Milking the family goat was a liberty until more ruthless planning made it a duty to contribute the yield to the GNP.* (RUU, p. 79, emphasis added)

This quote from Illich's *The Right to Useful Unemployment* (RUU), provides a glimpse in how his critique operates. To those who are not familiar with Illich, this comes as a surprise. Many would assume that rather than start from (or indeed use analogies of) narratives normally attributed to benign institutions (in this case a clerical class chosen to spread the word of a decentralized, and presumably autonomous, mechanism inspired by nothing less than the United Nations) are turned into a narrative that stands for the very opposite. This is the effect that Illich seeks. However, he does not want to shock those who have taken some comfort in a number of institutional narratives that they deem to be implicitly critical of the *status quo*. At the same time, he wan⌐

make sure that any complacency in accepting these narratives must be tackled at root.

The gist of Illich's argument must be read from how the assumptions that we have taken for granted are always tested. To start with, we are led to believe (and in turn we often claim) that to be free is conditioned by a transactional relationship. Politically this emerges from precedents of social contracts which, in our various political systems, take the form of a bargaining in an agonistic scenario whose actors are individuals, organizations and resultant structures. At a more intimate and individual level, from our infancy we are made to experience education as a schooled system through formalized assumptions of knowledge. Whether at home or in the classroom we were brought up to accept schooling as a conditional and contractual element in the attainment of social association, liberty and personal achievement.

This contractual reasoning stems from an economy whose forms of exchange require a hierarchy of knowledge and needs dictated by state- or privately-owned industries like education, healthcare, and social services. In his analysis, Illich finds it easy to refer to organized religion, because faith and conviction have historically been organized in the structures of established churches by the same way that ideology became the mouthpiece of party politics before it got cloned into managerialism. Given that ecclesiastical structures have predated and broadly informed the emergence of our current political systems in their secular form, Illich's critique cannot be ignored or easily dismissed. Nor should it be construed as some qualm from a disgruntled cleric with an axe to grind with the world through his own ecclesiastic lens. Illich is not simply drawing parallels. Instead, he presents us with structures that remain intrinsically tied to each other, not only in matters of politics but more alarmingly in how knowledge becomes a matter of systemic being and how, in turn, being is revealed through the myopic lenses of schooled forms of knowing, making and doing.

To reclaim the paths of a humanistic horizon takes an uncomfortable route to those who insist on the clear immediacy of the contemporary State in its established form. This is because a reclaimed humanistic horizon represents a recognition of the immanence of knowledge. That is to say, knowledge must be deschooled by being re-presented by its intrinsic value of being.

:aths full engagement with the dialectical character of a ground l into a horizon. As it asserts objective truth, this horizon sustains)jective values of its hermeneutic ability and the power of diverse

Those who are exercised in the discourse that vacillates within the perceived interstices found in modernity and its claim to a continuous actuality, might be tempted to presume that Illich's is yet another pre-modernist iteration. However, upon reading and engaging with the intellectual genealogy of Illich's work, his humanistic approach to the world asserts the modern in its original sense of the *actual*, as mediated by a free and intelligent grammar that refuses to become a positivistic ground of certainty. Rejecting certainty means refusing to play on with the heteronomous demands made by the transactional guarantee by which a positive economy seeks to discard autonomy under the pretext of liberty itself. As Illich confirms, in line with a long tradition of immanent thinking: to beat the hegemony of the guarantor of certainty, and to liberate freedom from the clutches of heteronomous liberty, an approach to freedom must be done inversely, just as the theologian trailing a *via negativa* seeks divine existence from a position of doubt and even rejection.

This is confirmed by how Marcuse puts the possibility of freedom within the reaches of utopia, which should not be read as bestowing liberty with an impossible task, but on the contrary, by asserting the possibility of freedom as a form of autonomy.

> The abolition of material poverty is a possibility within the status quo; peace, joy, and the abolition of labor are not. And yet only in and through them can the established order be overcome. Totalitarian society brings the realm of freedom beyond the realm of necessity under its administration and fashions it after its own image. In complete contradiction to this future, autonomy over the technological apparatus is freedom in the realm of necessity. This means, however, that *freedom is only possible as the realization of what today is called utopia*. (Marcuse 1988, p. xxvi, emphasis added)

Dreamers

The case for utopia runs on a non-identitarian track, knowing that in their autonomous and often paradoxical nature no amount of parts could ever share a unified, let alone unique, identity that fits into a homogenous whole. Accepting this state of affairs, one begins to verge on the possibility of a society, which Illich calls *convivial*. In *Tools for Conviviality* (TFC), Illich frames conviviality within a society characterized by "the balance between those tools which create the specific demands they are specialized to satisfy and those complementary, enabling tools which foster self-realization." (TFC, p. 24)

Many would argue that to knowingly make a utopian case based on immanence, paradox, and autonomous parts is to consign one's case into the abyss of impossibility. Utopian thinking is risky. Someone making a case for utopia looks absurd. Cases for utopia are like unwanted pregnancies—they risk abortion. The choreography and spin that have come to characterize middle ground political practices have systematically proscribed utopian thinking. To avoid such criticism, the slick, well-groomed and often young-looking 21st century centrist politician refrains from promising anything by which he or she would be held accountable. Spin-doctors would invariably tell any budding politician that it is far too risky to indulge in such talk. Verging on the utopian, let alone the promise of radical change, remains out of bounds. Talk of immanence is too obscure. Autonomy sounds too radical and smacks of extremism.

This state of affairs is not limited to politics. As exchangeable accountability is beatified and elevated to the altars of market-driven morality, its pietistic incursions have reached the shores of education and research which have increasingly been subscribed to that which replaces the mark of intelligent inquiry with a hallmark of academic management. Like any other moral order, the run for accountability exceeds itself. It installs a continuous iteration of identitarian thinking where the promise of theory, hypothesis, or contemplation is at best looked with suspicion and at worst derided and forbidden. Leading the "knowledge industry," academia begins to hold its rank and file to account. This is executed by the precision of an established and clearly expected practice that must be documented and vouched for as proof of activity, especially where the work concerns theory or speculation. Talk of "academic production" is no longer abstract. It is measured against identifiable results that fulfil what is misperceived as an academic "promise."

While traditionally, an academic promise was never concretized in that it subsisted in the immanent qualities of theorizing itself (where one could hypothesize without being held to account, and where experimentation was encouraged) this promise is now premised on those perfunctory qualities by which theoretical work becomes conditional on an elusive capacity of *cost* that is readily exchanged in fundable parts. In the academic promise of the knowledge industry, no theory can go without application even when the talk in boardrooms and faculty meetings alike is increasingly occupied by the need for "creativity and innovation." No one is immune. Even artists and performers have to negotiate their way to recognition within a "creative industry" where utopian thinking might well be an attractive and fashionable commodity, but whose existence is proscribed by tangible terms of *fundable* inquiry. For art to be entered into the social, affective and pedagogical ledgers of accountability it must name a price. As a unit of production, creative practice must be sold as a *scarce* unit; a scarcity by which the agency of profit could then function as a measure of knowledge in all its glorious hierarchical hagiography. Strangely enough, hagiographies could still make a profit in the knowledge industry, just as the selling of indulgencies managed to fill the Vatican's coffers with enough wealth to sustain a corrupt and immoral church while overflowing the heavens with supposedly redeemed souls.

On the horizon of production, dreamers and utopians are dismissed for failing to deliver on their promise, even when their promise was methodologically designed as a platform for hypothetical analyses. "The modern university has forfeited its chance to provide a simple setting for encounters which are both autonomous and anarchic, focused yet unplanned and ebullient," says Illich. Instead, modern universities choose "to manage the process by which so-called research and instruction are produced." (DS, p. 36) With hypotheses dismissed for being ungrounded, and for measured predictability to enjoy almost exclusive recognition, knowledge and creativity give up their autonomy to a dogma of functionality. This is best illustrated by how knowledge and creativity are now ranked against hierarchies of "need" in an effort to justify the existence of certain disciplines in academia. To make it to the pantheon of academic, artistic, political and other forms of *recognition*, one's dreams are only acceptable if they command a price and are made scarce enough to rise in demand.

Nevertheless, just as the omnipresence of practical power appears too close for dreamers to be able to resist it, there is a point in history where one must speak as a utopian, invoking the *oú tópos* as the place that is not there but which could be there if we care to imagine and want it. In practice, to declare a utopian promise, whether aesthetic or scientific, gnoseological or ontological, political or moral, may well have become too risky in the 21st century *polis*. Yet the risk must be had, as it would be even riskier to give up on utopia's promise. Few may want to do so, and the only way is to strategize both one's method and its execution for it to stand a chance of a hearing. In other words, the utopian must be had.

A Promise

Those who dismiss utopians come from all corners of the political spectrum, from the right, the left and the center; progressive, moderate, radical and reactionary alike. Friedrich Engels meticulously dismisses what he regards as utopian programs, so much so that he enters social theorists like Proudhon, Saint Simon and Fourier in the canon of political thinking as "utopian socialists." (Engels 1977) However, unlike contemporary critics of utopia, Engels is not after measurement per se, even though he appears to do so when he assumes that politics is mostly beholden to the success or defeat of reason. Not without irony, by this he makes himself a candidate for becoming a utopian in the eyes of those who came after him—namely us women and men of the 21st century.

Although Engels would somehow suggest that the utopian socialist is a harbinger of outlandish ideas, his approach comes from the measurement of theory against the social and economic conditions which to him provide those parameters by which one should do politics *scientifically* and bring about radical change. This kind of measurement is different from what today is experienced as a legitimizing slide rule, even though what Engels says could be easily read against the contemporary dogmas of accountability. Unlike current critiques of utopia, Engels's does not hide its ideological position. With regards to utopian socialists, Engels argued that their systems wouldn't work—not because of their promise, but on the grounds of how this promise is delivered; which is where his ideological position is invested in the analysis of such theories. To say that the needs of the *now and then* must tally with the particular contexts by which history becomes a measure of deductions made *a posteriori* would have to mean one thing today. However, this would have meant almost the opposite at a time when Engels assumed that reality was more than just a managerial assemblage of accumulated "facts" presumed on the political stalemate of class construction. Reading Engels, one would need to bear in mind such distinctions:

> The solution of the social problems, which as yet lay hidden in undeveloped economic conditions, the Utopians attempted to evolve out of the human brain. Society presented nothing but wrongs; to remove these was the task of reason. It was necessary, then, to discover a new and more perfect system of social order and to impose this upon society from without by propaganda, and, wherever it was possible, by the example of model experiments. These new social systems were foredoomed as Utopian; the more completely they were worked out in detail, the more they could not avoid drifting off into pure phantasies. (Engels 1977, p. 119)

In Engels's critique, utopians are read as having theoretical positions that would have to face up to the impracticality of what they propose. His critique is equally executed within the realm of theory and more so in how socialism as an ideology responds to the rational questions that faced 19th century society. Not surprisingly, in today's critique Engels himself would be regarded a utopian because he is seen as someone who frontloads his measure by an ideological position. This also means that Engels never rejects the idea of a promise in his political program—an aspect of politics that in the 21st century is frowned upon as being akin to a secret utopian agenda.

As Jacques Rancière explains, the modern critique of utopia is a direct attack and dismissal of the political promise. To Rancière, this turn comes at a specific time when the utopian is extended to any form of political promise. Historically this was clearly marked by the French Presidential elections in 1988, where the French people elected François Mitterrand without asking whether his "hundred and ten promises" made in 1981 (when he was first elected) were actually delivered.

> The new outlook of our candidate-president was supposedly that of someone who had finally seen the light, finally rounded the cape and entered the new century. For the original evil was the promise itself; the gesture which propels a *telos* of community, whose splintered parts rain back down like murderous stones. Politics was now going to renounce its long complicity with ideas of future times and other places. It would now *end as a secret voyage to the isles of utopia*, and henceforth view itself as the art of steering the ship and embracing the waves, in the natural, peaceful movement of growth, of that production which reconciles the Greek *phusis* with the everyday art of pushing forward one step at a time; that production which the last, mad century ruined with its murderous use of the promise. (Rancière 2007, pp. 5–6, emphasis added)

This state of affairs is now recognized widely in other instances of political life since the years of Mitterrand's Presidency. What followed looked pretty much like a relay race, which in effect turned politics into a sport of sorts where in the main we have seen the so-called *virtues* of the center's takeover. Though one often attributes an intensification of ideology to these years, particularly with the Reagan-Thatcher legacy, this evidently led to the opposite. In the 1980s Rancière was already reading the signs of this kind of secular centrism. He was then able to describe with utmost precision what is now commonplace in contemporary politics, even though one could never tell what would follow.

Since then the world witnessed the fall of the Berlin wall, the reunification of Germany, and the dissolution of the Soviet Union. Reagan-Thatcherism ultimately led to Blairism. Mitterrand and Helmut Khol were followed by Chirac and Blair, while Germany took a while to see the rise of Khol's successor in Angela Merkel who successfully ditched the Blair-like

Gerhard Schröder. This kind of leadership marked an era that coincided with a further expansion of the European Union. This expansion was sold on the perceived victory over the legacy of Cold War discourses to a political class that embraced a managerial form of antagonism that in turn inaugurated new forms of political secularization. Incidentally this also saw a radical, albeit short-lived, transformation within Southern European post-fascist democracies, particularly in Portugal, Spain, Italy and Greece, where political crisis marked the dissolution of their post-war historical parties, then followed by severe economic crises that were made worse by fluctuations and a forced "harmonization" warranted by the emergence of the European common currency, the rise of the Euro (see Varoufakis 2017).

Quandaries

While hopes in newfound economic and civil freedoms were greeted throughout the last two decades of the 20th century, the major casualty across the globe has been and remains what Rancière (2007, pp. 5–9) describes as "the end of the promise"—that is, the end of the political ability to dream and think in utopian fashion. As capitalism in Asia replaced former communist command economies in Russia and China, the promise that prevailed was that of more consumption and the provision of cheap commodities on a massive scale. This is still ushered in by monolithic forms of governance controlled by an economic oligarchy, as in Russia, or through a state communist nomenclature, as in China. In the meantime, on its home grounds of Europe and the United States, capitalism found itself in a quandary of its own making. Here the secular state, now held hostage to a managerialist turn, practically neutered any promise in the making of politics.

The United States witnessed a paradox in terms of the hopes promised by an Obama administration effectively undermined by "Tea Party" Republicans seeking to perpetuate their neoliberal confessional credo, which resulted in Donald Trump's presidency. Europe witnessed a similar assault on its secular traditions from two fronts: that of secularized managerialism on one hand, and a surge of nationalism on the other, whose emblem Brexit has become. Rather than eliminate the confessional state of "scientific communism," the end of the Cold War seems to have subverted the laic grounds on which traditionally, liberal democracies would have guaranteed an equal footing on which ideologies and ideas could be played without interference. This meant that the politics of *laïcité*—which Western Europe broadly expected to bring into the former Eastern bloc—met a fatal end.

This anti-laic latter-day secularism amounts to "a politics exercised altogether in the present, with the future being nothing but an expansion of the present, paid for, of course, by the requisite austerities and cutbacks. Such is the new sense of time," remarks Rancière, "to which we are now said to be acceding. At last, they tell us, we are entering the twentieth century—several decades late." (Rancière 2007, p. 6) Given that Rancière's paper was first delivered in 1988, one must bear in mind how just now, three decades later, any resistance to such an approach has been robustly set back and the same mentality has not abated even when new political formations have emerged in movements and new governments like *Syriza* in Greece.

Yet these new formations had to face up to, and compromise with, the economic violence by which a dystopian order has long been sealed in Europe and which ultimately saw their demise—as it has done with Syriza, which in 2019 found itself replaced by a rejuvenated *Nea Dimokratia*—the very same party that led the government against which *Syriza* emerged and defeated. As this book was started just after a compliant and emasculated *Syriza* government was voted back in to enact a program that it was supposed to oppose, one wonders where this leaves other political formations, such as *Podemos* in Spain (which, like *Syriza* is seriously losing ground to the old political hegemony of the social democratic *Partido Socialista Obrero Español* and the conservative *Partido Popular* which it originally challenged), or what appeared to be a rejection of the Blairite narrative in the British Labour Party with the election of Jeremy Corbyn as leader (threatened as it where by the confusion that emerged around Brexit), and the huge support that Bernie Sanders gained against all expected odds in the US primaries (which, after three years, is now appearing to become a shadow of its first iteration).

It would be foolish to assume that the backlash against the lack of political promise by the managerial élites is a phenomenon found only on the Left. The emergence of the nationalist right and what we are witnessing in terms of the reactionary consolidation of anti-immigration and racist sentiments in, amongst other, the old Eastern European (former communist) countries, leaves one puzzled by where an "end of politics" for Rancière in 1988, has left us in the end of the first two decades of the 21st century. This must also be read against the resurgence of political and religious formations that have emerged in the Middle East, where the picture is close on becoming as murderous as Europe and Asia during the two world wars in the 20th century.

At the risk of stating the obvious, to read Engels's critique of utopian socialists from the lens of 21st century skepticism towards utopia makes more than interesting reading. It would have been in Engels's wildest nightmares to think that the critique of utopia could even move outside the political realm of ideas and ideologies. As those who abdicated from ideologies found themselves clueless on how to cope with the rise of deadlier forms of confessionalism, in the 21st century the secular state—that problematic offspring of the "great bourgeois revolutions" of the 17th, 18th and 19th centuries—seems to have lost its ability to deal with the classic achievements of *laïcité*'s birthplace, France. This supposedly laic state is a far cry from what has now become a secularization that broadly transformed politics into a platform of policy making in the first place. It might explain why events like the *Charlie Hebdo* massacre in 2015 failed to galvanize and resurrect the old political promise beyond the charlatanry of a bunch of political leaders holding hands in the middle of Paris while conveniently kept away from crowds of protesters.

* * *

The death of the political promise left us bereft of the most fundamental promise that democracy holds—what Ivan Illich calls *conviviality*, and to which here we will return, time and again, as that promise by which this odd polyglot Catholic Jewish priest working between the New York's Upper West Side, Puerto Rico, Mexico and Germany, took the risk of being ridiculed and critiqued. And this, when in his works he sets out to disestablish not only faith from a religion trapped in its own institutional and clericalist certainties, but also as he goes on to deconstruct what progressives, liberals and conservatives alike have hitherto agreed to be unassailable: schools, hospitals and a range of services that were and remain broadly considered as the democratic *givens* of human progress.

As Illich was critiqued for what were at best considered as rather utopian alternatives, it was the same Ivan Illich who actually dared to dream beyond what was simply given by his religious and secular detractors. Thus, not only was he dismissed for being utopian, but he was also scorned for thinking beyond the given parameters of what was supposed to be fixed by church and state in their parallel zeal to help others through forms of development as force-fed by Roman Pope and American President alike.

For a Catholic priest in the 1950s and 1960s to be critical of the church's missionary zeal in Latin America, following suit in President Kennedy's earnest policy of help and development (mostly dictated by a fear that emerged from the Cuban revolution), it would have seemed not only odd, but very unlikely that his words were heeded let alone left to voice what in the 1970s resulted in a series of powerful critiques that cut across the most fundamental "achievements" of modern society. Let us not forget that in its Cold War permutations, modern society was supposedly based on dreams and ideas that were equally hailed by the competing triumphs of capitalism and communism, emblematically racing beyond the skies with Gagarin and Armstrong beatified as the new saints of "space-age" modernity.

Abbreviations: Works by Illich

TFC   *Tools for Conviviality*
DS   *Deschooling Society*
RUU   *The Right to Useful Unemployment*

References

Berlin, I. (1998). "Two Concepts of Liberty." In *The Proper Study of Mankind: An Anthology of Essays*, H. Hardy & R. Hausheer (eds), pp. 191–242. London, UK: Pimlico.
Dewey, J. (2000). *Liberalism and Social Action*. Amherst: Prometheus Books.
Engels, F. (1977). Socialism: Utopian and scientific. Marx, K., Engels, F., *Selected Works*. Vol. 3, pp. 95–151. Moscow: Progress Publishers.
Fukuyama, F. (2006). *The End of History and the Last Man*. New York: Free Press.
Illich, I. (2001). *Tools for Conviviality*. New York: Marion Boyars. (TFC)
Illich, I. (2009). *The Right to Useful Unemployment and Its Professional Enemies*. New York: Marion Boyars. (RUU)
Illich, I. (2012). *Deschooling Society*. New York: Marion Boyars. (DS)
Marcuse, H. (1988). *Negations. Essays in Critical Theory*. London: Free Association Books.
Rancière, J. (2007) *On the Shores of Politics*. L. Heron (trans.). New York: Verso.
Varoufakis, Y. (2017). *And the Weak Suffer What They Must?: Europe, Austerity and the Threat to Global Stability*. London: Vintage Books.

· 4 ·

TRADITION

To read and discuss Ivan Illich's work requires a readiness to move around and beyond fixed categories with relative freedom and a degree of playfulness. This is what he did in all aspects of his work, whether written, taught, disputed or practiced. Illich problematized social forms of living, such as education and health, often to the surprise and anger of many who never dared question these aspects of human life which over the centuries have been established and institutionalized.

Epoché

What is even more remarkable, and to some surprising, is that Illich could engage and critique such matters because he partakes of methods and approaches that he attributes to the *tradition*, or what Catholic philosophers have typically identified with a *perennial* approach to almost every aspect of life as that which grows from within a lineage of other moments of understanding (See Copleston 2003). By claiming tradition, Illich is unequivocal. He identifies a specific lineage in those philosophical, theological and political narratives outside of which his work would lose its core meaning. Tradition holds central significance throughout the entirety of Illich's work, even when this does not appear to directly confront his readers.

Like that of the Medieval theologians and the Ancient Greeks before them, the tradition that Illich adopts as a horizon often involves the method of *epoché* (ἐποχή), where, in tackling matters that look unlikely, one would first suspend that which appears to be likely or indeed compromised by the ifs and buts of common parlance. This method, as Husserl (2014, p. 55) explains, "is directed precisely at the discovery of a new scientific domain and one that is supposed to be attained precisely *through the method of bracketing*, but then only a specifically restricted domain." It is worth recalling that the method of epoché was the mainstay of theological application. The method of bracketing concepts was intended as a way of moving the same concepts and problems away from the processes that would alienate them from what they should or could mean.

Illich captures this moment of epoché when he states: "I want to celebrate my faith for no purpose at all!" (CCD, p. 22) This makes no sense without dealing with how he sustains tradition in his methods of distancing himself from the actuality of a case, by either looking at the case from a very different angle through a different language or a distant historical model, or by pushing the concepts to their limit in ways that were effective inasmuch as they were highly original and unconventional. To tie an argument simply to a purpose, being a presumed objective that is already defined, would impede one to even start. This is especially so when the matter at hand is engaged with matters of faith, and where the last thing one wants to do is to render faith as some utilitarian bargaining chip for a better deal or indeed salvation. Thus, while sustaining the tradition through its methods, Illich also sustains the tradition into the present, while pushing it into the future. He never anchors it to a dead past, let alone behold it to some preordained second coming.

While holding to such challenging thoughts, what I would ask of Ivan Illich's reader is to suspend at least two pairs of opposites. The first is the fallacy that the traditional stands opposed to the new by assuming that the former is somehow conservative while the latter is supposedly progressive. The second dualism may well be an extension of the first, where politically speaking we take a position on the right or the left, as attributed to conservatism and progressivism respectively; though as we all know, this is often belied by the practice of politics as traded on the grounds of the vested interests of the Establishment.

To be in tune with Illich's approach requires that one moves away from such categories, beyond which he seeks other spaces of arguing and partake of other contexts that externalize themselves from the normative entrapment of the expected. For example, when he speaks of development, he argues that "[d]evelopment is not judged against a rule but against an experience." (CCD, p. 18). Yet here he is not opting for a quick shortcut into opinion or solipsistic reflection. Instead, he takes the experience of *subjects* onto horizons that are neither idealized nor measured by the empirical tools by which, so often, practicism reifies human experience. Illich explains that "this experience is not available through the study tables but through the celebration of shared experience: dialogue, controversy, play, poetry; in short: *self-realization in creative leisure*." (CCD, p. 18 emphasis added).

After Deschooling ...

Anyone approaching Illich's work while carrying a baggage of dualisms will get confused and ultimately becomes disorientated, both intellectually and more so politically speaking. To the ears of some readers, Illich seems to be saying one thing when in effect he is stating the opposite, or steers away from what we have been schooled to think or do.

To take one of his best-known works, *Deschooling Society* (DS), the reaction that this book attracted when first published in 1971 was typically confused, to say the least. There are those who remain prone to react immediately, even after so many years of argument and counter argument. Objections to *Deschooling Society* heavily relies on *placing* this work somewhere within the realms of a mainstream critique of education on the left, right, or the center, where there is no place for it at all. Many find it difficult to do so and in detracting from Illich's main argument, those who reject deschooling hardly realize that the problem is caused by their misplaced insistence on a simplistic rendition of *a* concept and not on *the* concept per se. The difficulty to locate Illich's work is not found in the work per se, but in the expectations by which some would approach the notion of locating a work, that is, *any* work. Such expectations base themselves on premises which Illich modified or even abandoned, partly because his approach tended to evolve very quickly and because he always sought to engage in further dialogue especially with those who took exception to his ideas.

Even before a book like *Deschooling Society* is read, the term "deschooling" on its cover is alluring enough to raise a hostile feeling from those who are not ready to let go of their own schooled satchels, let alone their established baggage. Strangely, even after so many years, the book still gets stuck at the gates of the intellectual establishment's "need" to place a concept where it "belongs." As one tries to even use the term deschooling, many would argue that Illich's claim is now surpassed, even when, one suspects, they have never read a word of Illich's work and his subsequent follow-up to the reaction that both his book and the projects that it inspired have received over the years.

While "deschooling" (the word) gets to be used and misused *ad libitum*, and those who dare use it now are summarily dismissed as some Illichian Johnny-come-lately, *Deschooling* (the book) gets an assortment of polarized reactions. It is hailed by the neophyte as one of the best books ever written on education just as it is derided as idealistic and impractical by the self-proclaimed "experienced educator." As if this were not enough, it is also rejected by those who believe that the establishment of the school must remain unquestioned. In like fashion, some would welcome *Deschooling Society* as pre-modern, where education becomes a form of nostalgic belonging, hardly showing any comprehension of Illich's take on modernity in its Christian context. Others would go spare over what they misconstrue as an attempt to tear down the notion of universal education. As one reads Illich comprehensively, none of these arguments make any sense.

None of the above begins to qualify, let alone add anything to what Illich regards as the inherent problem that afflicts education at its core. Neither is it right to contend that *Deschooling Society* is somehow another iteration of critical pedagogy. This claim betrays a misunderstanding of critical pedagogy itself. Though a good and dear friend of Paulo Freire's, Illich worked in parallel with (rather than against or as an extension of) the latter's take on education. "I remember Paulo with immense affection," says Illich, "but also as somebody who more and more wanted to save the credibility of educational activities at a time when my main concern had become a questioning of the conditions which shape education in *any* form, including *conscientizacão* or psychoanalysis or whatever it might be." (IC, p. 207)

Illich considers schooling from a very different perspective. He neither concurs with, nor rejects Freire's pedagogy. Unlike many progressive educators who regard schooling as an extension of rights and a path to emancipation, Illich argues that even when schooling is prompted by a progressive agenda, it remains a mechanism of scarcity. Scarcity restricts and puts a price on everything, and education is no exception. Scarcity commodifies education into a measured activity whose nature and provision are decided by other than its supposed constituents. Yet Illich's friendship with Freire was never in question. "Paulo was for me a very solid point of passage and remains a dear friend." (IC, p. 207)

Two years after *Deschooling Society*, in *Tools for Conviviality*, Illich insists that the conditions of a post-industrial society confirm that "[u]niversal education through compulsory schooling is not possible." (TFC, p. ix) The educational constructs held from within the institutionalized assumptions of schooling—as in structures by which we live, such as healthcare, social work, transport, consumption, water, *et cetera*—need changing at source, from their very inception. The overstated and rather unwelcome focus on the term "deschooling" is partly to blame for a huge misinterpretation of Illich's critique of education. As a term, deschooling often shares the same fate with the word socialism in the United States where many a liberal and conservative pundit would use it to kill any conversation.

Illich is against what I would characterize as innocent-looking establishments that gather "kids" in the name of a universal provision where, in effect, they reinforce a type of socialization by which society and the school become synonymous. His critique is directed at those practices by which schools turn children into a human resource, and where the school's value is inflated to the extent that it becomes the custodian of social reality. This is done at the expense of education which, in a schooled narrative, loses its multi-dimensional possibilities, and therefore forsakes the radical sense by which teaching emerged in its deschooled origin. As Sam Rocha reminds his readers, as attested by several traditions teaching precedes schooling, rather than just reflect it.

> Teaching precedes schooling, anthropologically and metaphysically. Humans relied on teachers long before schools existed. Even before civilization brought humans into permanent settlements where schools could emerge, teachers were at work. The person of wisdom, the parent, the exemplar—all of these and more are embedded into the Socratic and rabbinic models of the teacher. Socrates taught Plato long before Plato founded the Academy. Jesus taught in the synagogue, yes, but he also taught on the mount and the sea. Even on the Cross, Christ taught the thief. *As an art, teaching is so ancient as to be pre-institutional, if it is not positively anti-institutional.* The teacher who dares to teach, the professor who risks a profession, the master who shows more than she tells—*over such figures, no school has any power, much less a monopoly.* (Rocha 2017, p. 78, emphases added)

In a schooled society, learning, education and schools are conveniently exchanged, synonymized and thereby distorted by the lack of a dialectical process. This leaves teaching at the receiving end of a systemic act that decimates its essential role. Diminished in this way, teaching as an art becomes a luxury reserved to those schools where education is afforded only relative freedom to allow teachers to exercise a portion of their creative, let alone, subversive and radical ability to lead the young through questioning the world.

I choose to refer to school children and students as "kids" (a word which as far as I know is not used by Illich) to emphasize the *herding* element of schooling which moves away from any positively construed notion of pastoral care. In a schooled context, pastoral care is measured and socialized. It is operated on an agenda that presupposes care and learning through set rules claimed to be benchmarks and standards of "excellence" but where what excels is the measurement by which it gains legitimation.

This is a far cry from the examples which Rocha singles out in the pre-institutional traditions of learning found in the rather subversive approaches that were taken by Socrates and Jesus (who, incidentally, were both executed by the state on the charge of corruption and blasphemy), or those who chose to teach outside the interests of a schooled society. As this tradition has been systematically suppressed, teachers find themselves grappling with the dilemma in which their vocation has been trapped. Rocha sums this perfectly when he reminds us how, "[t]eachers today sometimes seem unaware of the subversive potential of their vocation."

> It may appear that teaching is lost, but this absence is possible only within a schooled vision of teaching. Among professional teachers, the deeper and more ancient roots of their vocation have not wholly vanished from sight. Many teachers, both those who quit the profession as conscientious objectors and those who hang on doggedly, know the voice that calls them to teach comes from *a deeper and more intimate place than the school bell*. The law of the teacher is the same law to which Martin Luther King Jr. appealed when he gave his national lesson in Washington, DC. This is the law written on the heart of the person, the inviolable law that so many schools and nations fear and seek to control. (Rocha 2017, p. 79, emphasis added)

One often forgets that established interests shape schooled societies. They are teleological projects conceived on a massive scale by which society is planned and projected. In a schooled society the primary concern is not that of the child per se, but the learner who is expected to follow an agenda by which the child becomes a resource and the teacher an instrument that manufactures it. Those who are "left behind" in the schooled paradigm of society are likely to be considered as irrelevant to the economy. (Irony excepted, it would be amiss to forget George W Bush's *No Child Left Behind* policy and the philosophy that prompted it, which for all intents and purposes was originally conceived by Bill Clinton's education policy.)

Far from the school per se, a schooled society is characterized by the identification of interests by which human beings become quantifiable units: kids to be counted and measured in their ability and contribution to a set agenda. Clearly it would be irrelevant as to how the "kids" succeed, whether the system is learner-centered or didactic; whether at home or within the public or private sectors; whether they learn by rote, creatively, online or off line, in small groups or large classes. A schooled society is output driven. Its sociological value is tied to a functionality by which theorists, administrators and teachers alike are expected to deliver a curriculum that is clearly set against criteria, mostly to do with economic efficiency, social cohesion, and future projections. Worst still, when it comes to emancipating discourse, schooled societies are not challenged but modified in an attempt to "rebalance" a state of affairs operated on the tracks of a sociology of knowledge (see Baldacchino 2018, pp. 26ff and 63ff).

While universal schooling is presented as a right, the universalization of education remains a matter of socio-economic planning that is projected against hierarchies of manufactured needs, which, we are told, should help the individual find his or her place within society. This comes at a price that is measured, projected, and properly costed. Through schools and other means of organization, education begins to trade in a scarce resource. Being scarce, this resource begins to command a price according to the market that is out there. As a scarce and merchandized commodity, education begins to prompt efficient modes of production (call it "teaching and learning") that puts an identifiable price on skills and knowledge: "What makes skills scarce on the present educational market," says Illich "is the institutional requirement that those who can demonstrate them may not do so unless they are given public trust, through a certificate." (DS, p. 88)

... What?

This begins to explain why educationalist literature is busily engaged with the knowledge and creative industries, hailed and dreaded in equal manner by those who have to identify, cost, and strategize emerging new needs (and demands) within educational institutions ranging from Kindergarten to College. In his essay *After Deschooling, What?* (ADW) Illich is prescient when he states that, "if schools were disestablished for the purpose of more efficient delivery of 'knowledge' to more people, the alienation of men through client relationships with the new knowledge industry would just become global." (ADW, p. 48)

A schooled society is an economic mechanism that supplies a number of identifiable and projected demands. Politically speaking, this walled *polis* traps everyone, children and adults alike, into a relational assumption that a traditional-progressive dualism could never unravel. This is because liberals, progressives and conservatives alike tend to regard schooling as a practice intended to enable society to assess and cater for the socio-economic priorities of the day. Whether such priorities are informed by moral or economic values, industry, social coherence, or even democracy, makes no difference.

> At first, new knowledge is applied to the solution of a clearly stated problem and scientific measuring sticks are applied to account for the new efficiency. But at a second point, the progress demonstrated in a previous achievement is used as a rationale for the exploitation of society as a whole in the service of a value which is determined and constantly revised by an element of society, by one of its self-certifying professional élites. (TFC, p. 7)

This is why those who either regard Illich as an advocate for a critical pedagogy with a revolutionary agenda of open schooling on one hand, or as the traditionalist who seems to make a case against emancipation through education on the other, tend to either get confused or summarily dismiss his position. Their mistake is found in their tendency to hold onto a dualistic and polarized description of the world. Illich is neither for nor against the case for emancipation through schools. In effect, his position renders such assertions irrelevant because his critique is already placed *before* the school is even entered into the equation.

Illich's real beef has to do with a condition where what can be understood and owned as a form of learning is already lost by the aprioristic assumptions made about learners. In the mind of those who seek to *institutionalize* learning, the confusion between education and schools, and that between education and learning, is a gratuitous myth and more so an assumption by what some would prefer to see the debate over education expediently resolved without much change or transformation. He argues that "[t]he relation between what can be learned from ordinary living and what must be learned as a result of intentional teaching differs widely with place and time." (TFC, p. 58) Then he adds:

> It depends very much on rituals. All Muslims learn some Arabic as the result of prayer. This learning evolves from interaction in a context bounded by tradition. In much the same manner, peasants pick up the folklore of their region. Class and caste also generate opportunities to learn. The rich acquire "proper" table manners or accents and insist that these cannot be taught. *The poor learn to fend in dignity where no education could teach the rich to survive.* (TFC, p. 58, emphasis added)

As Illich would say later, particularly in response to the reaction that *Deschooling Society* attracted when first published, that his claim is not to abolish schools from society but to disestablish both school *and* society. Yet this would mean nothing unless there is a serious critique of how teaching and learning have evolved into a form of administration. In *After Deschooling, What?* Illich argues that "[d]eschooling will be only a displacement of responsibility to other kinds of administration so long as teaching and learning remain sacred activities separate and estranged from fulfilling life." More importantly he states that, "deschooling must be *the secularization of teaching and learning.*" (ADW, p. 48, emphasis added)

Clearly, deschooling is meant as the disestablishment of an edifice where teaching and learning are operated as confessional tools of alienation. As in a confessional state where church and state remain entangled in each other's rules, pretty much as in religion and the church in a schooled society education administers a preordained canonical system of knowing. Like the priests and mandarins of a confessional state, teachers administer an identifiable Canon, affirming x and y as the singular premises on which z becomes a universal hallmark of an educated person. Illich's critique implies that unless this administration is laicized, teachers and learners will never cease to play the role of priests to the faithful. This is where Illich has a lot to contribute to the necessary questioning of learning per se, particularly when teaching and learning often operate along self-declared universal norms by which we are all expected to confess an educational creed (See also Biesta 2006; Baldacchino 2018).

The Laic and the Ecclesial

In Illich's insistence for a distinctive form of *laïcité* within the educational sphere, one can see how his critique does not come from the usual canons of critical pedagogy, as derived from Marx, Gramsci, Fromm, Mannheim or Freire, nor from the assumptions of liberal and progressive theories, let alone their direct counterparts. His influences reveal an unexpected provenance, which Illich recognizes in works related to the sociology of religion (see Luckmann 1967) and the impact of reform on Christian thinking (Ladner 1959; see also Rubinoff 1971 and Illich, CCD). To such sources, one must add his research in 12th century writing, from which he gains special attentiveness to a much deeper intellectual tradition found in the juncture between secular and church histories. The Church is never far from his mind whatever he happens to be reflecting upon, especially when he draws our attention to the need for disestablishment and its laic approach. After all, Illich was an ordained priest, a Monsignor earmarked to become a high dignitary if not bishop, and some would argue that he could have made it to Cardinal if he played by the rules—which he obviously did not (see Hartch 2015, pp. 12ff).

In 1970, in his introduction *The Church, Change and Development*, where he edits a number of essays and letters by Illich, James Morton succinctly captures all of this while being quite prescient about the current situation in the Catholic Church:

> [T]o a Church that is increasingly polarized, perhaps only a man who is himself deeply committed to revolutionary change and yet rooted in a perception of the church that transcends party lines for a deeper unity, indeed for a common table to which a man comes from the barricades to break the joyful bread with his tactical opponent, perhaps it is this kind of man at this moment in history who can speak to the Church. (CCD, p. 8)

This is why any reference to, or argument for *laïcité* in Illich's work cannot be taken as a side issue. It urges attention from a profound understanding of the world that is laic, because it pertains to the *laïkós* (λαϊκός) which denotes that which pertains to the people taken from an ecclesial (*read also*: convivial) perspective. More poignantly, Morton adds that

> Contrary to enthusiastic attempts to mirror the Gospel in the current popular milieu—whether the "secular" and self-confident rationality of systems analysis and team problem-solving of 1965, or the "religious" playfulness of this year's groovy/hairy/scented festivals—Illich uses the apophatic logic of classical negative theology to mark the consistency of revelation. Parallel to the enigma of the burning bush (…) Illich constructs a grammar in which *silence* is the highest mode of communication, *poverty* the vehicle for carrying the most meaningful, creative and richest act, and *powerlessness* the means for demonstrating authoritative control; a language finally in which the autonomy of the *spontaneous and the surprising* is established over against the planned, of the ludicrous as opposed to the useful, and of the *gratituous* [sic.] in the face of the purposeful. (CCD, pp. 8–9)

The laic and the convivial give Illich's commentary a sharper edge over anyone who dares critique the canon, be it religious or political. This theological context, especially in its apophatic origins, must be considered when Illich turns to education, and more so his critique of schooling: "Equal educational opportunity is, indeed, both a desirable and a feasible goal, but to equate this with obligatory schooling is to confuse salvation with the Church." (DS, p. 10)

It is important to bear in mind the parallelism that Illich draws between the need to disestablish education and the secularization of teaching and learning. Like religion in churches, education trades in salvation as an ultimate goal of the school. The problem is that this reduces the promise of a better future—be it terrestrial or celestial—to an exclusive privilege that is only granted to a community of identifiable and certified members. This is where Morton's account of Illich's "language (…) in which the autonomy of the *spontaneous and the surprising* is established over against the planned, of the ludicrous as opposed to the useful, and of the *gratituous* [sic.] in the face of the purposeful" (CCD, p. 9) frames Illich's work by a deeper meaning. In reclaiming Illich's understanding of the laic from within his concern towards the *ecclesia*—as that sphere which is often distanced from the *agora*, and thereby those residing in the market square without necessarily belonging to the assembly—takes his discussion of education beyond being just *another* critique of education's institutional shortcoming.

To privilege a manner by which one obtains something is to create an exclusive opportunity for the few. This makes sure that what it provides remains scarce. Far from an excess of use or over-consumption, scarcity is created by privileged ownership. It is in the interest of those who are privileged through exclusive access that a service is kept scarce. So, the myth goes that just as one would not be saved outside the church, one would not succeed in life unless he or she goes to school. Terrestrial salvation comes as an institutional promise that confesses and administers the agreed canon of a schooled society. This will be duly conferred by an education that follows the same canon that defines salvation, and to which one receives full membership by giving full allegiance in return, as happens in every graduation and commencement.

> School has become *the world religion of a modernized proletariat*, and makes futile promises of salvation to the poor of the technological age. The nation-state has adopted it, drafting all citizens into a graded curriculum leading to sequential diplomas not unlike the initiation rituals and hieratic promotions of former times. (DS, p. 10, emphasis added)

...this creates a monopoly in terms of who decides what we need as human beings and what makes us *ripe* to join the *educated*. Conveniently, just as individuals go to church to ascertain what their spiritual needs may be, they also go to school for their intellectual needs; they subscribe to a health insurance company to have access to a doctor and a hospital that will tell them what is wrong with their health; they frequent and stick to specific supermarkets to find what food is best for them. Likewise, they watch cable television and surf the Internet for their entertainment; they fully subscribe to social media to have their say in a virtual community of friends; they follow a diet of sporting events for their sense of belonging, support their college or local football or baseball team to fulfil their membership of an identifiable community; they vote and even register as member of a political party, and they seek to follow and dutifully conform with ever-new institutionalized practices so they could better identify their needs.

However, before someone accuses Illich of pushing people out of the professional sphere and into the hands of the village quack, one needs to bear in mind what he is criticizing. Illich is not criticizing medicine as a science, or education as a practice that remains critical to our understanding. Rather, what he puts under severe scrutiny is how the institutionalization of these practices and of everyday living slowly redefines and ultimately distorts and controls a corollary of human needs.

It is very much a matter of direction and who takes ownership of what or even whom. Yet Illich insists on the centrality of the person: the person who learns, who is healthy, who lives a fuller life. It is here that institutions fail; starting from schools which dictate to us what we should be learning, and ending with the dentist who seems to own his patient's teeth and insists that cavities need to be filled and look good when in effect the owner of those teeth is the patient who may want healthy teeth but is not concerned with the aesthetics of dental care. It makes no difference whether the dentist is serving the client in some expensive down-town private clinic in Madison Wisconsin, or whether he happens to be employed by the National Health Service (NHS) in leafy Royal Leamington Spa England. Those who should be owning their teeth are the patients, and they are neither clients nor serfs, but human patients.

I should add that often Illich is well-known in such sectors as health and social care, and unlike most educators, health and social work professionals hold his work in higher esteem especially when it comes to understand the patient's position and role in the institutionalization of care. This is where one finds that only recently are women no longer frowned upon when they opt for a home birth, just as Illich has shown in his various examples of how, at some point, home births became the privilege of the few rich and the domain of the poor who have no choice but to give birth at home.

Processed Emancipation(s)

In so many ways Illich was advocating *choice* before it was hijacked by the market-specialists who now use such language in order to attract more customers and make more money. The flip side is that as nationalized institutions start to run in partnership with private enterprise, this language of *choice* is being consolidated, but for reasons that have been institutionalized—where we speak of "choice" at the same time that we speak of "accountability" and "value for money." Here the state becomes a mega corporation and as citizens, we are reduced to customers. We may be told that we come first, but only as customers and less as citizens. Thus, whether in a state-owned NHS hospital in Warwickshire England or Kirkcaldy Scotland, or in a private clinic in downtown Beijing, New York or Chicago, our needs are often balanced between what we choose and what comes *fully-formed* and indeed *informed* by the professional who decides almost always on our own behalf what we should be doing to stay healthy, to succeed professionally, to remain beautiful in old age, to live "the good life," and to go to Heaven!

This notion of human needs is gauged according to provision, which in turn defines what is to be scarce and therefore expensive. If we can afford to pay more for schooling, health, food, and just about everything accordingly, we are prompted and invited to do it in a certain way. Scarcity is an indicator of something valuable, and we hardly heed to what Marx (1990) had to say about the value put on a fetishized commodity, because in all possible manners we have already given our full consent. In fact, we *want*—as we are effectively *schooled*—to be part of the language of myth by which life itself is fetishized. This is almost taken for granted, especially when we know that by dint of scarcity this hierarchic provision does in time fulfil its own prophecy and create an order of satisfied customers.

Even when the cycle is apparently broken and new store chains begin to sell highly fashionable products at lower prices, this creates a new category of needs and a new set of values by which people's tastes and abilities are measured accordingly. Somehow the fetish is reinforced even when one manages to acquire the same commodity at a knockdown price courtesy of global chains like *Walmarts, Marshalls, Target, Maxx* or *Century 21*. The reason for this perpetuation of scarcity (even at knockdown prices) is that an inculcated hierarchy of needs is quickly learnt and absorbed by the consumer—the same consumer who is led to believe that he or she is gainfully autonomous by moving with fashion while paying less.

Likewise, emancipatory attempts become processed and turned on their heads by similar mechanisms. A good example in education is the creation of *free schools* in England by Conservative administrations. Then parents were encouraged to create autonomous schools (funded and supported by the state, and therefore free at the point of provision) in order to fulfil needs that are not provided by mainstream schooling. Yet even if all free schools were progressive schools based on the premise of an emancipatory and critical pedagogy, this new stream of schooling does nothing by way of taking out learning from the paradigm of scarcity. A system of free schooling tends to reinforce scarcity under the false pretext of a plural provision, which in effect is false because the ultimate measure of socialized selection happens wherever a child is being schooled. More so, there's a caveat to the "alternative" nature of free schools. Illich takes his readers through the process:

> Free schools are practical alternatives; they can often be run more cheaply than ordinary schools. (...) Not only are alternatives more widely advocated, they are often at least partially implemented: experimental schools are financed by school boards; the hiring of certified teachers is decentralized; high school credit is given for apprenticeship and college credit, for travel; computer games are given a trial run. (...) Yet all these alternatives operate within predictable limits, since they leave the hidden structure of schools intact. (ADW, pp. 42–43)

These supposedly autonomous bodies become even more effective than mainstream schools in reinforcing a system of measurement and certification that supports the *status quo* from which *free* schools were supposedly meant to *break*. This falls into a cycle by which expected needs are continuously fed against expected measures.

> Free schools, which lead to further free schools in an unbroken chain of attendance, produce the mirage of freedom. Attendance as the result of seduction inculcates the need for specialized treatment more persuasively than reluctant attendance enforced by truant officers. Free school graduates are easily rendered impotent for life in a society that bears little resemblance to the protected gardens in which they have been cultivated. (ADW, p. 43)

Reading *Deschooling Society* retrospectively, through the reflections and discussions that Illich sustained after its publication, and more so revisiting the wide reaction that this radical work got, one would make much more sense of Illich's deeper approach to education. From this, what is meant by a disestablished approach to education becomes clearer. At this stage, it is not that difficult to agree with Illich when he argues that, "[t]he public is indoctrinated to believe that skills are valuable and reliable only if they are the result of formal schooling. The job market depends on making skills scarce and on keeping them scarce, either by proscribing their unauthorized use and transmission or by making things which can be operated and repaired only by those who have access to tools or information which are kept scarce." (DS, p. 89)

Beneath God's Nose

Just as one needs to take a much longer view of how Illich's work has evolved—both in terms of its readership and in how Illich himself reacted to those who engaged with him—to contextualize Illich in expected parameters is almost impossible. This is because as soon as one begins to assume that such parameters are clear or familiar, Illich goes on to deconstruct many received assumptions by statements which come as a surprise even to those who assume to share the tradition that Illich so carefully ascribes to.

Fine examples by which readers are taken unawares are found in Illich's brilliant conversations, especially when captured in audio and video form, where the fast-talking polyglot is given the opportunity to speak and reveal the weave and waft of his complex and creative mind *alla prima*—as it comes, without the aid of cues or prompts (see Illich & Domenach 1972; Illich & Cayley 2014a, 2014b, and 2015). In his conversations with David Cayley, Illich reveals how in his work he seeks to walk beneath nothing less that God's "big" nose:

> Yes, beneath the nose of God. God has a nose as big as mine, seemingly. Lee [Hoinacki] who knows me very well, knows that I haven't tried to do anything else. That's the key for what I've written in my life. You know, people read *Deschooling* twenty years later. Let them look for Thomas Luckmann's book *The Invisible Religion*, and they'll see where it all began. When he speaks about "church" and "faith," I simply put in "school" and "education." At that time, I still identified education with the faith. I wouldn't at this moment. (IC, p. 242)

While some readers might find this surprising, what follows in Illich's approach is even more perplexing, particularly when one tries to read him from outside the realm of his theological world. Illich's is a world that he appears to constantly return to, though he never leaves it for one moment. Illich tells Cayley what he means by "the fact of Western Culture." It is a culture intrinsically articulated by a Christian tradition in whose revelation he finds himself trapped in an aporia by which "the attempt to insure, to guarantee, to regulate Revelation, the best becomes the worst." (IC, p. 242) He explains how Revelation got institutionalized and perverted in the Western polity that still embodies it. This is where Illich insists on the central point of the message of the Samaritan, which he associates with the contemporary Palestinian, in whose kindness Jesus's parable tells us of how enmity is overcome by the love of the stranger, and where even when we all become Samaritan *qua* Palestinian, we freely choose not to ever overlook and less so forsake the Jew lying in the ditch who requires love and a helping hand.

This reversal is only apparent by dint of its aporetic trope. Illich's route of kindness, otherness and love, is to be travelled as an *aporia* that never takes one side against another because it does not operate on dualisms. His aim is to embrace paradox, as this operates in "directions" that become entangled in each other. I would argue that we would find it hard to fully appreciate Illich unless we see this aporetic entanglement as essential to a freedom from dualism and its forced contestation. We would make even less sense of Illich unless we deconstruct the notion of a dialectic that is simply a contradiction between two sides that morph into a third case.

As I see it, Illich's world operates on a combination of dialectical, asymptotic and aporetic possibilities by which his thought and the world that he dreams of do not stop with or against a particular 'side'. One could almost suggest that Illich's is often closer to Spinoza than Hegel or Marx in that his universe is ordered by the possibility of a convivial multitude where contraries inhabit each other's exchanged extensions within one universe, in its inherent and immanent divinity, and which gives sense to contradiction by dint of its possible commonality. Freedom cannot be gained without the other, in that it does not assume a breaking off from the other but is an assertion of each other as other, and therefore the same. In an Epimethean sense this implies a hope that trusts faith "in the goodness of nature" (DS, p. 105). In this renewed sense of hope in faith's divine nature, Illich could well be saying what Spinoza confirms in his *Political Treatise*: "I have laboured carefully, not to mock, lament, or execrate, but to understand human actions." (Spinoza, 1951 I§4, p. 288)

The immanent sense by which Illich poses the convivial meaning to Spinoza's multitude gains a degree of relevance, if not centrality, to his work. Illich states that conviviality is "individual freedom realized in personal interdependence and, as such, an intrinsic ethical value." (TFC, p. 11) To assert this ethical value, Illich's approach denies the privileged ease by which dualistic and triadic contradictions traditionally pit sides against each other. This sense is found in his last paragraph of *Deschooling Society*, which is concluded by his chapter on Epimethean man, where, as we have seen earlier in this book, Illich chooses to discuss Epimetheus rather than his more famous brother Prometheus. Reminding us of Epimetheus's role in the story of Pandora's box (or *jar*, depending on how fussy you are on archaic Greek), Illich takes his readers into the scope and light of Epimetheus's sense of afterthought. In his vision of an Epimethean narrative, afterthought is that which helps us humans care for each other: "We need a name for those who collaborate with their Promethean brother in the lighting of the fire and the shaping of the iron, but who do so to enhance their ability to tend and care and wait upon the other ..." (DS, p. 116; see also Illich & Domenach 1972)

Illich views and names these human beings as Epimetheans. Unlike Prometheans who steal the fire and iron from Zeus to give it to humans, Epimetheans seek to help humans share their existence in the world by making use of what was salvaged by Pandora upon her realizing that nothing of what was lost would ever return except hope itself. This is a radical choice in that Illich 'returns' to a tradition he never left, and by which he asserts the aporias of the old theologians and their classical forebears. Illich's aporia takes the form of an assertive ambiguity:

> I live also with a sense of profound ambiguity. *I can't do without tradition, but I have to recognize that its institutionalization is the root of an evil deeper than any evil I could have known with my unaided eyes and mind.* This is what I would call the West. By studying and accepting the West as the perversion of Revelation, I become increasingly tentative, but also more curious and totally engaged in searching for its origin, which is the voice of him who speaks. It's as simple as that ... childish, if you want, childlike, I hope. (IC, p. 243, emphasis added)

Illich's conclusive qualifier in this conversation cannot be more theological yet equally political. Asked by Cayley whether the perversion and the preservation of Revelation go together, Illich's answer is "Absolutely. That is what the human condition is after the crucifixion. You can't take the crucifixion away if you want to understand where we have arrived at." (IC, ibid.)

"Progressive Conservative"

With the crucifixion presented, as it were, as a concluding qualifier, one could be misled in thinking that Illich is boxing himself into a singular category. The most obvious category would be that of the priest, more so the Catholic priest of Jewish and Gentile parentage who may well have been in conflict with the church, but who retains the *ordo*, or the dogma (understood as a systematic form of monism) of those principles that mark his tradition. Yet this would invariably flare up the dualism that struggles within a passionately progressive yet conservative mind, by which one could then again rest assured or indeed kept at a distance from what he rightly calls his "profound ambiguity."

This may sound close to the designation of a *progressive conservative* by which Angelo Roncalli, otherwise known as Pope John XXIII, has been described when he decided to call the Second Vatican Council which was to change the Catholic Church by taking its message back to its radical foundations. However, this does not exactly make full sense when reading through Ivan Illich's work. While the case of Roncalli, and to some extent his successor, Giovanni Montini, (better known as Paul VI, who had closer dealings with Illich), could go on to sustain an argument where conservative and progressive categories become insufficient, what remains key to Illich's self-confessed ambiguity is in how he remains steadfast within the tradition by taking the Gospel's kenotic pretexts to their radical conclusion. As his lineage remains deeply Catholic, it is also fiercely loyal to the world in which everyone belongs. Again, we can see how he takes Catholicism to its logical conclusion.

This is a central point of both politics and ethics, which the former Anglican Archbishop of Canterbury Rowan Williams made about Pope Francis and the perception of his position within the Catholic tradition:

> This is a point that has relevance well beyond the limits of the Church. We are all easily lured into what might be called "package deal" ethics: if you are committed to one cause you will probably be committed to a particular set of causes, even if there is no clear logical connection. The danger then is of reducing ethics to style, to a set of superficially matching accessories. It is an important jolt for us to have to come to terms with those who look for a deeper kind of consistency – whether they are radical libertarians uniting a pro-choice position with a deeply individualist social morality, or Catholics uniting an

orthodox sexual ethic with root-and-branch hostility to market economics or nuclear arms. It was one of the choice ironies of the era of the Second Vatican Council that the stoutest defender of the inherited position on birth control — Cardinal Alfredo Ottaviani — was also one of the fiercest advocates of nuclear disarmament. Having to think through the connections between our moral perspectives so that we can have intelligent arguments about them is a rather urgent need in the current climate, where policy and principle are so often created reactively and opportunistically. (Do I have any political party especially in mind? Perish the thought.) (Williams 2015, pp. 3–4)

Intriguingly, as Illich himself would recall, it was because of the church's inability to "condemn government for keeping atomic bombs" that he decided to leave his position as advisor in the Second Vatican Council (See Hartch 2015, pp. 64ff).

> I gave [Cardinal] Suenens a little caricature which somebody had drawn up for me. In that cartoon you see five popes, with their characteristic noses, one behind the other, all pointing one finger at one of two objects standing there — an already slightly flaccid penis with a condom filled with semen hanging on it, and an atomic rocket, ready for take off. In the balloon was written, "*It's* against nature!" I am proud to have been and to be associated with, and to be loyal to, an agency, a *worldly* agency, which still has the courage to say, even today, "It's against nature." The finger might be pointing at the wrong object. (IC, pp. 100–101)

In looking "for a deeper kind of consistency," as Williams puts it, one could see how Illich retains his loyalty to a tradition which often makes it different for most of us to understand how and why, in its decisions, the church moves at the speed of glaciers.

Philosophia Perennis

So, what is this tradition that leaves popes and prelates pointing haplessly at flaccid sexual organs dressed in condoms with some disdain? As mentioned earlier in this chapter, to look for a deeper consistency one must take all of this into account while also recalling a philosophical approach that the tradition adopts in its Aristotelian-Thomist configurations of a *philosophia perennis*. Such a desire for a perennial approach of human understanding should be read from the commonality that is held in finding a way to the notion of the Truth. Never a relativist, Illich sustains his deep engagement with a tradition that needs to be understood from within its own aporetic values and therefore from the radical freedoms that it articulates, notwithstanding the reactionary history by which its dogma has been imposed.

Clearly, in the case of Illich's work, this tradition also matters to what he saw as a *method*, which, with the crucifixion as a central signifier, continues to raise questions. If Illich's reader decides to conveniently put aside such an insight, much of the significance of Illich's work will be lost. And I would hasten to add that this would be lost more to non-Catholics than Catholics, who would regard Illich as moving beyond the perceived limits of their faith and traditions.

This is the conscious ambiguity by which Illich does not simply think or write, but also lives as someone who deliberately and consciously chose to reject the political privilege that the church has offered him while retaining the perennial privilege bequeathed him by the tradition that he loved so much. This however could be open to several misinterpretations. I would hasten to add that this perennial privilege must be read as a desire for a kind of continuity that one could (or indeed should) interrupt. As that consummate Catholic philosopher, Frederick Copleston reminds the readers of his monumental *History of Philosophy*, a *philosophia perennis* "did not drop down from Heaven, it grew out of the past." And "[a]gain, if there is a *philosophia perennis*, it is only to be expected that some of its principles should be operative in the minds even of philosophers of modern time, who may seem at first sight to stand far from St. Thomas Aquinas." (Copleston 2003, p. 2)

Beyond his strong and insistent claim to tradition, the hardest to square with Illich's work is his approach to history through the crucifixion, especially when most of the time Illich is not writing as a theologian (or is he?). To those who may be somewhat familiar with Catholic discourse this could come across as an offshoot of liberation theology, which though plausible, is not entirely the case. To those who might read Illich's claim from a wider Christian perspective, it might even come across as an effort to bring down the crucifixion from the altars to take to the community. This might give a sense that verges on the Protestant traditions by which personal freedom and piety emerge from within a convivial context as a communal church that rejects a traditional hierarchy. Thirdly, there could be an argument which remains outside the Christian tradition, and where Illich's references are often read as a discourse that may well be grounded in a theological origin, but which moves beyond it.

I would argue that while there may well be a number of plausible arguments, in all three positions there is a distortion of Illich's own, original, approach to what caught his critical interest in the world. Reading Illich from any of these perspectives would fail the reader from appreciating the singular way by which he seeks to present a case that intrinsically defies those identitarian habits by which we so often cut corners and articulate one position in terms of what appears to share some elements of others. In rejecting this identitarian approach, I would argue that Illich comes closer to Adorno and Horkheimer (1990) in their dialectical logic, than to Gustavo Gutierrez (1998) in his radical theology.

On the first possible connection—which often mistakes Illich for being a theologian of liberation—one could say that Illich *does* engage in forms of theological thinking that regard the crucifixion as a profound image of struggle and where the Christ-event denotes a form of defiance towards power. Given Illich's declared attachment to the tradition and his friendship with liberation theologians like Gutierrez and Helder Camara, liberation theology may well appear to have an influence on his work. However, this cannot be taken as an easy shortcut into reading his theological work. To say so is highly problematic, not only in view of his relationship with the church and some of the missionary work that evolved in Latin America in the 1960s (see CCD, pp. 23–45 and CoA, pp. 53–94), but also because Illich's work defies any attempt to draw strict connections with such a lineage. Interestingly, insofar as one could regard Illich as a radical, his position differed (sometimes *radically*) from such an expected lineage. As Todd Hartch's historical study of the relationship of Illich's work with theology and the church shows, Illich's relationship with liberation theology was neither directly consequential and less so consistent or harmonious (See Hartch 2015, esp. chapters 4 & 6). More so, Illich's work is never marked by a consistent support towards any particular group, though he always seemed closer to some theologians more than others.

Secondly, with regards to a protestant reading of his work, Illich's sense of belonging to a small "c" *catholic* outlook in almost anything he did or studied, draws a neat distance from the notion of an unmediated engagement with the divine *logos* that became human. His sense of communion places the individual at the center of a convivial context that articulates *in se* a mediated approach to both faith and politics. Hence any argument for a small "p" *protestantism* in Illich's work becomes a *non sequitur*, especially when the immanence by which he partakes of the notion of reality strongly articulates a critique of capitalism and with it the Protestant ethic that moves it. Illich deems what mediates a community as being convivial, where, as we have seen above, freedom is gained by tools that would, "limit this freedom only in favor of another member's equal freedom." (TFC, p. 12)

Thirdly, it would be difficult to secularize Illich from his theological references because the notion of what is secular or laic in the trajectory of his work (two terms which, as we have seen, are not always synonymous), cannot be approached as a simple act of negation or omission. In its original state, secularization is often shaped by what is being secularized. In dialectical terms, one could distance Illich from theology as well as any other foundational appropriation of the tradition—be it progressive or conservative—while at the same time the theological underpinning of his work cannot be dismissed or ignored.

As Rowan Williams reminds us, the designation of progressive and conservative, left or right, "can be an alibi for lazy thinking" particularly when we forget the methodological contexts by which we draw such distinctions.

> "[C]onservative" and "progressive" imply that we all know there is one road for everyone on which we may move forward or backwards, rapidly or slowly. It doesn't hurt to be reminded from time to time that *this assumption can be an alibi for lazy thinking*. The Catholic tradition of ethics and theology sets out a model of what is abidingly good and life-giving for human beings which does not depend on this model of a single road towards a given future. It is about making choices that bring you closer or otherwise to a particular vision of human well-being; and those choices do not necessarily map directly on to other, familiar taxonomies. (Williams 2015, p. 3, emphasis added)

In Illich, *laïcité* as a form of disestablishment is not an ideology but a profound methodological route by which one gains the necessary distance, indeed the *epoché*, that would give us ample space to engage with the plural nature of the world. To understand Illich, what matters is how distance and bracketing would, in effect, trace one's trajectory onto a tradition that will in turn inaugurate a process of disestablishment.

Without understanding his close engagement with tradition, Illich's direction remains estranged from customary expectations. Specific assignations of exclusive belonging would be problematic, not only with regards to how we read Illich but more so vis-à-vis the subjects that he covers. Somehow, when confronted with Illich's work, I keep recalling Arendt's argument about plurality when she argues that it is because we are all the same (via *natality*) that we are different (via *plurality*) (Arendt 1998, pp. 8–11).

The Convivial Challenge

Key to Illich's work is the manner by which he frames the human condition within conviviality. To be wholly engaged in a sense of community is to recognize the immanence—that is the sense of interiority—by which one understands how moments of liberation and emancipation cannot be severed from *sacrifice*.

Liberation is a form of action that does not simply represent an outlook that prevails over another. If there is to be an overtaking of the manner by which a community comes to be, this must, as tradition shows, bring together both a contemplative and an active life; or to put it simply, both theory and practice. Yet action and contemplation could only intersect at a moment of sacrifice, which could take various forms—be they religious or political, personal or public—and where there is always a sense of *emptying*; a letting-go of the presumptions of both certainty or superiority. Tradition bears this out radically through an understanding of liberation that comes by virtue of *kenosis*, a *lowering* that, far from being a form of belittling, is a way to achieve the inner nobility of what we recognize in our shared juncture between contemplation and action, awareness and reform qua *re*-form.

This is where the Crucifixion becomes a central signifier of Illich's puzzle. It is an event in history that sustains the tradition while opening it to what is to come from the vantage point of the ultimate kenotic moment, indeed the ultimate sacrifice. From the lens of kenosis, the tradition is not just a lineage of images or texts, dogmas or edicts. The tradition remains profoundly embedded in a history that we elect together as a horizon of affirmation, characterized by continuous questioning; indeed, a faith prompted by doubt and curiosity. It is only by such a kenotic approach to what we are and who we consider ourselves to be in our convivial ways that history will have meaning for us as individuals within a community. Histories that emerge from collective hubris, and therefore a sense of superiority and exclusion, only elevate the vested interests of the few. In effect such histories are myths intent on justifying oppression while rejecting the very sense of community on which they claim to take pride.

True to a perennial reading of history, the attention to what is convivially possible must come from those outlooks that remain centered on the place of kenosis. As will be discussed in the chapter on reform (see Chapter 6, below) the relationship between history and kenosis emerges on an assumption of *origin* that is understood as a perennial affirmation of iterative beginnings sustained by possibility. For an iteration of origin to articulate a horizon of diverse possibilities, it requires that we create and sustain a continuous narrative of forms through the arts, letters, sciences, politics and religion in order to articulate reform as *re*-form—that is, as a continuous *return* to that by which a sense of renewal surpasses the mono-directional notion of progress as understood in its positivistic definition. Likewise, this equally rejects any assumption of origin which is held hostage to conservative and reactionary myths by which history is reduced to a one-dimensional and destructive affair. Ultimately kenosis is a way of being that recognizes in history a perpetually diverse horizon of plural events.

While Christians would have to argue that kenosis is crowned by the episode of Jesus's crucifixion, as otherwise the Resurrection—whether corporeal or spiritual—would make no sense, the kenotic aspiration by which a convivial society could become possible is not unique to the Christian tradition. Rather, it has to do with a world outlook where poverty is central to the narrative of living. Addressing the Episcopal Church's *Christian Social Relations* Conference in Puerto Rico's San Juan in 1967, Illich argues that the church "challenges us to deeper poverty instead of security in achievements; personalization of love (chastity) instead of depersonalization by idolatry; faith in the other rather than prediction." (CCD, p. 19)

The kenotic tradition is already strongly preconfigured by Judaism, to which Illich is equally attached and without which one could never move towards (and even beyond) Christianity itself. In *The Great Transformation*, Karen Armstrong presents the prophet Amos as an embodied example of kenosis:

> Amos felt that his subjectivity had been taken over by God. He was not speaking his own words, but Yahweh's; the prophet had left himself behind in passionate empathy with his God, who had experienced the injustice committed by Israel as a personal humiliation. (Armstrong 2006, p. 89)

Given that Christianity followed on from the Jewish tradition, knowing how kenosis played a continuous role during moments of historical change, particularly where secularism emerged from Christianity itself, shouldn't be difficult. This is attested by how the kenotic approach re-emerges in the politics of modernity—particularly through the emergence of socialism; and that of philosophy at the very moment when modernity returns to its own ascendancy (see Lyotard 1989). While in the former the claim was for convivial communities that would gain their ground, with the demise of socialism the very notion of a ground is challenged by the fluidity of interpretation (Vattimo 1995 and Gadamer 1976) and a new kenotic moment is identified (Vattimo 1988) as a substitute of the certainties by which humanity continues to face violence, oppression and a quest for forms of disestablished meanings.

One is tempted to remark that what causes this cycle of disestablishment is the perennial condition by which human thinking continues to emerge in perpetual ascendancy albeit confessed in full doubt. This is a major challenge, especially when the assumptions of certainty—as we have seen above with regards to scarcity and its effect on the shaping of education, health and commodities—becomes a matter of being, indeed an ontological problem. As Illich states in *Tools for Conviviality*:

> Most people have staked their self-images in the present structure and are unwilling to lose their ground. They have found security in one of the several ideologies that support further industrialization. They feel compelled to push the illusion of progress on which they are hooked. They long for and expect increased satisfaction, with less input of human energy and with more division of competence. *They value handicraft and personal care as luxuries, but the ideal of a more labor-intensive, yet modern, production process seems to them quixotic and anachronistic.* (TFC, p. 44, emphasis added)

The ambivalent relationship with tradition—*made* or otherwise *found*—is evident in the dilemma that Illich portrays with the relationship between an assumed present and a mystified past. Tradition comes to mediate what we perceive to be the world and how we seek to live in it. This would cut both ways and is mostly approached with a nostalgic reaction to a "past" that never was. In as much as history makes sense to us and provides us with the tools by which we could create meaning, tradition is an essential part of that history which is not simply a series of stories that tell us what actually occurred or may have happened. As another Williams, this time not the Archbishop of Canterbury, but the Welsh Marxist novelist, critic and academic Raymond Williams (1967, p. 16) put it, "tradition is not the past but an interpretation of the past: a selection and valuation of ancestors, rather than a neutral record."

More than the past or history per se, what matters in tradition are the *valuation* and *selection* of the tools that were left to us by our ancestors. But this cannot be assumed as given, especially when the present is squeezed between myths of progress and displaced nostalgia. In this selection we cannot claim to remain neutral, let alone disinterested. A neutral assumption for tradition would only leave us with an unquestioned meta-narrative, approached without tools and simply assumed by *other* traditions that leave us tool-less—which, in Illich's world outlook, would also mean that we are left powerless.

Reading through Illich one finds how to clarify and bring together those selected aspects of the tradition by which tools are created or provided to help us do something and to be *who we are*, rather than *what we are made to be* in order to fulfil the needs of the system's machinery. He does this by bringing tradition back to us in ways that we have never imagined as being possible. This is not a closed historical heritage, but a tradition from which one partakes a diverse yet immanent sense of meaning. More importantly, meaning's immanent diversity presents us with methodological possibilities that help us gain the necessary distance from matters at hand; matters that are often too close and too ingrained in our ways of thinking and doing.

Abbreviations: Works by Illich

ADW   *After Deschooling, What?*
CCD   *The Church, Change and Development*
CoA   *Celebration of Awareness*
DS   *Deschooling Society.*
IC   *Ivan Illich In Conversation.*
RNF   *The Rivers North of the Future*
SW   *Shadow Work.*
TFC   *Tools for Conviviality.*
VT   *In the Vineyard of the Text*

References

Adorno, T. W. (1990). *Negative Dialectics.* London: Routledge.
Adorno, T. W. & Horkheimer, M. (1990). *Dialectic of Enlightenment.* New York: Continuum.
Arendt, H. (1998). *The Human Condition.* Chicago, IL: The University of Chicago Press.
Armstrong, K. (2006). *The Great Transformation. The World in the Time of Buddha, Socrates, Confucius and Jeremiah.* London: Atlantic Books.
Baldacchino, J. (2018). *Art as Unlearning: Towards a Mannerist Pedagogy.* London: Routledge.
Biesta, G. (2006). *Beyond Learning: Democratic Education for a Human Future.* Boulder, CO: Paradigm Publishers.
Copleston, F. (2003). *A History of Philosophy. Volume 1. Greece and Rome.* London: Bloomsbury.
Gadamer, H. G. (1976). *Philosophical Hermeneutics.* S.E. Linge (ed. & trans.). Berkeley: University of California Press.
Gutierrez, G. (1988). *A Theology of Liberation: History, Politics, and Salvation.* Maryknoll, NY: Orbis Books.
Hartch, T. (2015). *The Prophet of Cuernavaca: Ivan Illich and the Crisis of the West.* New York, NY: Oxford University Press.

Husserl, E. (2014). *Ideas for a Pure Phenomenology and Phenomenological Philosophy. First Book: General Introduction to Pure Phenomenology*. Indianapolis, IN: Hackett.
Illich, I. (1970). *The Church, Change and Development*. F. Eychaner (ed.). Chicago: Urban Training Center Press. (CCD)
Illich, I. (1974). *After Deschooling, What?* London: Writers' and Readers' Publishing Cooperative. (ADW)
Illich, I. (1981). *Shadow Work*. New York: M. Boyars. (SW)
Illich, I. (1993). *In the Vineyard of the Text: A Commentary to Hugh's Didascalicon*. Chicago, IL: University of Chicago Press. (VT)
Illich, I. (2001). *Tools for Conviviality*. New York: Marion Boyars. (TFC)
Illich, I. (2012a). *Celebration of Awareness: A Call for Institutional Revolution*. New York: Marion Boyars. (CoA)
Illich, I. (2012b). *Deschooling Society*. New York: Marion Boyars. (DS)
Illich, I. & Cayley, D. (1992). *Ivan Illich in Conversation*. Toronto: House of Anansi Press. (IC)
Illich, I. & Cayley, D. (2005). *The Rivers North of the Future: The Testament of Ivan Illich*. Toronto: House of Anansi Press. (RNF)
Illich, I. & Cayley, D. (2014a). *The Corruption of Christianity: Ivan Illich on Gospel, Church and Society*. Cayley, D., Podcasts. Accessed: May 4, 2019, http://www.davidcayley.com/podcasts/category/Ivan+Illich
Illich, I. & Cayley, D. (2014b). *Part Moon, Part Travelling Salesman: Conversations with Ivan Illich*. Cayley, D., Podcasts. Accessed: May 30, 2019, http://www.davidcayley.com/podcasts/category/Ivan+Illich
Illich, I. & Cayley, D. (2015). *Life as Idol*. Cayley, D., Podcasts. Accessed: May 3, 2019, http://www.davidcayley.com/podcasts/category/Ivan+Illich
Illich, I. & Domenach, J. M. (1972). Video interview. *Un certain regard* series. Institut National de l'Ausiovisuel. Accessed: May 5, 2019, https://www.ina.fr/video/CPF86658011/ivan-illich-video.html
Ladner, G. B. (1959). *The Idea of Reform Its Impact on Christian Thought and Action in the Age of the Fathers*. Cambridge, MA: Harvard University Press.
Luckmann, T. (1967). *The Invisible Religion. The Problem of Religion in Modern Society*. New York: Macmillan.
Lyotard, J. F. (1989). *The Postmodern Condition: A Report on Knowledge*. Manchester: Manchester University Press.
Marx, K. (1990). *Capital: A Critique of Political Economy*. London; New York, NY: Penguin Books.
Rocha, S. D. (2017). *Tell Them Something Beautiful*. Eugene, OR: Cascade Books.
Rubinoff, L. (ed.) (1971). *Tradition and Revolution*. Toronto: Macmillan of Canada; New York: St. Martin's Press.
Spinoza, B. (1951). *Political Treatise. The Chief Works of Benedict de Spinoza*. New York: Dover Publications.
Vattimo, G. (1988). *Dialettica, differenza, pensiero debole*. [Dialectics, difference and weak thought]. *Il Pensiero Debole* [Weak Thought]. G. Vattimo & P. A. Rovatti (eds.) Milano: Feltrinelli, pp. 12–28.
Vattimo, G. (1995). *Oltre l'Interpretazione*. [Beyond Interpretation]. Bari: Laterza.

Williams, R. (1967). *Modern Tragedy*. Stanford, CA: Stanford University Press.
Williams, R. (2015). Pope of the masses: Is Francis really the people's champion? *New Statesman*. 10 September. Accessed: 10 October 2015, http://www.newstatesman.com/politics/religion/2015/09/pope-masses-francis-really-people-s-champion

· 5 ·
LEARNING

In *Tools for Conviviality*, Illich argues that "[a] society constructed so that education by means of schools is a necessity for its functioning cannot be a just society." (TFC, pp. 41–42) He comes to this conclusion after stating that the premise of a just society is liberty, though here liberty is not abstracted into an absolute and irreducible state, but where "a just society would be one in which liberty for one person is constrained only by the demands created by *equal liberty for another*." (TFC p. 41, emphasis added) Illich would appear to equate liberty with equality, though to say so needs further qualification.

In formulating the notion of *equaliberty*, Etienne Balibar (1994, p. 50) argues that this equating is "indispensable to the modern, 'subjective' recasting of right, but is powerless to guarantee its institutional stability," adding that a mediation is required, which could well take "the antithetical forms of 'fraternity' (or community) and 'property.'" In a way, Illich would have agreed, though in his case, the mediation would probably be closer than fraternity through what he identifies with the conviviality by which such a form of liberty is sustained by equality and vice-versa. "Such a society requires as a precondition an agreement excluding tools that by their very nature prevent such liberty," Illich adds, and this will be "true for tools that are fundamentally purely social arrangements, *such as the school system*, as well as for tools that are physical machines." (TFC, p. 41 emphasis added)

Equality, Liberty and Meaning

Equality could never sustain liberty in a context where advantages and privileges find themselves embedded in systems that may initially appear to be egalitarian but ultimately run counter to any sense of fairness, let alone social justice. Just as liberty does not stand on its own as an irreducible category, equality per se cannot remain unqualified, particularly when freedom is articulated in a context of human and social relationships that aspire to be convivial in tenor and more so in practice. In this context, Illich places the school as a good example of the challenges to equaliberty, though the school is only one of many tools that facilitate inequality:

> In a convivial society compulsory and open-ended schooling would have to be excluded for the sake of justice. Age-specific, compulsory competition on an unending ladder for lifelong privileges cannot increase equality but must favor those who start earlier, or who are healthier, or who are better equipped outside the classroom. Inevitably, it organizes society *into many layers of failure*, with each layer inhabited by dropouts schooled to believe that those who have consumed more education deserve more privilege because they are more valuable assets to society as a whole. A society constructed so that education by means of schools is a necessity for its functioning *cannot be a just society*. (TFC, pp. 41–42, emphasis added)

Illich blows up several myths, some of which often come from quarters that one would expect to be on the left of politics where the premise of equality is assumed as a point of departure and ultimately as a precondition for liberty. Conversely, in bringing together equality and liberty, Illich is also critiquing those who, from a positioning of the right, would sustain that liberty is a precondition of any assumption of equality and fairness. In throwing in the caveat of a convivial society where both liberty and equality cannot be untangled, Illich not only runs in parallel with Balibar's notion of equaliberty, but he also qualifies it in a way that he stands beyond what is customarily expected from across the political horizon.

Illich owes this approach to Thomas Luckmann. In his sociological discussion of the anthropological condition of religion, Luckmann asks, "How are subjective processes objectivated in society? How are social objectivated phenomena institutionalized and what are the functions of institutionalization?

How do institutionalization and objectivation, once they have produced social realities, affect the subjective processes in which institutionalization and objectivation are rooted?" (Luckmann 1967, p. 44) As Illich has often recognized Luckmann's *The Invisible Religion* as one of the major influences in his critique of education and schooling in *Deschooling Society*, one could, through a reading of Luckmann, begin to better understand Illich's perspective on the school system as one of those tools which are conceived as fundamentally pertaining to "purely social arrangements." (TFC, p. 41)

Luckmann begins to engage with the implications that he sets by his question "How are subjective processes objectivated in society?" by arguing that in the first place, "[o]bjectifications are the products of subjective activities that become available as elements in a common world both to their producers and to other men." (Luckmann 1967, p. 44) However, here he is not simply proposing subjective experience as a mere reflection, but as pertaining to a spatiotemporal reading of the world that is neither restrictive nor simply symbolic of a straightforward state of affairs. Bearing in mind that he is speaking of religious social formations in the sense of the human organizational product of religious thinking, Luckmann qualifies this by stating that "[w]hile expressions are available only in face-to-face situations, objectivations serve as indices of meaning outside such limitations of space and time." This makes such observations "social" and "since the construction of symbolic universes as systems of meaning occurs by means of objectivations, it is evident that we cannot consider them as a summation of isolated subjective processes." (Luckmann 1967, p. 44)

As Luckmann moves on to ask how institutionalization occurs, and as this becomes a question of meaning as well as social organization, one would recall how in Illich the idea of institutionalization is not simply equated with a matter of social organization. Institutionalization transcends the expected mechanistic approaches by which humans buy into what operates on their subjectivities in ways that are far from being simply estranged or alienated—which is what structuralists have invariably argued. Reading Luckmann, one realizes where Illich is coming from: "The objectivation of a symbolic universe as a system of meaning presupposes that the subjective experiences entering into its construction be meaningful. The meaningful quality of subjective experience, however, is a product of social processes." (Luckmann 1967, pp. 44–45)

So far so good, although one cannot assume that Luckmann the sociologist is simply finding a way to fit in the process of meaning from a simple constructivist assumption. Luckmann also wears a hermeneutic hat and he does not need to deny that he is focused on religion and its anthropological condition. Thus, he argues that "[s]ubjective experience considered in isolation is restricted to mere actuality and is void of meaning. Meaning is not an inherent quality of subjective processes but is bestowed on it in interpretive acts. In such acts a subjective process is grasped retrospectively and located in an interpretive scheme." He then adds what I would consider as a crucial qualification: "The interpretive scheme is necessarily distinct from ongoing experience. If we may use the term in its most elementary sense we may say that the interpretive scheme 'transcends' ongoing experience." (Luckmann 1967, p. 45) This is where Luckmann distinguishes himself as not only a sociologist of religion but as someone who is ready to engage with (not without the risk of) entering the spaces of interpretation while moving away from the merely experienced by which more than an empiricist has found him or herself dragged down the currents of positivism. This is how he approaches the delicate balance between subjective experiences and their subsequent objective travelling within and over the institutional terrain. It is also important to note that later he qualifies his argument, stating that "a human organism could not detach itself, on its own, from ongoing experience and interpret it in the light of past experience." (Luckmann 1967, p. 46)

> Interpretive schemes result from sedimented past experiences. The relation between experience, its meaning and interpretive scheme is reciprocal and dynamic. The meaning of experience is derived from the relation of ongoing processes to the scheme of interpretation. Conversely, ongoing experiences modify the interpretive scheme. The very possibility of successive experience being sedimented in a scheme distinct from any actual experience rests upon a certain degree of detachment. Such detachment cannot originate in a simple succession of isolated subjective processes. Now it is true that a genuinely isolated subjective process is inconceivable. At the very least, each ongoing experience has a temporal horizon of past and anticipated experiences. (Luckmann 1967, p. 45)

It is advisable to keep Luckmann on one's side while reading through Illich's critique of education. This is because Illich treats schools as human organisms that are neither detached nor reduced to categories (like liberty, equality, justice) that are isolated from each other in either meaning or social relation. Like Luckmann, Illich puts great weight on the interpretive processes by which the analysis of these organisms is played; which is where he is often misconstrued when others try to read him from perspectives that seem to ignore (purposively or naively) his interest in the condition by which social organisms such as the school, share the same context by which religion remains an anthropological and by implication a human condition. This constitutes a *philosophical* anthropology that recognizes the transcendental qualities by which humans are valued and in turn value each other.

Theory, Choice and Common Sense

Damned Assumptions

Everyone has an opinion on the relationship between learning, education and schooling. Based on common-held expectations, the common—rather *damned*—assumption is that learning is mostly attributed to growth and to the idea of moving from a state of not knowing to a state of knowing, from one stage of development to another. Learning is commonly expected to be "progressive." To state that one "is learning" or that one "has learnt" means that one moves sequentially from x to y to z; from a state of not knowing y, to a state of knowing that y is $x+1$ or $z-1$.

Conditioned on this sequential assumption education is broadly regarded as articulating a diversity of forms of learning through identifiable organized processes, though what that actually means varies according to how one would view this process—mostly from one's own experience; and whether the process itself confirms or defies such a sequential logic of growth. This also means that education might have to do with *how* and in what *context* we *do* or *must* learn to know y. This gives way to nuanced arguments over why we concluded that y is $x+1$, and whether it is true to say that this is the same as $z-1$ or indeed $z-x$, depending on the value of x and z.

However, this becomes contentious when it attempts to define what learning and schooling may or may not have in common, given that the latter assumes and somehow limits the former. This is especially the case when a curricularized assumption of education is forced as some sort of legal conditioning on who is considered to be "a *learned* person," that is, as someone who has had enough *learning* to be measured adequately against the standards set by a schooled society. Questions on education are often normative and pretty loaded with answers. An argument for or against certain kinds of education is judgmental and unavoidably controversial. It is almost natural—though not necessarily correct—to relate one's view of education to one's own experience. What does it mean to be educated? What is a bad education and what would a successful education imply? In some languages and cultures "being *educated*" also means "being *polite*" and knowing how to distinguish between private and public spheres of behavior. The wider the range of options, the wider and stronger range of opinions will thrive.

When it comes to schooling the issue moves from the generic to the personal and on to the public sphere. As the ultimate institutionalized moment of one's own learning and by which one is deemed to "have an education," schooling designates the public dimension of what it means to learn and become educated. Here the notion of choice is used only to veil what invariably is an *ought* in the manner of an educational imperative. The generic and personal spheres of learning and education become institutionalized, even when schooling may well be a domestic affair as in the case of home schooling. We know that theories and debates on learning, education, and schooling are complex and they cut across and go in all directions. Some would simply dismiss what I have just sketched and seek to provide other ways of describing how *learning*, *education* and *schooling* work together. Both positions would make equal sense. But here I do not want to enter a debate on whether we are actually speaking of a three-legged stool or a bench that is far sturdier.

Even when elaborate theory and argument are involved; even when progressive, liberal and critical positions take turns in confronting what they see as traditional and conservative forms of education; what matters in one's experience of learning, education and schooling is conveniently missed. Far from making do with a commonsensical view of education without resorting to analysis and argument, the point is that whether discussed in a pub, in a PTA meeting, in the classroom, on social media, or during an international symposium, a case for (or against) education cannot be ascertained by any measure or reason. If anything, not unlike art, when one defines education or learning, let alone schools, one would be better off starting from what they *are not*. Better still, when dealing with learning, education and the school, the argument would be more useful if we were to start from where they *shouldn't* be.

Opinionated Evidence

In a discussion on BBC Radio 4 between a Minister of Education and a parent who was campaigning for more flexibility for British families to have the choice to take their children out of schools during term time for other than emergencies, a BBC anchor premised his first question to the parent by stating that unless "one is brainless" we all agree that everyone should go to school (See BBC 2015). The parent agreed, as did the Minister who in turn insisted that "evidence shows" that a week missed from school could badly affect a child's performance in her exams.

Sustained by this kind of "evidence," a claim to "common sense," and a priority for testing, this discussion offered no space for real dissent when it came to education, let alone schooling. There was not even a moment when one could broach the idea or pose the question as to why should everyone be schooled in such a sustained manner. Why shouldn't there be flexibility and real choice when it comes to schooling and what parents want for their children? Is it so *brainless* to think that regular sustained schooling may not be essential for education or learning?

At this stage in the history of education I cannot see how there will be any other answer to such questions. It would repeat the tautology that without schools a child's education will suffer because learning is impaired and will not take place. As I call this argument a tautology, I realize that my thinking is trapped in the three-legged stool analogy by presuming that we cannot leave behind the notion that learning, education and schooling complement each other because they form part of the same *thing*.

If we care about schools, education and learning, a lot of our assumptions have to give way to lateral methods by which we approach them. We cannot assume that one leads to the other seamlessly, even when this perception has long entered into popular folklore. There are many reasons for this. Firstly, this confusion is historic and it effectively weakens the very same argument for what learning, education and schooling, in their different implications, could well mean. Secondly, we cannot forget that schooling, as it is presently organized and made to function, is entirely constructed on socio-economic and political assumptions, and therefore it goes on to perpetuate the same socio-economic issues that we have to confront. Thirdly, though it is a service located within the public sector, education seems to have to endure a continuous state of change which often does more harm than good. Fourthly, the point of schooling let alone universal education, is never questioned and less so dismissed as only one of many possibilities for what learning is assumed to be.

While politically it is more than expedient to accept schooling as a social imperative (because we know that such talk is broadly hegemonic), to claim that this imperative is what strengthens the case for learning, education and schools is to weaken them in their permutated contexts. The major obstacle to this opening is that society itself has become schooled. This means that there is no way that one could move out of a cycle where one's education and learning are unquestionably institutionalized in the first place.

The Three-Legged Stool

If we begin to disassemble the proverbial stool and its three legs, we are not only faced with a degree of difficulty (because we are equipped with inappropriate tools), but we are very unlikely to do so because we think that this will ultimately question our own education. In questioning the three-legged stool, we are accused of deconstructing ourselves, because education has become an *ontological* question. We are left with a tedious question that amounts to whether we can, at any point, think or act outside one's own state of being, when in effect, one could only define oneself by the very same state of being. Hermeneutically speaking, schooling has become the only narrative by which one could interpret it, which seems to imply that only through schooling could one deschool society.

As we follow Gramsci and speak of education as belonging to a hegemonic system—if not being a hegemonic expression in itself (see Gramsci 1967, pp. 217ff)—we tend to forget that hegemonies, as Laclau (1996) reminds us, are a matter of subtle dialectical procedures whose logic operates on truth values that are not only tautological by intention, but whose meanings are antinomic by dint of what lies behind their contrarian logic. This becomes evident even when we begin to take apart the process by which liberal and social democracies claim to have achieved those forms of emancipation by which the individual and universal spheres come to be mutually related. Similarly, the case for education as that ontological referent of learning within a schooled society is in and of itself not only historical, but also dialectically bound to what we claim to consent freely through common sense. Here the problem is not common sense *per se*—which some regard as too hasty and uncritical—but the realization that this method of common sense lacks the very spontaneity, freedom and unmediated agility by which we could ever claim it.

To argue, like the BBC anchor, that one would be brainless to state that not everyone should go to school, is to come to accept that even common sense must be schooled. This predicates freedom on a conditioned *choice* that may well be educated but which remains unfree, where being educated implies a measure that is assumed on socio-economic and political ends. As we speak of a schooled society, we mean a society that *becomes* the School. Schooled societies leave us with no choice of exiting let alone the right to avoid society's space even when we are supposedly educated enough to claim such an ability (and freedom).

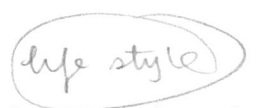

This, Illich argues, comes to the point where "a desirable future depends on our deliberately choosing a life of action over a life of consumption, on our engendering a life style which will enable us to be spontaneous, independent, yet related to each other, rather than maintaining a life style which only allows us to make and unmake, produce and consume—a style of life which is merely a way station on the road to the depletion and pollution of the environment." (DS, p. 52) Reading this against the scenario offered by Luckmann in his philosophical anthropology of human organizations it seems to me that Illich's point here is not *when* we *will* but rather *if* we *could* or even are *allowed* to make such a choice.

Kant's Futuring

To begin to challenge the "common sense" argument for education, here I follow in Illich's method and jump back by a couple of centuries, to Kant. In *On Education*, Kant initially appears to presume what education is and should be with far too much certainty. His approach to education appears to be tightly teleological, underlined by the certitude of a moral assumption by which learning moves from the necessary discipline to "sit still" until one gets to a notion of judgment which also appears to conform to the same practical reason that prompts it; a notion of judgment premised by the good. Yet, as one reads through, Kant also comes up with surprises, no less odd, yet no less contemporary to the 21st century reader.

At some point Kant speaks of discipline where he appears to advocate for a blunt form of schooling. He then moves on to insist on the need for experimental education where one gets the feeling that Kant even anticipates some of what Illich had to say about learning. Today it would sound odd to state that "[o]ne of the greatest problems of education is how to unite submission to the necessary, restraint with the child's capability of exercising his free will—for restraint is necessary." (Kant 1900, §29, p. 27) But then again, Kant's actual question is: "How am I to develop the sense of freedom in spite of the restraint?" (ibid.)

"Restraint?", one might ask. Why couch discipline in such a manner when one wants to speak of freedom? While it is tempting to suggest that this is just a turn of phrase from a bygone era, it would be a mistake to do so. This is because Kant is after something more substantial that has to do with the problematic of learning and how often education and learning are presumed to lead from each other, when in effect if they were to simply follow a causal sequence this would only yield a mechanistic process. Those who are somewhat familiar with Kant also know that the primacy of freedom here does not come as an *outcome* of restraint or discipline. Freedom prefigures everything and is assumed *a priori* through the primacy of intelligence and how we, as rational beings, predicate (and are in turn predicated by) the truth. Thus, while reading Kant might need some guidance, there is also an expectation that education must be untangled from a causal notion of learning.

Kant argues that "[o]ne principle of education which those men especially who form educational schemes should keep before their eyes is this—children ought to be educated, not for the present, but for a possibly *improved condition of man in the future*." (Kant 1900, §15, p. 14, emphasis added) This does not seem to be particularly radical. The point, however, is that Kant makes this argument by way of negating any causal approach to education. It is how Kant describes this future that even today will make considerable difference to those insisting on learning as a fixed category of progression. He goes on to explain how a possibly improved future comes "in a manner which is adapted to *the idea of humanity and the whole destiny of man*." (Kant 1900, §15, p. 14, emphasis added)

> This principle is of great importance. Parents usually educate their children merely in such a manner that, however bad the world may be, they may adapt themselves to its present conditions. But they ought to give them an education so much better than this, that a better condition of things may thereby be brought about in the future. (Kant 1900, §15, p. 14)

In anticipating the future, Kant is suggesting that education cannot create a future in the manner of the present. This is again a point that Kant brings in when he implicitly critiques the replication of experience, where rather than learn the coordinates of space and time, these come to us *a priori*. One must not forget Kant's argument that we come cognitively equipped with the concepts of space and time, which means that we are able to transcend that which is given in experience. In other words, we are critical beings rather than simply experiential learners.

If one were to read *On Education* without recalling Kant's aprioristic concept of space and time, this point is missed for what might even appear to be a conservative stance in Kant's presumption of education as an expected point of amelioration. The latter is easily confused—or misinterpreted—to be a necessary restraint by which a kind of passive progress emerges from discipline, followed by experimentation, and back to forms of a moral order of education that is mostly presumed by an *ought* that would reinforce learning. In Kant's idealist logic, the ordering may feel odd and back to front to the empiricist's position that expects learning to follow as a consequence of experience and its accumulated processes of evaluation. A closer reading, which would abide by the sequence of the idealist's logic (that does not simply follow mechanistic forms of causality but which anticipates the cause by its end, its *telos*) Kant's theory of learning is already premised by a critical narrative that is far more radical than we customarily expect.

Reading Kant on education often gives the feeling of a conservative assumption of unquestioned, quasi Whiggish, form of progress qua amelioration. Yet a hermeneutic reading of *On Education* confirms the opposite. Far from following a conservative route to education, he follows up on the power of judgment. While he argues that "[t]he prospect of a theory of education is a glorious ideal, and it matters little if we are not able to realise it at once" (Kant 1900, §8, p. 8), he does not imply that we should give up on seeking new forms of transformation that transcend the current context. The point of theory in Kant is never mechanical. Less so is it detached from reality.

We get a glimpse of how Kant transcends the expected divisions between theory and practice, understanding and experience, when he moves to the point of questioning whether education is an art or a science. It is the question that any contemporary of Kant's would ask about everything. "Education is an art which can only become perfect through the practice of many generations." (Kant 1900, §11, p. 10) Yet, the generational issue is flawed, as he already indicates from the start. This art must have two alternatives: it is either mechanically reproduced by instrumentally perpetuating the agenda of the now to the future, or it is a matter of judgment—by which human beings are able to mediate the particular with the universal. As he puts it in his third *Critique*: "Judgement makes possible the transition from the realm of the concept of nature to that of the concept of freedom." (Kant 1974, §IX, p. 41) This cannot be clearer, in that the power of judgment that we exercise through reason allows us to move from what we experience to what we conceive and thereby own freely as rational beings. But what does judgment really mean beyond a simplistic assumption of *learning b* from experiencing *a*, as opposed to anticipating and thus negating the limitations of *a* by asserting *b*?

"All education which is merely mechanical must carry with it many mistakes and deficiencies, because it has sure principle to work upon. If education is to develop human nature so that it may attain the object of its being, it must involve the exercise of judgment." (Kant 1900, §14, p. 13) The implication is that rather than have an art that is either mechanical or endowed with the power of judgment, the art of education becomes a dual track of both science *and* judgment. To that effect, "the mechanism of education must be changed into a science, and one generation may have *to pull down what another had built up.*" (Kant 1900, §14, p. 14, emphasis added)

Educational futures cannot be presumed on simplistic assumptions of learning, which are almost always guaranteed by those who presume growth as a condition of life. We know from Dewey, that growth can only be presumed on (and through) immaturity, (Dewey 1966, p. 41) which is to say that if growth is assumed to happen anyway, we are not only misleading ourselves into progressive myths, but we are also putting learning across as being no different than a cumulative form of programming.

The reason is not only "scientific" as Kant would put it, but also as a form of "futuring," as existentialist philosophers of the radical imaginary such as Greene would recommend while citing Sartre (Greene 1978, p. 172). To be able to articulate the judgmental possibilities by which education, as a critique, could open and achieve a *future* is not simply teleological. To break with the cycle and presume to have a better future is radical enough to claim that education could never become an instrument, neither to justify the present and less so to project a future on the assumptions by which the present is mortgaging the younger generations into its systems of reification and scarcity.

Lewis and Marx

Kant's position is partly echoed by C.S. Lewis, who in his book *The Abolition of Man*, comes up with what, initially, also appears to be a rather conservative take on learning. In taking issue with an unmediated approach to literature by two teachers he calls Gaius and Titius, Lewis appears to critique a method of education that leaves the Canon behind, only to appeal to the immediacy of experience.

> I think Gaius and Titius may have honestly misunderstood the pressing educational need of the moment. They see the world around them swayed by emotional propaganda—they have learned from tradition that youth is sentimental—and they conclude that the best thing they can do is to fortify the minds of young people against emotion. (Lewis 1947, p. 8)

"My own experience as a teacher tells an opposite tale," says Lewis. "For every one pupil who needs to be guarded from a weak excess of sensibility there are three who need to be awakened from the slumber of cold vulgarity. The task of the modern educator is not to cut down jungles but to irrigate deserts." (Lewis 1947, p. 9) Lewis presents the idea of an approach that would change the world not by bringing down meaning to practice, but to take the practice and the unmediated into the meanings by which education acts as "the right defence against false sentiments" and by which it inculcates "just sentiments." This happens if we stop "starving the sensibility of our pupils" as this makes "them easier prey to the propagandist when he comes." (Lewis 1947, p. 9)

Distancing the educational argument away from a facile dualism of sentiment against reason, Lewis moves to the notion of *just* and *noble* sentiment, and therefore to a judgmental approach which does not simply bridge the particular with the universal, but that follows identifiable ideals by which one could ennoble the sentiment that originally might prompt one to learn. This is a conscious approach towards a path of nobility that Lewis claims to be common to all traditions, which he identifies with "the *Tao*."

> Those who know the *Tao* can hold that to call children delightful or old men venerable is not simply to record a psychological fact about our own parental or filial emotions at the moment, but to recognize a quality which demands a certain response from us whether we make it or not. I myself do not enjoy the society of small children: because I speak from within the *Tao* I recognize this as a defect in myself—just as a man may have to recognize that he is tone deaf or colour blind. (Lewis 1947, p. 12)

Contrary to any impression that the concept of the Tao might give, there is nothing mystical about Lewis's position. He is seeking to reaffirm a standard, or indeed a ground against which one could measure what would allow us to move beyond the now. In this respect, he is adopting a similar measure to Kant's:

> We live in an age of discipline, culture, and refinement, but we are still a long way off from the age of moral training. According to the present conditions of mankind, one might say that the prosperity of the state grows side by side with the misery of the people. Indeed, it is still a question whether we should not be happier in an uncivilised condition, where all the culture of the present time would find no place, than we are in the present state of society; for how can man be made happy, unless he is first made wise and good? And until this is made our first aim the amount of evil will not be lessened. (Kant 1900, §19, p. 21)

Lewis seems to echo Kant's approach, albeit in an altogether different wording, which up close seems to share the sentiments that Kant expresses two centuries earlier.

> [A]ll the time—such is the tragi-comedy of our situation—we continue to clamour for those very qualities we are rendering impossible. You can hardly open a periodical without coming across the statement that what our civilization needs is more 'drive', or dynamism, or self-sacrifice, or 'creativity'. In a sort of ghastly simplicity, we remove the organ and demand the function. *We make men without chests and expect of them virtue and enterprise.* We laugh at honour and are shocked to find traitors in our midst. We castrate and bid the geldings be fruitful. (Lewis 1947, p. 16, emphasis added)

Yet to bring Kant and Lewis together seems to make too much sense for comfort. I say so by dint of their discomfort with anything that appears too clean and commonsensical. Somehow, in laying out the sense by which they confront the obvious, one could be doing them a disservice in presenting them as being all too obvious, when in fact their work never is; which is where I want to bring in a third interlocutor, not much known for his educational theories, yet often overused (and abused) by educational theorists, especially when they squabble between themselves over who represents most clearly his radical and critical edge: Karl Marx.

This is a somewhat surprising side of Marx with which many may not want to engage, mainly because here he appears to go against the grain of his own comrades, and against an entire party—the German Worker's Party and their program, better known as the *Gotha Program* of 1875. The problem is not with Marx's rift with his comrades (something that characterized his political work on many fronts). The surprising aspect of this rift is on the matter of the disagreement itself, which at first sight appears to be a disagreement on a universal right. Here we are invited to a stark reminder of Marx's unique ideological versatility, in that unlike Kant and Lewis, who by and large could be taken as the consenting heirs of the bourgeois revolution that in many ways reinforces the rationalist tradition, Marx rejects almost wholesale those assumptions with which anyone would, at first, come to some agreement. While it seems safe enough to assume freedom and education as claims to what the bourgeoisie, in its rationalist approach, would have asserted as a state of right, upon reading Marx such a reassurance begins to vanish.

Contrary to the followers of Ferdinand Lassalle, Marx takes exception to the German Workers Party's demand that "the intellectual and ethical basis of the state" should begin with the right for a universal and equal elementary education by the state, expressed and exercised through "Universal compulsory school attendance" and "Free instruction."

> "Equal elementary education"? What idea lies behind these words? Is it believed that in present-day society (and it is only with this one has to deal) education can be equal for all classes? Or is it demanded that the upper classes also shall be compulsorily reduced to the modicum of education—the elementary school—that alone is compatible with the economic conditions not only of the wage-workers but of the peasants as well? (Marx 1977, p. 28)

What seems to be the problem with the Gotha Program's claim to a universal education that is *freely* provided by the state? Why doesn't this square with the ideals of equality, which one would presume to be a cornerstone of the workers' revolution? Why shouldn't elementary education be that instrument by which such a right is claimed and through which the workers would gain a degree of emancipation?

On a closer look, Marx's problem is not with education per se, but with the state, particularly what he would see as the myth of a *"free* state." One could see how in regarding the polity as a mechanism that is not simply assumed by a dynamism of legal power, a constellation of real powers that move within the complexity of capital are revealed. Marx could never accept the idea of freedom as one that simply consents to legal equality. In effect Marx squarely rejects the very idea that there could ever be a free state, in that the idea of the state held by the people is simply a fallacy. Ultimately any socialist should know that the state is contingent upon a future where it must wither away. Here Marx's futuring appears more radical than Kant's, though not without a tinge of idealism, it takes an equally hopeful leap. In Marx's case, the *ought* is never placed on the onus of learning but on that of a sense of autonomy which even education per se could never anticipate with either certainty or clarity. This is *yet-to-come*.

This radical break from the bourgeois reassurance of a rational future, which is suggested in both Lewis and Kant's investment in education, is further confirmed by Engels's own rejection of equality. As Engels tells Auguste Bebel in his cover letter to which he attaches Marx's *Critique of Gotha*, any notion of a socialist society as being simply a state of equality is a misconception. It is a "one-sided" notion that harks back to the French old ideals of liberty, equality, and fraternity. Engels regards this as "an idea which was justified as a *stage of development* in its own time and place but which, like all the one-sided ideas of earlier socialist schools, should now be overcome, for it only produces confusion in people's heads and more precise modes of presentation of the matter has been found." (Engels 1977, p. 35)

When Marx takes on the notion of a free state, he is objecting to the one-sidedness of the concept of equality by which Engels feels uncomfortable. "Free state—what is this?"

> It is by no means the aim of the workers, who have got rid of the narrow mentality of humble subjects, to set the state free. In the German Empire, the "state" is almost as "free" as in Russia. Freedom consists in converting the state from an organ superimposed upon society into one completely subordinate to it; and today, too, the forms of state are more free or less free to the extent that they restrict the "freedom of the state." (Marx 1977, p. 25)

Marx would never be contented with what Kant invests in education and which somehow Lewis sustains in the practice of engaging with the child's sensibility. Granted that Marx is taking a much wider vista than Kant or Lewis, in his critique he is signaling that education by its own is not enough, just as a free state means nothing unless it is qualified by the inherent struggle that needs to change it. Taken as commonsensical and almost always assumed to be universal—a universality which Lassalle's followers have clearly legitimized by bourgeois revolutionary declarations that go back to the Jacobins—this sense of freedom attributed to education is, to Marx, a fallacy.

> "*Elementary education by the state*" is altogether objectionable. Defining by a general law the expenditures on the elementary schools, the qualifications of the teaching staff, the branches of instruction, etc., and, as is done in the United States, supervising the fulfillment of these legal specifications by state inspectors, is a very different thing from appointing the state as the educator of the people! *Government and church should rather be equally excluded from any influence on the school*. Particularly, indeed, in the Prusso-German Empire (...) the state has need, on the contrary, of a very stern education by the people. (Marx 1977, p. 28, emphasis added)

Within the Spheres

This excursus into Kant, Lewis and Marx leads us back to Illich, who in his characteristic way approaches education in a manner that takes us further into history, as he openly attempts to challenge us to revisit the present. In the notes for a lecture that he gave at Teachers College in New York in 1979, Illich takes on what he calls the "social spheres" within which education remains trapped. Just as astronomy was caught in the grounding of the "celestial spheres" for centuries, so is education stuck in a paradigm by which it has become a sphere in itself. Yet while in astronomy there were enough scientists, philosophers and even theologians to debunk the celestial spheres as mythical—people who even lost their lives for doing so, such as Giordano Bruno—Illich argues that education remains trapped in a universe run on spheres.

For this reason, Illich seeks to encourage research *on* education, citing analogically, Scholasticism and how it remained compromised by the unquestioned *truth* of the celestial spheres from where it was even assumed that God mechanically moves the universe. He reminds his audience how Aquinas contends that, "science was free to investigate, first if heavenly spheres were driven by a soul, second, precisely how many spheres there were, and third, to what degree these spheres and their epicycles were eccentric." (IMP, p. 106)

Aquinas insisted that the three-dimensional nature of these spheres, as well as their uniform movement and substantive nature could never be questioned. They pertained to the divine, just as a universe centered around the Earth almost stopped Galileo to confirm with Copernicus, that the Earth was never static. More remarkably, Illich goes on to argue that education as a discipline still behaves as if the spheres are still at the foundation of physical and theoretical reality. They may be social or psychological spheres, yet the foundational assumption of the spherical mechanism of finitude remains at the core of education. Not unlike Copernicus, who gave way to the affirmation of a heliocentric arrangement but never questioned the celestial spheres, educationalists remain stuck in a time that has no after. Unlike those scientists and astronomers who "deal with a before and after," educators "still lack such a historical perspective on their own work." (IMP, p. 106)

> Today, these men's common, firm and critical conviction about the existence of such heavenly spheres is almost beyond belief. Yet, Keynesians and Marxists, Curriculum planners and Free Schoolers, Chinese and Americans, are all convinced that *homo* is *educandus*, that his well-being—nay, existence—depends on services from an educational sphere. (IMP, p. 106)

Illich is making a very clear indication towards those who could or should reject the foundational assumptions of the spheres, even when they have moved into a progressive or reformist position. He singles out the Keynesians and Marxists, who incidentally still reign supreme in the delineation of educational theory, maybe better known as liberals and critical theorists of education. He even includes those who see themselves as prophets of de-schooling, but who like Copernicus and Kepler, and unlike Giordano Bruno, did not renounce the grounding of observation from the paradigm of the heavenly spheres. Illich warns against education's fatal insufficiency. An insufficiency of research that remains inward looking. "I am under the impression that the educational debate, no matter how radical, is still only concerned with a rearrangement of social spheres on the model of pre-Kepler stargazers," Illich claims. He adds, continuing to run on the analogy of the discipline of astronomy, that while "correct observations on shared imagery and shared competence are still used," these continue to "fit a redundant paradigm." (IMP, p. 110)

New cycles and epicycles are added to the spheres without ever questioning the finality and finitude by which the spherical paradigm limits education per se. This relates to the scenario of the American and British educational spheres of the late second decade of the 21st century, where at the same time that free schools lay claim for autonomy, the underpinning of educational policy and critique remains limited to the schooled assumption of a common core; where a curriculum which is liberally assumed to be wide and malleable, still claims its core to be unquestioned—*de facto*, by the structure in which success in education is reduced to a few options that could be counted on one hand; *de jure*, by the universality by which education is conceived, funded and run on the strict negotiation of need and calculated provision of public and private money. This renders education into what it provides as scarce and thus distributed and consumed as such.

Even when approached from liberal, progressive and radical positions, education witnesses no effort to be taken out of the erroneous bounds of the basic spheres per se. The control of its operation renders the educational spheres for what they are: schooled prospects that engage neither in the futurity that Kant dreamt of, nor the nobility by which Lewis heightened the necessary sensitivity of learning per se. The spherical limits that are subsumed in the educational paradigm as critiqued by Illich, position Marx against the Marxists who seem to assume that education is redeemable from within its social spheres. In his critique of the Gotha program, Marx signaled a danger to his future followers by drawing his example of Lassalle's Jacobin myopia that missed the point of socialism needing to be move away from the paradigm of the spheres. From its analogy of astronomy and the celestial spheres, Illich's critique of education finds strong echoes in Marx's *Critique of Gotha*.

In some reversed historical context, Marx could have used Illich's words and still claim his position. A good example is when he critiques the idea of fair distribution as proposed by the Lassalleans. "What is 'a fair distribution'?" Marx asks. "Do not the bourgeois assert that the present-day distribution is 'fair'? And is it not, in fact, the only 'fair' distribution on the basis of the present-day mode of production?" Lassalleans were not unlike Kepler and Copernicus. As they changed the positions of the class system and reordered the planets, the earth, and the sun, they assumed that the spheres of bourgeois law remain legitimate by exponentially establishing a socialist agenda of fairness and redistribution. In contrast, Marx identifies the finitude of the legal sphere and remarks: "Are economic relations regulated by legal conceptions, or do not, on the contrary, legal relations arise out of economic ones? Have not also the socialist sectarians the most varied notions about 'fair' distribution?" (Marx 1977, p. 16).

Just as Kant and Lewis do not call for the assumptions of an educational sphere that would secure a future for the child and a place for the child's sensibility, Marx makes a radical plea for distinction when he argues that "'Elementary education by the state' is altogether objectionable." (Marx 1977, p. 28) Likewise for Illich one cannot presume education on an unchanged paradigm, even when the presumptions appear to be radical or critical enough to claim fundamental change:

> This construct of an educational sphere is thoroughly consistent with other similar constructs, especially the spheres of economics and politics. The process through which each of these spheres has been disembedded to the point of achieving a radical monopoly that paralyzes its corresponding vernacular homolog can be studied separately for each one. (IMP, p. 112)

Illich's reference to the "vernacular homolog" is highly relevant in terms of the models of analysis that he uses later in *Shadow Work* (SW). As education becomes a homolog of the political and economic spheres, it partakes of the finality and limitation by which, as other spheres, politics and economics impose themselves on everyone's vernacular expression of the world. In this we find how while the convivial way of experiencing the world becomes infinite (as indeed astronomy now takes it portents beyond the limitations of the spheres that restricted Copernicus), in the self-imposed spherical limitations of educational research we are limited to what is found in education, resulting in an inward-looking zone of comfort by which the school remains central and core. In contrast, Illich provides a way out. "[R]esearch on the educational sphere can claim a certain priority," claims Illich. "Studying the process through which this sphere, in its ideological construction and in the degradation and replacement of vernacular languages by taught mother tongue after the invention of the loudspeaker, permits unique insights into the analogous elements that went into the constitution of other social spheres." (IMP, p. 112)

In this reclaimed sense of a universe of particulars, the vernacular emerges in its autonomy against and beyond the imposed standardization of one political and economic sphere. Illich dares these spheres and moves beyond the claims made by Kant, Lewis and Marx. His view of research on education moves beyond the expected categories by which even his work is often pigeonholed:

> Education as a subject matter and as a discipline has been defined by the construct and constrained by its basic assumptions up to now. This cannot be otherwise for research in education. But research on the relations of the educational domain to the global ideology of a society, together with the history of these relations. constitutes the kind of study which ought to be called research on education. (IMP, p. 112)

Far from rejecting education as a discipline—or reduce it to a "professional" sphere—Illich presents the academic character in its comprehensive diversity. He exits education from its spherical self and floats it into an infinite universe of vernaculars.

Abbreviations: Works by Illich

DS   *Deschooling Society.*
TFC *Tools for Conviviality.*
IMP *In the Mirror of the Past.*
SW   *Shadow Work.*

References

Balibar, E. (1994). *Masses, Classes, Ideas. Studies on Politics and Philosophy Before and After Marx.* London; New York: Routledge.
BBC (2015). School term-time holiday fines 'unworkable', says LGA. Accessed: 2 November 2015, http://www.bbc.co.uk/news/education-34591050
Dewey, J. (1966). *Democracy and Education.* New York: The Free Press.
Engels, F. (1977). Letter to Bebel. Marx, K. & Engels, F., *Selected Works.* Vol. 3, pp. 31–37. Moscow: Progress Publishers.

Gramsci, A. (1967). *La formazione dell'uomo. Scritti di pedagogia.* G. Urbani (ed.). Roma: Riuniti Editori.
Greene, M. (1978). *Landscapes of Learning.* New York: Teachers College Press.
Illich, I. (1981). *Shadow Work.* New York: M. Boyars. (SW)
Illich, I. (1992). *In the Mirror of the Past: Lectures and Addresses, 1978–1990.* New York: M. Boyars. (IMP)
Illich, I. (2001). *Tools for Conviviality.* New York: Marion Boyars. (TFC)
Illich, I. (2012). *Deschooling Society.* New York: Marion Boyars. (DS)
Kant, I. (1974). *Critique of Judgement.* J.H. Bernard (trans.). New York: Hafner Press.
Kant, I. (1900). *Kant On Education (Ueber pädagogik).* A. Churton (trans.). Boston: Heath & Co.
Laclau, E. (1996). *Emancipation(s).* London: Verso.
Lewis, C. S. (1947). *The Abolition of Man. Or Reflections on Education With Special Reference to the Teaching of English in the Upper Forms of Schools.* New York: Macmillan.
Luckmann, T. (1967). *The Invisible Religion. The Problem of Religion in Modern Society.* New York: Macmillan.
Marx, K. (1977). *Critique of the Gotha Programme* (Marginal notes to the programme of the German Workers' Party). Marx, K. & Engels, F., *Selected Works.* Vol. 3, pp. 13–30. Moscow: Progress Publishers.

· 6 ·
REFORM

If at times, Illich's work is described as being either wildly radical or suspiciously conservative, this comes down to a fundamental misunderstanding of his approach to reform. While the *radical* attribution is misplaced in terms of what it means to go to the historic root of matters that have been hitherto "normalized" by an ideologically skewed reading of history, the *conservative* accusation reflects a serious difficulty in "placing" Illich's take on matters like labor, gender, education, health, and the ecology; an approach which appears to fall out of kilter with what is broadly related to liberal and progressive narratives.

In her book *Divine Disobedience: Profiles in Catholic Radicalism*, Francine du Plessix Gray recalls Illich telling her:

> I am attacked by both the left and the right because I insist on rigorously correct behavior. (…) You reform by staying within the system. I believe in good manners, in playing the rules of the game. If you don't like the rules of chess, stop playing but do not try to reform the rules of chess. (Du Plessix Gray 1970, pp. 274–275)

This must also be read from how Gray defines and appreciates radicalism as a return to the roots, but which would surprisingly mean that while conservatives would frown on these radicals' open disobedience, progressives would quickly learn that such radicals also attest to a conservative claim: "The non-violent revolutionaries such as the men I write about wish to return to ancient ideological principles—be they principles of the Gospel or of the Constitution—which they feel have been sullied by time and by the blind obedience of docile majorities. In this sense the rebel heroes of this book are deeply traditional, deeply conservative men." (Du Plessix Gray 1970, p. x). This is typified in Illich's words when, describing his center in Cuernavaca, he states: "CIDOC [Centro Intercultural de Documentación] is in its deepest sense a contemplative place, not a conspirational place, and this is scandalous to both the left and the right." (Du Plessix Gray 1970, p. 275)

Idolatrous Hypotheses

Perhaps, a foremost example of how Illich's work moves outside expected ideological spheres is found in his profound criticism of the idolization of *life* as a construct. His deep concern comes from how the word "life" has come to denote a self-serving concept in discourses on human reproduction and the ecology. A superficial reading of this critique would easily mistake Illich for "taking sides" in the debates that still prevail over abortion, even when it is evidently grotesque to do so. Equally problematic would be any shallow take on his discourse on the environment, where climate deniers might hastily assume that Illich is being "with them" when he questions some of the approaches taken by environmental activism.

Illich's legacy in the discussion of life as a construct is best captured by Barbara Duden in the Introduction to her book *Disembodying Women*. She argues that "[p]oliticians and jurists, theologians and physicians are engaged in a major effort of social creation whose object is 'life.' As a result of this effort, a new idea has become universally accepted: just as the Blue Planet—'seen' from space—is the environment of all life, so woman is the environment of new life." (Duden 1993, p. 2) Echoing Illich's critique of the managerial way by which everything becomes institutionalized, Duden adds that "[a]lmost overnight, these beliefs have become growth industries for new professional establishments, from ecological systems engineers to bioethicists, to manage. Concurrently, the term *life* (and *a life*) has become an idol, and controversy has attached a halo to this idol that precludes its dispassionate use in ordinary discourse." (Duden 1993, p. 2)

In his scathing commentary on the manipulation of the word "life," which he calls an "amoeba word," echoing Poerksen's analysis of "plastic words" (see IC, pp. 252ff; Poerksen 1995), Illich took on no one less than Cardinal Joseph Ratzinger (who would then become Pope Benedict XVI), sharply contesting his translating of "a scientific statement into ordinary language," where, by declaring the zygote as a person in the name of *life*, he "completely falsifies what the laboratory warrants." (IC, p. 259) His beef with Ratzinger extends from his concern over a construct becoming an idol. As he put it, the word *life* "has become a way of speaking about what were once respectfully called persons." (IC, p. 256; see also Duden 1993, pp. 21–23) In 1989, addressing a conference of the Evangelical Lutherans of America, Illich states that "[a]s currently used, the English words 'life' and '*a* life' feed the most powerful idol which the Church has had to face in the course of her history." He voices his fear that a lack of rooting in Biblical language would trap the Churches in "engag[ing] the myth-making power which they possess as late twentieth century institutions to foster, consecrate and sanctify the abstract secular notion of 'life.'" (IMP, p. 220)

> Carrying out this profoundly 'religious' and equally non-Christian enterprise, they thereby make it possible that this spectral entity progressively replace the notion of 'person' in which the humanism of Western individualism is anchored. 'A Life' is amenable to management, to improvement and to evaluation in terms of available resources in a way which is unthinkable when we speak of '*a* person.' (IMP, p. 220)

Such myth-making lends itself to an idolatrous state of affairs which translates a word into an instrumental perversion of divine attribution. The attribute is divine because for Illich, life is only construed as such at that specific moment when Jesus (whom as a Christian, Illich considers as the incarnate God) declares himself to Martha, "I am life" (see IC, pp. 255ff). To bring life as the moment of divine incarnation into an equivalence with anything that could be managed is to pervert Jesus's statement. "As a perversion of the statement by the incarnate God, 'I am life,'" says Illich, "the construct *life* belongs to hell, if there be one, and we would have to invent it if there weren't to say where it belongs." (IC, p. 266) By this very sense of profound protest against an idolatry that reduces life to an equivalence that renders everything in the universe to a *creature* of life, Illich would go on to scandalize his Lutheran audience by cursing the very word: "To Hell with Life!" (IC, p. 277). As he would later explain to Cayley, his discomfort was such that in the same way that he was forced to curse "life" then, he now finds himself uttering: "To hell with God as a hypothesis!" because the idolization of life reduces God into a mere hypothesis.

In this thread, the argument follows suit in Illich's critique of those who assume that somehow human *responsibility* implies that humanity has a right to presume to own and liberally manage nature and the universe. This is done by exerting power over nature just as doctors and theologians, in declaring a zygote to be a life and thereby a person, have presumed to take control and to manage what they would claim to own as a person inside a woman's womb.

> While Medicine manages life from sperm to worm, Churches have acquired a new social standing by framing these medical activities within the semblance of an ethical discourse. Bio-ethics provides a new and prestigious job market which gives preference to unemployed clerics with university degrees. I am therefore fully aware of the difficulty I face when I choose life as my exemplary instance of a notion which takes on spectral but unquestioned existence through an institutional commitment to new domains of management. (IMP, p. 223)

Colored Circles

This makes uncomfortable reading on both ends of an arc of habituation by which we have been trained in spanning the spectrum of human reproduction, in that the premise taken by Illich refuses to uphold Ratzinger's assumption of the zygote as a human person while at the same time Illich also argues that the sense of ownership over what resides in a woman's womb is an act which violates the woman's body by effectively disembodying her. Again, Illich is characteristically defying all those expected dualities by which we have been schooled to look at just about anything that we care to presume to construct our reality. As if inviting us to relive Augustine's struggle with Manichaeism, Illich endears in cultivating an outlook that forfeits the comforts of habit. He invites us to, instead, seek other forms of speaking; to discover other imaginaries that would need to be removed away from the scopic assurances of a world that we insist on *watching* with voyeuristic mania though hardly ever *seeing*, let alone knowing, with humility and awe.

At a semiotic, though in no less tangible level, our invasive forms of watching, amounts to the alienation of a woman from her body, in the same way the world is summed up in the emblematic idolatry of an image. Illich shows how this is done in the name of a construct called "life," captured in the constructed imagery of a pink fertilized human egg and that of a blue planet Earth as emblems of total estrangement.

> These two colored circles are results of the transformation of activities, which are called scientific so that they can demand high funding, into images which can be used in propaganda, and now become thresholds, doorways, to something which nobody sees, something which makes sense for nobody—life here and life there; a life pink, general blue; pink light, blue light—the ultimate for which any sacrifice can be justified. (…) These two images are the threshold through which *life* justifies total global management. It's justified because of the sacredness of this nothingness. (IC, pp. 265–266)

In the same vein, Illich argues that the cry against global warming often risks resulting into superstitious "rain dances" (IC, p. 283) which somehow sustain the same logic by which the environment is exploited and destroyed. Whether by design or inadvertently, the claim to own (and eagerly exploit) or save (and risk disembodying) the ecology could well result in forms of *hedonistic* arrogance that equate human existence with an ostensive power over everything in the name of *life*. This ends up distorting and appropriating what should only be attributed to God—or any notion of universal multitude—that is reduced to the whims of a human hypothesis. The presumption to exert managerial power over an ecology of life—whether the planet's or the fertilized egg—is an arrogation over the living, whichever way it is perceived, as divine or in the plenitude of the universe. This form of estrangement, this total disembodiment of the living, transpires from a sense of seeing by owning and prying by violating (See also Duden 1993, esp. chap. 2, 5 and 15; Illich 1998). More so, it reveals that to play the counter-game on the same premises of an idolatrous assumption of *life* renders both claims and counterclaims to be futile and nothing less than a self-indulgent frenzy of disputes that lead to nowhere.

A further example which would leave many readers in some, if not total, consternation (unless they set aside their ideological baggage of expectations) is the scorn that Illich received from a number of prominent feminist academics when he published his book *Gender* (see G). Then, he was reprimanded for being reactionary and male-centered, as he offered an historical take on gender where, as in his discussion of domestic labor and the vernacular, his analysis took an approach that was seen to be completely out of kilter with feminist and gender studies literature. Illich's alleged transgression was to take a leap back into narratives and instances of history that methodologically allowed him to adopt several forms of arguing which appear to have nothing to do with the present, knowing very well that this would enable him to return to the present with a fresh approach. This was not appreciated by some gender scholars who misconstrued his method as being a reactionary turn, almost as if it were intent on resurrecting those forgotten notions of gender that are commonly regarded as the source of a history of discrimination. While there is hardly any disagreement over the historicity of gender exploitation and patriarchy, Illich's detractors mistook his distinctive engagement with this history as an affront to their own ideological histories, when Illich's method always aimed to move out of the stricture of the ideological spheres by consistently looking out for other possible forms of explanation that would in turn offer different solutions to the vicissitudes of human exploitation.

Cayley succinctly argues that despite what is claimed by his critics, Illich "does not fantasize (…) about a return to the past." Rather, he offers "a disciplined and documented account of what gender was, *standing outside the present* and seeing it with a vision sharpened by the knowledge of a profoundly different past." (IC, p. 32 emphasis added). As I will explain further in this chapter, the decision to *stand outside* is key to Illich's method, from where we find that the categories by which we remain beholden to presumed ideological certainties and expectations are rendered irrelevant in how he engages with anything that he dares to investigate.

Back to Duden, one would appreciate how the subtle distinctions that she makes are rather lost on the ideological entrenchments by which an approach to issues of such fundamental import is often distorted. While emphasizing that she is not seeking to espouse any "of the positions that typically appear in current controversies over life, abortion, euthanasia, genetic engineering, or the environment," and while she makes it clear that she is not intent on formulating any "opinion on the legal regulation of abortion or on access to prenatal care, nor (…) with the social, ethical, or medical evaluation of chemical, genetic, or surgical interventions," Duden limits her focus on showing that, "historically (…) the human fetus, as conceptualized today, is not a creature of God or a natural fact, but an engineered construct of modern society." (Duden 1993, p. 4) Her aim (which I would regard as running in synchrony with Illich's original approach) is to "discuss the many-layered process involved in the synthesis of this fetus, the invention of fetal norms and needs, and the pseudoscientific directives that ascribe the responsibility for the management of a life—as defined for optimal measurement and supervision—to women." (Duden 1993, p. 4) Those who would still insist on interpreting this from within their reductionist spheres would never grasp how scholars like

Duden and Illich have managed to break out of the straitjacket of an ideological history.

> There are people who are pro-life: some oppose abortion, others vivisection, capital punishment or war. Their opponents want the choice to interrupt pregnancy or life-saving treatment. As Will Campbell said to me three years ago: 'life is tearing the Church apart.' And yet, *no one dares to oppose the use of this verbal amoeba* in public controversy. Least of all churchmen. Some burn incense to life. Others have become specialists in peddling pseudo-biblical pieties about the 'value' of life. (IMP, p. 223, emphasis added)

To miss out on how an historical method must exit the stricture of ideological predication reveals another major source of confusion on the part of those attempting to co-opt Illich's position into their own. As he states in *Shadow Work*, when discussing vernacular values in contrast with values which are deemed to have economic measurement and thereby prone to be administered, Illich always expects "some self-appointed tutor of the so-called proletariat" who would accuse him of "avoiding the critical issue by giving importance to noneconomic niceties," and to whom Illich directs the question:

> Should we not seek first the just distribution of commodities that correlate to basic needs? Poetry and fishing shall then be added without more thought or effort. So goes the reading of Marx and the Gospel of St. Matthew as interpreted by the theology of liberation. (SW, pp. 72–73)

Returning (to) Form

Understanding Illich's approach to reform comes with the need to pay closer attention to a body of work that he deemed to have significant influence on the evolution of his ideas, the foremost being Gerhard Ladner's seminal work *The Idea of Reform* (1959). To Ladner, the idea of reform prompts the question "whereby the terms contained in the definition are transposed from the history of ideology to that of preterideological existence." (Ladner 1959, p. 35) To claim such an existence—that is, one that moves outside and beyond (*preter*) the bounds of ideology—is to claim *another space* for reform. Illich regards himself as Ladner's "grateful pupil" (VT, p. 31), which means that upon reading Illich it would be difficult to ignore how, in addition to a preterideological existence, Ladner's definition of reform also plays the role of a "provisional conceptual tool (…) which may not always fit the historical material exactly," where "various types of renewal ideas did, of course, mix and blend with the idea of reform." (Ladner 1959, p. 35)

Ladner defines reform "as the idea of free, intentional and ever perfectible, multiple, prolonged and ever repeated efforts by man to reassert and augment values pre-existent in the spiritual-material compound of the world." (ibid.) Here, one is immediately confronted by an approach that looks "back," in that to *re-form* is to invite one to return to *form* (noun) as well as to *form* (verb) again. This approach pertains to a specific way of reading what it means to lay claim on a reality that conceptually would neither hedge its bets on causal expectations (whose empirical validation is expected to legitimize pragmatic methods) nor would it claim identifiable and historically validated expectations (that are designed to fulfil a set of agreed-upon teleological projects). As both claims would correspond to that sense by which liberal and progressive reformists have respectively placed their onus on change, this would explain how an idea of a *return to form* plays itself outside both definitions of reality. This might give the impression that in lying outside such realms one would have to tinker with two extreme ends that somehow result in an endgame which zeroes in on either a radical dismissal or a reactionary withdrawal.

To read "reform" as a "return to form" requires an approach that moves beyond the categories by which we are used to frame our customary approach to change. Far from an endgame, Illich and Ladner approach the process of history by remaining in its own element, keeping it away from the identitarian solutions to which all ideological certainties are attracted. As indicated by Illich's critique of educational research, the aim to move beyond such certainties belongs to the desire to break out of an outlook that is still beholden to a universe that is trapped into the fixedness of presumed spheres (IMP, pp. 105ff). As we speak of a return, we speak of a space that moves outside and beyond the spheres of a history of ideological certainty. Beyond the history of ideologies, a wider narrative belongs to what is denoted by the "preter," the beyond, into which (and indeed *by which*) we exit out of a hedged assumption of a formalist view.

This does not mean that ideologies should be externalized from history, or that there is such a thing as ideological neutrality. On the contrary, this is an approach which, while fully aware of the ideological spheres that have constructed history, the very idea of history must not be confined to a structure that is exclusively moved by ideologies *qua* forms. Nor should ideology represent a singular entry into history as that would result in a formalist fallacy.

It would make sense to say that Ladner's take on form is stoutly anti-formalist. To read a concept like that of reform *inversely* comes with a challenge which firstly, must reject an incremental assumption of progress tied to expectations that claim to move away from the very condition that prompts them; and secondly, it must exit the boundaries of their spheres of certainty, be they political, social or economic.

To better illustrate how we can approach reform from the idea of a return to form, one could borrow Illich's use of the notion of "shadow." *Prima facie*, the concept of a shadow appears to be mimetic and derivative; pretty much construed as the reflection of a concrete body or reality. Instead, if one reads Illich's notion of shadow inversely, the possibilities of a re-form takes unexpected turns, where reality is approached through a series of formative reiterations and where it is possible to reach a point in history where one finds a degree of equivalence between the shadow and what it purports to reflect—as indeed we find in his discussion of shadow work and wage labor. Illich clarifies this by approaching social phenomena such as labor and domesticity, which, within the bounds of causal and teleological progress, would appear nonsensical:

> I propose 'shadow work' to designate a social reality whose prototype only is modern housework. Add the rising number of unemployed to the increasing number of people kept on the job only to keep them busy, and it becomes obvious that shadow work is by far more common in our late industrial age than paid jobs. By the end of the century, the productive worker will be the exception. (SW, p. 113)

To presume a reformist argument in this representation of a domestic realm which purposively lies outside the industrialized legitimation of labor is not easy, especially when the aim is to articulate a political stance that is clearly moved by ideological and pragmatic expectations. Yet here, Illich is following on from a perspective of reform that extends from various ideas of renewal found in an array of secular and religious narratives that regard reform as moments where liberation runs across a horizon of events that *re-form* and thereby give form again to women and men's liberty. The implication gets closer to what Ladner identifies with an idea of newness "understood as identity or equivalence of a new condition with a perfect original state." (Ladner 1959, pp. 46–47) While this might sound Platonic, especially when it is cited as being reflective of Greek patristic reform (Ladner 1959, p. 47), in the way it plays in Illich the shadow does not portend a perfectible origin. Rather, it indicates a state of affairs by which the new condition comes out of a dynamic that has nothing to do with perfection of a form *in se* but in a sense that seeks to recover the domestic context, and thereby the recognition of a *domiciled* space—as a return to a *home*—by which a social reality recalls its own sense of ownership, and therefore by no means benign but surely cast in a shadow and thereby lost.

> My interest is in that entirely different form of unpaid work which an industrial society demands as a necessary complement to the production of goods and services. This kind of unpaid servitude does not contribute to subsistence. Quite the contrary, equally with wage labor, it ravages subsistence. I call this complement to wage labor "shadow-work." (SW, pp. 99–100)

Given that Illich is bringing to the argument what we customarily call "family life" (SW, p. 100), the sense of what is lost in this appellation (and human condition) is what is taken away through "the stress of forced consumption, the tedious and regimented surrender to therapists, compliance with bureaucrats, the preparation for work to which one is compelled." (SW, p. 100) Where does this leave us with the idea of reform? A partial answer is found in how Illich brings into the argument a sense of return to when shadow work and wage labor shared the same existential origin, and whose bondage, in the 19th century's bourgeois setup of the family, changed from that of a subsistence-centered household to that of the wage earner and his dependents. This is where, Illich argues, such a bondage "tied the *femina domestica* [housewife] and a *vir laborans* [male laborer] in the thralldom of complementary impotence typical for *homo economicus*." (SW, p. 113) In recognizing and articulating shadow work, one could see how Illich is working labor back into form, while never attempting to presume normatively that such a return would mean a desirable restoration. Here, reform *as* re-form becomes a method of analysis, by which we come back to our present and reclaim a newness of insight into the condition that would inversely aim at a better state.

Shadow-less Affairs

Key to Illich's idea of reform is that of the convivial, as it is rooted in a series of conversational practices that are best understood from their vernacular potential. The vernacular carries a generational portent. It stands diametrically opposed to any nationalistic reification of the *"volk"* into a pre-modern myth of a purported simplicity where the people is supposed to claim its biological strength as that which "is 'subject to blood' [as] it arises from the 'soil', [and] furnishes the homeland with indestructible force and permanence." (Marcuse 1988, p. 23) Far from a reactionary pre-modernist claim to a naturalistic notion of the people, the vernacular transcends the claim to a distinction from the modern. Unlike the "folkish," the vernacular asserts the possibilities of the *modo* as acts that are signified by the actuality of *what is there*. It thereby stands as a reminder of what has become distanced from what the evolution of constructive capital, in its sociological forms of knowledge, has been estranged from us by way of making it scarce and thereby prone to resort to a folkish view of "life."

Here, scarcity is cue. It comes from a differentiation—indeed what Illich calls an apartheid—that cannot be avoided. Unlike the mechanisms by which the folkish view perverted what it denounced as the deficiencies of a liberal state (and with it, what it saw as its socialistic extensions) the vernacular cannot lay any such claim as it sits outside the mechanisms of the sociology of knowledge. The idea of the *volk* cannot be confused with the vernacular. Illich explains that, "without apartheid based on sex or pigmentation, on certification or race, or party membership, a society built on the assumption of scarcity cannot exist." (SW, p. 99)

I would argue that the denied negation of the grounds by which society could reclaim its convivial approach to a world which in its vernacular difference would counter the apartheid required of scarcity, is generative. This is because in their genealogical cycles human beings have tamed their creative dispositions by means of a specific form of habituation. Habituation at best frustrates and at worst precludes the human potential of *overcoming*. Instead, it assimilates the return—and with it the power of nostalgia—into a schooled imaginary that fails to differentiate labor and its dynamic within the making of the self and the society that we create. This is the same imaginary by which we are urged to build a world by acts of positive construction. In addition, this is a reification of reformism, as both the sense of a return and that of nostalgia are instrumentalized in a way that progressive and liberal reformism is pushed back into a consolidation of causal and teleological services to constructivist certainties.

The modes of construction by which reform has been reified thereby go counter to any notion of renewal by reclaiming that which we lost to instrumentalism. Contrary to the Ladner-Illichian idea of reform as a multiplicity of returns and reiterations, the reformism handed to us by various traditions on the right and left, often becomes a form of suppressing by actively obliterating the vernacular segments which once preserved the relationship between shadow work and wage labor. Instead, the constructivist zeal by which many seek to liberate the individual into society, has reverted this relationship and ultimately presented us with a shadow-less form of human living—not dissimilar to what Marcuse (1986, pp. 170ff) calls one-dimensional thought. Illich confronts one-dimensionality with a clear purpose. In *Shadow Work* (which was published in 1981) he states that:

> Ten years ago, we tended to distinguish social options exercised within the political sphere from technical options assigned to the expert. The former were meant to focus on goals, the latter more on means. Roughly, options about the desirable society were ranged on a spectrum that ran from right to left: here, capitalist, over there, socialist "development." The *how* was left to the experts. This one-dimensional model of politics is now passé. Today, in addition to 'who gets what', two new areas of choice have become *lay* issues: the very legitimacy of lay judgment on the apt means for production, and the trade-offs between growth and freedom. (SW, p. 11)

Illich refuses to plot matters against a left and right polarity. He proposes a graph with three axes: x, y and z. The two ends of the x-axis are immediately identified as being the left and right, to which we have been beholden in the semantics of politics. Unless we exit the flat groundedness on which this left-right conception of the world has been plotted, we cannot approach anything without such measure, and consequently we would never break the cycle of the system of myth. To the x-axis, Illich presents us with a y-axis whose ends represent the *hard* and *soft* choices that correspond to options such as those of energy, though it would be too simplistic to leave it at that. "On the y-axis," says Illich, "I place the technical choices between hard and soft, extending these terms far beyond a pro and con atomic power: not only goods, but also services are affected by the hard and soft alternatives." (SW, p. 11)

Perhaps the most intriguing, and key innovative aspect of Illich's three-dimensional approach is found on the z-axis. At one end, he puts *homo artifex* as that artistic being which subsists in what it makes and does. On the other end, one finds the industrial reality of the *homo economicus*, where humanity finds itself caged within the alternatives presented by the flatness of an interpretative reality that is limited to left and right (See SW, p. 12). On the z-axis, the vernacular reality of subsistence gains centrality, not simply as an historical segment which Illich excavates, but as that which is the source of the shadow that, not without irony, reveals the otherness of wage labor on the industrial end of the *homo economicus*.

The core of this aspect of Illich's social and economic philosophy, is best approached from a closer attention to the relationship between labor and its shadow *qua* work.

> While for wage labor you apply and qualify, for shadow work you are born or diagnosed. For wage labor you are selected; into shadow work you are put. The time, toil and loss of dignity entailed are exacted without pay. Yet increasingly the unpaid self-discipline of shadow work becomes more important than wage labor for further economic growth. (SW, p. 100)

In the world of a shadow-less wage labor—which operates within the span that runs between left and right on the x-axis—the "real world" becomes myth. That is why schooling's impact remains of major concern in this state of affairs.

Abolished Worlds

In its establishment of learning, education practically suppresses the vernacular possibilities of human artifice. It goes without saying that whether we find a way for deschooling or not, the need to break the cycle of the social system of myth remains a matter of urgency. As one is engaged with the dialectical nature of emancipation and its bifurcated ability to fold on itself, Gianni Vattimo reminds us how "even at its best, the media-human sciences complex is emancipatory only inasmuch as it places us in a world less univocal, less certain and so also much less reassuring than that of myth." (Vattimo 1992, p. 26) Strangely, by dint of myth we are prepared for the expectancy of superseding those very myths by which the certainty of consistency has taken root, where the scaffolded directions by which cognitive growth is planned and manipulated, must be rejected and where a less reassuring world emerges.

This puts us in a world that Vattimo likens to that "for which Nietzsche invented the figure of the *Übermensch* (…) the same world to which philosophy responds by way of what may now justifiably be called the hermeneutic turn." (Vattimo 1992, pp. 26–27) This presents an intriguing parallel with Illich when he states that, "most current college-level reform looks like the building of high-rise slums. Only a generation which grows up without obligatory schools will be able to recreate the university." (DS, p. 38) The drive to do away with the high-rise slum is to recognize the inter-subjective capacity by which one takes on the full edifice and like the *Übermensch* reclaim one's space for transcendence for one's own self. In Illich's case, the ability to overcome the world inter-subjectively warrants the need to cultivate a horizon of conviviality.

In the edificial grammar of "high-rise slums," education becomes a fad of critical phantasms, while learning becomes increasingly trapped and distorted by the myths of development and progress. This reinforces the conservative fallacy which reclaims education in the name of a liberal agenda that is devoid of its once-republican radicalism, immaterial as to whether it would have been Jacobin or Jeffersonian, of the left or the right. Building more floors on top of this edificial grammar could only have one consequence: the incremental growth of a society of myth where everything that would have been mildly radical finds itself normalized. The once-radical history of schooling becomes trapped in itself, just like any claim to the public's *res*—its *affair*, its *res publica*. In this society of myth, education's *truth* seeks legitimacy only in the fabular ends by which it is externally instrumentalized. Just as in the trinity of *truth, beauty and goodness*, the members of that other trinity, *learning, education and the school*, find themselves alienated from each other. They suffer from the same disintegration which followed the collapse of Jacobin republicanism; the same collapse that shook the foundations of Kant's faith in the Enlightenment and pushed Beethoven to strike off his Napoleonic optimism by which he wrote his *Eroica*. Like the triadic expectation of truth, beauty and goodness, that of learning, education and schooling can never stop its continuous unraveling. Each element will go its way, as they lose their combined ability to articulate the plural realities of the vernacular order. Men and women lost their ability to transcend what used to determine them as a received triadic order between the understanding and conduct that was bridged by the sentiments by which they could create and therefore subsist. This is where the vernacular comes in more prominent play.

As a man who lives through the descent of the republican idea, Ralph Waldo Emerson's vernacular approach stands as a reminder of how circularity is played into the myth of permanence: "You admire this tower of granite, weathering the hurts of so many ages." Then, almost inviting us to remain in awe of what we come across thanks to the schooled edifice of a subliminal myth, Emerson adds, "Yet a little waving hand built this huge wall, and that which builds is better than that which is built." (Emerson ND, vol. 1, p. 194) To gently remind us what we should have known, Emerson also recalls what the interpretative elements of reality are all about. His hermeneutic is subtle, and not unlike Nietzsche's, his premise remains situated in how we position ourselves within it.

Neither Emerson nor Nietzsche would offer any excuses for those who seem to prioritize the edifice over those who built it. What we have been taught to assume as a fact is just a making that is dismantled by the very same hands that built it: "The hand that built can topple it down much faster." (Emerson ND, vol. 1, p. 194) As Nietzsche asks in *Twilight of the Idols*, "How the 'Real World' at last Became a Myth":

> The 'real world' — an idea no longer of any use, not even a duty any longer — an idea grown useless, superfluous, *consequently* a refuted idea: let us abolish it! (…) We have abolished the real world: what world is left? The apparent world perhaps? … But no! *with the real world we have also abolished the apparent world!* (Nietzsche 1982, pp. 40–41)

What worlds have we abolished? What has remained "real"? Illich cannot give a straight answer to this question. Getting to know Illich's way of thinking, one would soon realize that if he were to attempt to give a *straight* answer, he would not be able to. He clearly implies that what we expect or regard as straight answers could only amount to deceptive replies. To set the scene for the reader to better grasp this approach I cite his penultimate few sentences that conclude *Shadow Work* where he presents us with how "[t]he sentimental glorification of the victims of apartheid: women, patients, blacks, illiterates, underdeveloped, addicts, the underdog, the proletariat, provides a way to solemnly protest a power to which one has already capitulated." He leaves us with no comfort, adding that "[t]his sentimentalism is a dishonesty for which there is no known substitute in a society that has ravished its own environment for subsistence." (SW, p. 116)

Illich's audiences frequently find themselves in a dilemma. While they love the man's spirit with the fervor of a saint's devotee, they fail to receive what they wrongfully expect of him. I hazard to guess that Illich's reply to such devotion would not be dissimilar from Jesus's pronouncements on John the Baptist: "What did you go out into the wilderness to see? A reed swayed by the wind?" (Luke 7:24)

Far from arrogant or elitist, Illich's work demands the commitment, love and dedication of a 12th century monk who labors on his work day and night while praying and devoting his service to God, and by implication, to the liberation of humanity from its daily burdens. By dint of his unique sense of reform, Illich captures the radical imagination by a sense of *renunciation* (as he frequently remarks, citing Thomas Aquinas) that would reject the pleasures of a quick answer or saving grace.

In many ways, what appears to be a radical political stance in Illich's work is not moved by a sense of revenge or indignation, but by an intense pathos that turns into an empathic set of pronouncements which are more likely to retreat when asked to produce a list of actions or demands. His radicalism is not found in direct action, but in the practice of *retreat*—indeed a sense of iterative return which deceives those who see it as giving up, when in effect it is a form of philosophical arguing, political discoursing, and a practice of regrouping which underpins the very notion of a perennial sense of reform *qua re*-form.

Abbreviations: Works by Illich

DS   *Deschooling Society*
G   *Gender*
IC   *Ivan Illich In Conversation*
IMP *In the Mirror of the Past*
SW   *Shadow Work*
VT   *In the Vineyard of the Text*

References

Duden, B. (1993). *Disembodying Women. Perspectives on Pregnancy and the Unborn.* Hoinacki, L. (trans.). Cambridge, MA: Harvard University Press.
Du Plessix Gray, F. (1970). *Divine Disobedience. Profiles in Catholic Radicalism.* New York: Alfred A. Knopf.
Emerson, R. W. (ND). *The Works of Ralph Waldo Emerson. Four Volumes in One.* New York: Tudor Publishing Company.
Illich, I. (1981). *Shadow Work.* New York: M. Boyars. (SW)
Illich, I. (1983). *Gender.* London; New York: M. Boyars. (G)
Illich, I. (1992). *In the Mirror of the Past: Lectures and Addresses, 1978–1990.* New York: M. Boyars. (IMP)
Illich, I. (1993). *In the Vineyard of the Text: A commentary to Hugh's Didascalicon.* Chicago, IL: University of Chicago Press. (VT)
Illich, I. (2012). *Deschooling Society.* New York: Marion Boyars. (DS)
Illich, I. & Cayley, D. (1992). *Ivan Illich in Conversation.* Toronto: House of Anansi Press. (IC)
Ladner, G. B. (1959). *The Idea of Reform Its Impact on Christian Thought and Action in the Age of the Fathers.* Cambridge: Harvard University Press.
Marcuse, H. (1986). *One-Dimensional Man. Studies in the Ideology of Advanced Industrial Society.* London: Ark Paperbacks.

Marcuse, H. (1988). *Negations. Essays in Critical Theory*. London: Free Association Books.
Nietzsche, F. (1982). *Twilight of the Idols and The Anti-Christ*. R.J. Hollingdale (trans.). London: Penguin.
Poerksen, U. (1995). *Plastic Words. The Tyranny of Modular Language*. Mason, J. & Cayley, D. (trans.). University Park: Penn State University Press.
Vattimo, G. (1992). *The Transparent Society*. D. Webb (trans.). Cambridge: Polity Press.

· 7 ·
CONTINGENCY

Ivan Illich's last testament, *The Rivers North of the Future*, is a text embedded in a firm belief in redemption through God-made-man—what some theologians refer to as "the *Christ-event*." Just as Emmanuel Levinas cannot be distanced from the Talmudic narratives through which he articulates his philosophy, Illich could never be read outside the Christ-event's ensuing tradition into which he was ordained. This would explain why Illich never shies away from paying testimony to those theological horizons on which he invites us to travel, while narrating the story of the cross and its divine grace, even when his audience is never exclusively religious, if at all. As I will argue in this chapter, we need to understand Illich's choice of narrative from what Hans Blumenberg (2010, p. 5) calls a "metaphorology," which "seeks to burrow down to the substructure of thought, the underground, the nutrient solution of systematic crystallizations; but it also aims to show with what 'courage' the mind preempts itself in its images, and how its history is projected in the courage of its conjectures."

Golgotha's khôra

Illich's way of embedding history in the incarnation and crucifixion of Jesus the Rabbi from Nazareth inaugurates him as priest, philosopher and public intellectual. Yet this is not simply reduced to a metaphor understood as a symbology by proxy. In the pragmatics of the metaphor that Illich adopts, history enters an added dynamic which transcends, yet never renders absolute, its own particularisms. As Blumenberg explains, metaphors "have a history in a more radical sense than concepts, for the historical transformation of a metaphor brings to light the metakinetics of the historical horizons of meaning and ways of seeing within which concepts undergo their modifications." (2010, p. 5)

I read this as cue to how, whether the narrative happens to be specific to an identifiable worldview or not, in its metaphorological *practice* it bears a transformative effect on everyone, immaterial of creed, ideology or outlook. Levinas's philosophy is never exclusively Judaic in its portent, even when its narrative specifically presents itself from a Rabbinic lineage. Illich's story of the Christ-event is not the sole property of a Catholic paradigm within which, as it happens, it often makes uncomfortable reading. Bearing this in mind, on the trajectory that Illich presents through the story of the crucifixion, one attains a deep sense of radical freedom by which everyone—Christian, Jew, Muslim or none—would need to exit the city and find one's way to a place which, in the Christian story, is the Golgotha.

Illich argues that the Golgotha is not a *sacrum* and cannot be read through religious science (IC, p. 268). He explains that a sacrum is a threshold, which appears to be the ultimate and the transcendent (IC, p. 264). He approaches the Golgotha from a theological standpoint, which in itself takes on a perspective that makes more sense from a metaphorological practice by which a far deeper sense is gleaned into history and how the sacred has been disembodied and removed from the living by the idolization of life.

> If there is something analogous to a *sacrum* in the Christian tradition, it is the tomb; and Christian holy places are built around an altar, a table, which stands on top of an empty tomb and is covered by a cupola. (…) The empty tomb had a powerful structuring influence on fifteen hundred years of Western history. I find the emptiness into which the blue and the red thresholds lead much more frightening, [here Illich is referring to the scopic disembodying of the blue planet and the red zygote] because what stands behind these thresholds is not just emptiness but nothingness. (IC, p. 268)

From a non-Christian perspective, an exiting into the Golgotha translates in the disestablishment of an idolized life. This does not simply aim at dismantling an institutionalized world, but is prompted by the powerful notion of an emptiness aimed at countering the elimination of the sacrum. Apophatically speaking, the empty tomb represents a fullness that is diametrically opposed to the expensive waste by which the free market gains its hegemony on the back of scarcity. The Golgotha is not to be understood through religious science because it is found within the elemental particularity of a vernacular sense of speaking. This is now reduced to nothing by a language with which church and state claim to have unified by means of a systemic suppression of dialectal diversity (See Chapter 2, above).

From this perspective I would suggest that outside the polity of institutions, the Golgotha becomes the *pagus*, the greater space that extends beyond the walls of the city, where the undocumented and those deemed foreign, the outcasts and those considered different, seek a language and with it a *modicum* of redemption. This brings no solace or romantic benignity. Golgotha is an aporia. It represents the freedom to occupy a site regarded by pagans and believers alike as the place where criminals find a cruel death.

Ironically as the people of the *pagus* (traditionally defined by the walls of established citizenry) the pagans were to be quickly moved outside the walls of the Abrahamic faiths when the latter prevailed. Yet it was the Roman pagan who then regarded the other—Christian and Jew alike—as being "the barbarian," and thereby an outsider to the legitimacy (and imperial overreach) of the *pagus*. Bearing in mind this historical sense of permanent alterity between insiders and outsiders, citizens and migrants, pilgrims and refugees, the metaphor of the Golgotha gains a richer meaning in how Illich presents us with the event of the crucifixion which allies the Abrahamic believer with the Roman pagan, especially when Christianity became the established religion of the Empire. As such, beyond the aporia of historical alterity, the Golgotha remains a constant, in that whoever happens to take over the city, the state and the church, as a space of execution it will always belong to the outcast.

Immaterial whether they happen to be citizens, pagans and barbarians Golgotha's men and women remain estranged from the institutional conventions that purport to give them humanity. This place, this unnamable and indefinable *khôra*, remains outside the inner and greater polis, and is always found somewhere beyond the boundaries of the city which, to the state and the church, configure the limits of legitimacy. Such limits both proscribe but also enable the articulation of goodness and truth, just as they rescind or make possible any entitlement to the beautiful or the divine (*qua* universal). However, as Illich retorts with forceful yet eloquent conviction, the crucifixion changed all this and transformed a rejected ground into a horizon of radical freedom; a freedom that goes to the root of what it means to emancipate oneself in a place that both state and church regard to be an agôn of shame and disgrace, uncleanliness and foreignness.

Discussing Illich's *Medical Nemesis* (MN), Lee Hoinacki states that "Illich revealed the center of his faith, the Incarnation, and the supremely apophatic expression of the God-man's life, his passion and death."

> The believer can come to the Cross through an art of suffering. That is supremely difficult, however. Although different arts of suffering were found, that is, practiced in all traditional cultures, that was in an era far distant from contemporary knowledge and experience. (Hoinacki 2003, p. 386)

Hoinacki is right. Contemporary knowledge and experience appear far too distant from the history within which Illich frames the claim for suffering. Yet, if we read him through the lens of a metaphorological practice, history as chronological distance gives way to history as a logic that shares a common-held vicinity by which Illich reclaims the vivid words and images of characters and thinkers from across the story of humanity, whether they happen to be 12th century monks, Puerto Rican immigrants in the Upper West Side, or 1st century Jews. He takes a methodological leap that would make equal sense to the enthusiastic young American missioner who is advised to go back home by his language teacher in Cuernavaca, as it would clearly connect with the atheist teacher or social worker in the poor suburbs of any metropolis. Most of all, as Illich's interlocutors, we will begin to understand why in 1st century Palestine, a small group of devout yet rebellious Jews decided to follow in their crucified rabbi's footsteps. Rather than just believe the Christ-event as Christians, through Illich's approach we transcend our formative limitations to figure out what it means to say with conviction that shame and disgrace, suffering and death, are strong signifiers of freedom. Exiting the city into the site of Golgotha is a way of finding and experiencing. Rather than a given *sacrum* of religious knowledge, it is a conscious choice of another place. This is consistent with the message of liberation by which Illich reaches out to everyone, immaterial of race, religion or lifestyle, as siblings in the person of the marginalized and rejected. What remains unique to the Illichian *extent* is found in how it insists on narrating the story of the Samaritan as a freedom to choose one's neighbor in the figure of those whom the community regards as the foreign and unclean enemy of the people.

Kenotic Tools

It is essential to understand Illich's overall position from how he engages with a philosophy that places considerable weight and emphasis on contingency, and by which this bears out a radical concept from within a tradition that goes to the root of the narrative of weakening and exiting, Illich presents contingency as an expression of "the state of being of a world which has been created from nothing, is destined to disappear and is upheld in its existence by one thing, and one thing only: divine will." (RNF, p. 65) In this will, one does not find overwhelming power, but kenotic love; a weakening of the divine which becomes one with the world—*enfleshed*, to use his favorite term.

From the divine's kenotic enfleshment, Illich draws the logical conclusion by which modernity would in turn take the world out of the same divine hands that held it. This might sound like a peculiar second thought, if not an inconsistency. However, Illich stays within the theological boundaries of his beliefs because in this retrieval away from the divine he sees the precondition of modernity "not because modernity is founded on the idea of contingency, but because it was only in a society in which people had strongly experienced a world as lying in the hands of God that it would be possible, later on, to take that world out of God's hands." (RNF, p. 69) In Illich's thought this is a dynamic relationship which disestablishes the intellectual and scientific boundaries that now limit the idea of contingency to that of an accidental state of affairs linked to a lack or scarcity, and thereby misconstrued as being in constant need of rectification through institutional necessity.

Discussing *In the Vineyard of the Text* (VT) Illich goes at some length to show how the 12th century gives him a vantage point to look with fresh eyes at what he sought in the notion of a tool by which one begins to experience contingency. He seems to reject his own claim made earlier in *Tools for Conviviality*, where he "believed that the idea of a tool as a means shaped to (…) arbitrary purpose had always been around," (RNF, p. 73) claiming that the emergence of a tool that gave us meaning happened much later. He explains how we have moved away from the notion of an *organon* found in Aristotle, (who exemplifies the *organon* as a "hand armed with a pencil") which would not distinguish the tool from its user. Then he goes on to argue that there was a breakthrough when the tool became a means. As proof of this breakthrough Illich cites two books written in the 12th century: *De artiis artibus* by an anonymous writer, and Hugh of St Victor's *Didascalicon* (see VT and Hugh 1991). In the latter, Illich explains how "Hugh writes about the science of mechanics," (RNF, p. 73) as he goes on to claim that this was the first time anyone has ever done so.

What value does a commentary on 12th century texts hold or promises to a time that straddles between the end of the 20th century and the beginning of the 21st? More so, what convergence, if any, could Illich find with the qualifying claim made by the crucifixion of a radical preacher living in Palestine during the third decade of the 1st century? At best, connections like these often feel and look like a brave leap in search of fortuitous historical associations. But as one becomes more attuned to an idea of reform and change as being integral to what Ladner (1959, p. 73), discussing St Augustine, calls a chain of "formative and reformative principles and acts," one finds that there is less of a leap and more of a reclaiming of horizons. These are horizons whose awaited recognition is less of a new ground and more of a *re-cognition* of what is continuously present. On such terms *change* remains a perennial condition.

With Illich, nothing could be fortuitous inasmuch as contingency cannot be reduced to a chain of coincidences. Following Blumenberg's historical account of the concept of contingency. (see RNF, pp. 65–67) Illich shows that in simply equating contingency with the accidental one would risk relegating it to a conceptual realm that is devoid of the immanence of its Christian origin notwithstanding its Latinized meaning found in Aristotelian logic.

> The idea that the world is contingent at every instant on God's will begins to be evident only in the eleventh century and is not fully fleshed out until towards the end of the thirteenth century. This is an event in the history of philosophy, but I believe that (…) what philosophers of that age expressed was a transformation in people's feelings. The world comes to be considered as something contingent, something indifferent to its own existence, something which does not bear within itself a reason or right to exist. (…) [T]his idea of living in a world which doesn't carry within itself the reason for its own existence, but gets it from an absolutely necessary, personal, ever-creating God belongs to the unique axiomatic certainties of the twelfth, thirteenth, and fourteenth centuries. At this moment, the world's very existence takes on the character of something gratuitous. The world which is around me, the cat over there and the four red roses which bloomed during the night are a gift, something which is a grace. (RNF, p. 65)

I read this as a way of recovering the dialectical potentials of contingency in its historical evolution (see, amongst other, Heller 1993 and Rorty 1989) with the intent of showing how such profound implications have become concealed and thereby systematically proscribed. More importantly, this is a dialectic that also changes its coordinates in that it does not simply presume to be either predetermined or accidental but moves beyond that sort of diarchy by being in turn re-cognized—that is, conceived once more—as an occasion for convivial togetherness.

> This moment of our being together, which I'm enjoying immensely, is not predetermined by some *karma*, isn't chance, isn't logically necessary, but rather is a pure gift. It's a gift from that Creator who keeps beings in existence, and by understanding things in this way, we can also see our own activity in sitting here in an entirely new light. (RNF, pp. 65–66)

The idea of a gift must be seen as other than simply a received commodity from a necessitarian order, be it divine or otherwise; but as that which we *realize* both in terms of an awareness but also in terms of making togetherness possible and thereby real. This is a free act of coming together, but also an event that belongs to how we come into this reality (and realization) of a being that *becomes* and *comes into* a world which has been left at the mercy of accidentality and thereby bereft of the contingent. In an earlier iteration of this conversation, as it was transmitted on CBC's *Ideas* interviews with David Cayley on the theme of *The Corruption of Christianity*, Illich's words are transcribed as follows:

> Contingency refers to a state of living in a world which doesn't bear in itself the reason for its own existence but gets it from an absolutely necessary, personal, ever-creating God. Things get their existence, their presence in the world from an act of the will of the Creator. We are both, in our essence, human beings, but it is a personal act of God's will to bring you and also that little cat, that kitten there, into existence and keep you both in existence. And in front of this act of God's goodness, I can do nothing else but bow in deep respect. (TCC, pp. 30–31)

Leaving aside the faith and metaphorical tools by which Illich continuously proclaims God's grace in the gift of contingency (particularly in how he regards the incarnation and crucifixion as tangible historic turns), another key to the centrality of this state of affairs is found in how contingency becomes another discursive signifier that gains a growing degree of centrality in understanding his work. One cannot but appreciate how Illich has a unique way of adopting concepts that move beyond the spaces where they are conventionally found. In addition, he invests such concepts with a wider value, transforming them into ideas that move within and beyond the boundaries of faith or language, history or religion. For the reader to make sense of this—especially if he or she does not happen to partake of Illich's theological enthusiasm—is to follow his thread out of these very same boundaries. Not without paradox, this requires that one moves within the same boundaries of the narrative metaphor itself, by using them as lines of possibility whose perennial value leads to effective reform. As we have seen earlier in the chapter on tradition, this is how Illich recovers the vernacular roots of our diverse possibilities.

From within this perspective, "to reform" means to distinguish between boundaries that close, and boundaries that signify a way of exiting the same enclosure. Understood from the idea of contingency, reform does not stand for a finite sense of progressive steps aimed at amelioration, but for its very opposite: a sense of possibility which is facilitated by the opportunities discerned from a contingent state of affairs—what John Duns Scotus attributes to a logical possibility which he encapsulates in the proposition "There can be a world, *mundus potest esse*" (see *Lectura* I 39, § 49, in Duns Scotus 1994, p. 116, with commentaries in pp. 28 and 116).

In Illich's way of thinking, concepts gain wider dynamic ways of being and doing. In regarding contingency within a framework of possibility, he ties it to the case of a convivial community and the entelechy of a horizon of diverse possibilities. From his unique approach, contingency is read as a possible condition that is found beyond its own demise: "once the universe is taken out of God's hands, it can be placed into the hands of people, and this couldn't have happened without nature having been put in God's hands in the first place." (RNF, p. 70)

After Contingency's Sunset

On a horizon that refrains from compartmentalizing philosophy and theology, history and faith, the laic and the confessional, this aspect of Illich's work is sustained by its profound appreciation of the apophatic method by which one comes to the *knowledge* (rather than *belief*) that God incarnated himself as a human being, thereby submitting himself to the free hands of other humans who would denounce and execute him as a mere criminal. As this remains, according to St Paul, "unto the Jews a stumbling block (*skándalon*, σκάνδαλον), and unto the Gentiles foolishness (*morían*, μωρίαν)" (1 Corinthians 1:23), the "offence" caused by the image of the Son of God's death renders the divine into the scandal that makes inane any attempt to rationalize it; by which in turn, humanity may well seem affronted, but where to the same humanity, a tool of freedom is gifted through the kenotic implements of disinterested love. Not unlike the time of the Hebrew prophet Amos, God's people return the favor by heaping more social injustice on the weak, the oppressed and the vulnerable:

> Thus said the LORD:
> For three trespasses of Israel,
> And for four, I will not turn it back—

> For their selling the just man for silver
> and the needy for sandals.
>
> Who trample the head of the needy
> in the dust of the ground
> pervert the way of the poor.
> And a man and his father go to the same girl
> to profane My holy name.
>
> And on pawned garments they stretch out,
> along every altar,
>
> and wine bought with funds from fines
> they drink in the house of their God. (Amos 2: 6–8; Alter 2019, pp. 1258–1259)

One could feel a historical precondition for Amos's articulation of Yahweh's wrath. Amos is not just the harbinger of divine anger. He is primarily the voice of the underdog; a prophet of social justice as his premise is that God has weakened himself when he continuously pardoned humanity for its transgressions. And yet the same humanity refused to treat others compassionately and never ceased to offend their own maker and protector. Amos's admonition is moved by a strong sense of social justice; an effort to realize the kenotic spirit by which a convivial society could become possible. Knowing that society refuses to listen to the message of love and compassion, Amos's attack is fierce and saves no one, neither secular nor religious leaders who in their might have taken advantage of the powerless in both the marketplace and the temple. In modern speak, Amos's words fit well with Illich's:

> They forget that people *eat*, and that people die when they are *fed*. These self-appointed keepers of their brothers make other people's survival depend on their own growing efficiency. By shifting from the production of guns to the production of grains they reduce their sense of guilt and increase their sense of power. (TFC, p. 44)

On reading their anger and frustration, one cannot help thinking that Illich and Amos are both signaling an end or at the very least a threshold that holds no hope for remission or redemption. There is a sense of helplessness in front of the power by which people use the contingent condition to strengthen the greed of hegemonic power; a condition that came from the freedom that they got when the "the universe is taken out of God's hands" so "it can be placed into the hands of people." (RNF, p. 70) Even so, contingency is never a curse, but a favor which is made possible, according to Illich (and probably Amos), because "it couldn't have happened without nature having been put in God's hands in the first place." (RNF, p. 70)

Beyond a theological point of view this state of affairs is more than familiar. It is by the power to take fate in our hands that we as human beings have submitted to the rules of contingency, thus claiming to consign it to the dustbins of history. We must not forget that such rules of contingency have come about because we have felt how they impact on our own rational imagination. By this we convinced ourselves that we are, by necessity, free and intelligent; just as we have also evolved the very notion of divinity in its historical dialectic of human thought and behavior. To deny that we have a claim on contingency would bring back the wrath of an absolute necessity—which, in religious terms, would equate with the wrath of God, while in secular parlance would imply a total sense of hopelessness and absolute destruction.

We have seen this in war and genocide: the industrialization of death in Belsen and Auschwitz-Birkenau, and the infinite power of destruction in the bombing of Hiroshima and Nagasaki. In all cases, human beings have taken full power of their freedom to destroy other human beings, and with their others, they—their brother's and sister's keepers—destroyed themselves and buried the sacred value of freedom. This perversion of freedom never stopped, and we now witness what Pope Francis describes as a "piecemeal third world war" (BBC 2014). As their brother's and sister's keepers, human beings are once again exercising the "right" to behead, burn alive, or crucify other human beings in full sight of cameras, claiming to do so in the name of an All Merciful God. In the name of the same God others refuse to give succor to the refugee on the pretext of cultural purity, religious and secular freedom, which they trumpet as a human right which they reserve for themselves. Many claim a "right" to denigrate and rebuke the immigrant for seeking better economic conditions. While this moral majority assumes self-righteous modes of existence, it quickly blames others for what it refuses to see in its own image. This is a condition for which Amos would surely implore divine wrath.

While this is caused by what Illich calls "the sunset of contingency" (that is, when we claim our freedom as a guarantee against the mishaps of a world where the only necessity is our freedom), beyond this sunset he still embraces a sense of possibility even when at times he appears to be desperate and on the brink of hopelessness. Whether seen from a secular, ideological or religious perspective, the power of this contingency, cruel and manipulative as it could be, gains relevance at this very point of absolute despair. Unless I misread Illich badly, he goes on to claim that the very condition created by contingency after its own demise has the potential to embody a liberating turn by which a universe "placed into the hands of people" gives a new meaning to another contingent condition that follows its own sunset. This is because such freedom was given to us by the same God that let go of the world. If read from a non-religious viewpoint, it is a freedom that we have achieved by dint of our own intelligence. Whether we see this as given to us by God or whether we insist on taking it out by our own free volition, it makes no difference to how the sunset of contingency marks a historical turn, although one must qualify this by Illich's own challenging paradox: "A contingent nature at its noon is gloriously alive, but it is also uniquely vulnerable to being purified and cleaned of its aliveness in the sunset of contingency." (RNF, p. 70)

This paradox helps one realize that from the distinct perspective by which Illich presents us with contingency in its original Christian outlook, there is a distinctly liberating turn, even for those who may not find relevance in his religious faith. If one regards his choice of narrative as being representative of an identifiable dynamic which even without a theological value holds court in the historical context of how contingency plays its role in the turn of modernity, one would do well to heed to what Illich has to say in terms of the ensuing state by which humanity has been confronted by this sunset.

Even as Illich the theologian and man of faith presents this from the perspective of the crucifixion, it is not difficult to appreciate his case for a kenotic appraisal of history, which modernity has witnessed in the life and ultimate sacrifice of individuals like the Mahatma Gandhi, Edith Stein, Martin Luther King Jr., Milada Horáková, Dorothy Day and many others. The approach to history presents a scenario where human beings realize the freedom gained from the sense of love and self-sacrifice that kenotic thinking bequeaths. While Illich's use of theological discourse may not be to everyone's intellectual or moral disposition, the argument that he makes with regards to contingency must be examined from a utopian stance (in the sense discussed earlier in Chapter 3) in an attempt to dispel the night that follows the sunset.

On such terms, Illich's theological pragmatic remains both relevant and reassuring, particularly in terms of how it represents, in and of itself, all that one would attribute to the possibilities which emerge from the moment of history's aporia. This, I would read in parallel with Blumenberg's comment on Goethe's *Theory of Colours* (1994), arguing that "[t]he Goethean pragmatics of knowledge is determined by the belief that man does not force his way into nature as an intruder but always already enjoys the richest communion with truth from the midst of nature and by virtue of its favor." (Blumenberg

2010, p. 29) In similar ways Illich is confronted by history as he leaps back into its cavernous gaps, seeking connections across which he finds ways to shed light on modes of Being that refuse to allow the positivist's *empirie* to limit their portent. This resonates with how Blumenberg beautifully describes Goethe's refusal to concede to Newton's theory of color, as an "Olympian rage against Newtonian physics." Goethe allows himself to venture "one last time, an existence of trust in Being," as he was "filled with the conviction that we only need to keep our eyes open to encounter the self-showing of truth." (Blumenberg 2010, p. 28; on Goethe see also Wittgenstein 1990 and Baldacchino 2017, pp. 206–213)

Metaphor and Agency

In its many iterations, the discourse of contingency, its deceptive 'disappearance' and its subsequent "change of hands" from those of God to that of humanity, cannot be distanced from the metaphorological practices that gave it such a multifaceted meaning and by consequence placed it at the center of those discourses which so often ignore it. Illich's metaphor of contingency's sunset gains a powerful insight into how historically this had an impact on technology and with it the onset of its new role in modernity. But Illich was never alone in this line of thinking, considering the history of contingency as a concept, notably running from Aristotle (1984a; 1984b) to Avicenna (2005), Aquinas (1991; 1993); Duns Scotus (1987; 1994), Hegel (1975), Nietzsche (1968; 1982), Dewey (1893), Pareyson (2000) and Rorty (1989), to name a few, and to which I would add that of Agnes Heller (1993) whose work provides strong parallels yet contrasting views to Illich's.

The place of contingency at the turn of modernity is accentuated by Heller, who argues that "[a]t the dawn of modernity, contingency-awareness arrived with a shock that could no longer be given a cosmetic treatment, relegated to the margins. Once a marginal phenomenon, contingency-awareness moved swiftly towards the centre." (Heller 1993, p. 4) Having explained that this shock originates in how contingency awareness culminates to a "point of a conflict which will be presently overcome"—that point being the moment of *aletheia*, "of unconcealment, the moment of truth" which in the Jewish-Christian genesis is emblematized in Adam and Eve's eating from the tree of knowledge—Heller argues that "from this moment onwards, men and women must choose on their own, and they must respond, that is, they must take responsibility. *Contingency is the loss of innocence.*" (Heller 1993, p. 4, emphasis added)

This begins to resonate with Illich's description of humans taking contingency into their hands and away from God's own, but the problem is *where* and *when* this happens. Heller adds that "contingency-awareness evaporates in the instant of shock. God's voice resounds loudly; although cursing and punishing them, he still remains the God of human creatures. He makes sure that their lives do not remain without purpose." (Heller 1993, p. 4)

Following Illich's historical-theological interpretation, could one say that as the shock of contingency brings back God's agency with the loss of innocence, it was with Christ's crucifixion and resurrection that it was returned to human beings, only to take on redemption as a sign of removing it from God's hands? Heller's choice of historical context is not that alien to Illich's, though what she draws from it is not a sunset inasmuch as another dawn, which she articulates as follows:

> The shock came, and it was immense, because modern natural sciences were invented by Christians in a world where the teleological explanation of the universe and of each and every person's life had been taken for granted since time immemorial. For long, it had been a matter of heresy even to touch the chord of a possible contingency. The moment of truth, of *aletheia*, of unconcealment appeared—in the dominating Christian interpretation of Genesis—as the hereditary sin. Men and women were anything but contingent in medieval imagination; on the contrary, they were guided by Providence, and so was the whole universe. As far as our knowledge goes, never before had a dominating world-view been so entirely impregnated by the idea of providence, never before was teleology so universally conceived and accepted as in medieval Christianity. In this cosmos, no leaf could have fallen from a tree without having been so willed by God. (Heller 1993, p. 5)

Heller's interpretation is qualified by the distinction that she draws between cosmic and historical contingency, which implies a series of teleological differences as to where contingency is placed in terms of its agency, meaning that contingency itself occupies different places in the metaphorological accounts of the various histories that invoke them.

The commonly held claim which Heller reiterates about the place of contingency in the Middle Ages sits in some contrast with Illich's. From Illich's perspective one would assume that with the onset of modernity and going with the assumption of what an actual sunset of contingency means and what ensues from it, would bring us back on a commonly held route that opened its way to modern takes on contingency. But this remains unclear unless

Illich's take on contingency (as broadly reflecting, but then evolving beyond, Blumenberg's) is framed within its relationship with his idea of reform and disestablishment.

This requires us to revisit contingency in its conceptual evolution in the Middle Ages from a lens that, inasmuch as it is philosophical in composition, it remains semantically theological. In this spirit, a close look at the concept of contingency in the theologies of Christian medieval thought, particularly in the work of John Duns Scotus, would confirm how Illich's break with the assumption that "being guided by Providence" must mean that "men and women were anything but contingent in medieval imagination," (Heller 1993, p. 5) is but an opening to a deeper understanding of contingency that promises a greater wealth of possibilities.

A major qualifier that needs to be kept in mind when approaching concepts such as contingency from the perspectives that Illich tends to proffer as they come informed by his close reading of medieval theology, is best illustrated by a group of scholars who produced a remarkable study and full commentary of Duns Scotus's *Lectura I 39* on *Contingency and Freedom*. In their detailed introduction to this study, Vos Jaczn et al state the following:

> In logic many things change. As we have seen, the chronological order loses its logical priority; the tightly knit correspondence between *Sein und Zeit* is unraveled, because the structures of being are not revealed to us by time. The structured nature of being demands an approach in terms of structural moments. The theory of 'instances', which assumes 'ante' and 'post' to be related structurally, stands out as a striking example. If theologians in later times say: "We must not understand this order chronologically but logically," *they appeal to the Scotian method of analysis*. (Vos Jaczn et al., in Duns Scotus 1994, p. 34, emphasis added)

Illich's subscription to forms of reasoning that remain distant from the causal measures of the *empeiría* (a distinction that he consciously draws from philosophical and theological traditions that originate in Parmenidean logic) is not that distant from the horizon traveled by the Scotian method of analysis. Opting to travel logically, rather than take expected chronological trajectories, comes close to what Blumenberg has to say when discussing the moral insights that were inherited from the Stoics,

> Teleology no longer signifies the universal concord of cosmos and logos for the fulfillment of human existence (εὐδαιμωνία); instead, it guarantees the conspicuousness and penetrative force of those truths on which salvation depends, beside which all other truths sink back into the semidarkness of mere verisimilitude or the inaccessibility of *res obscurae*. (Blumenberg 2010, p. 19)

On the logic of salvation, the argument that contingency cannot subsist in the implied necessity of a set goal (*telos*) for and by which fulfilment is possible, is invalidated by a shift in what teleology signifies. Instead of an ordering of causality, a teleology of salvation sustains—or rather, *subsists in*—those truths on which other possibilities come in play. This also implies that inasmuch as teleology is decoupled from necessity, necessity itself is no longer regarded as the direct elimination of contingency as they become *synchronically* possible. One must read this possibility in the sense by which Duns Scotus would argue that it is not incompatible for God and contingency to be synchronous by dint of the freedom that is given in the act of creation. It would also mean that the possibility of contingency is not only present in Medieval thinking, but it retains strong compatibility with a contingent universe that is created by a necessary God.

> The far-reaching impact of [Scotus's] theory of synchronic contingency becomes clearest in the concept of the will. God's will and man's will act within an ontological frame which *embraces innumerable contingent states of affairs together with necessary states of affairs*. The freedom of a will which, willing something at a specific moment, can will something else or the opposite or the very same moment, can only be maintained within a contingent universe. (Vos Jaczn et al., in Duns Scotus 1994, p. 26, emphasis added)

Closely following Blumenberg, Illich excavates a wealth of Medieval thinking on contingency to reveal what could be seen as a quasi-antinomic character. Contingency appears to have two characters which present us with a difficulty in trying to make one compatible with the other. It has to do with a sense by which we conceive of agency as necessary while running in parallel with contingency which in Aristotelian logic is deemed to be necessity's opposite. One finds some resonance in Heller's account of historical contingency, which unlike cosmic contingency, is drawn to a particularistic state of affairs where, if any, a teleological explanation takes a number of radically different trajectories. Heller sums this up through representative metaphors of "the zero and the infinite" as that of cosmic contingency, and the "being-thrown-into" for historic contingency (see Heller 1993, pp. 3ff) While this doesn't draw a neat parallel between Heller and Illich—which, as argued above, would present us with some contrast in terms of how they approach medieval philosophy—the idea that contingency presents us with two instances, if not two *logics*, is evident in the binary track that they both follow.

Drawing from the Franciscan tradition to which Duns Scotus belonged, Illich explains why the binary notion of a necessary God in a contingent universe becomes perplexing to the modern mind:

The will of God, Duns Scotus says, is its own cause. This emphasis on the freedom of God which one finds in the Franciscan tradition of Bonaventure, Duns Scotus, and Francis himself, and *which is so unsatisfactory to the modern mind*, has two sides (…). Bonaventure, for instance, brought God nearer to me by making him more like me. And absolute resignation before the will of God is something profoundly beautiful. But, it is also true that the emphasis on the supremacy and inscrutability of God's will in Franciscan philosophy is finally pushed to the point where this will becomes arbitrary. Contingency at this point takes on the meaning which it still has today in English and French: mere chance, or instance. All one can say about what happens is that it happens because it happens (RNF, pp. 66–67, emphasis added).

The point in question puts contingency right at the center of Illich's approach to a world which, as it takes itself from God's hands, remains intrinsically bound to the necessary existence of God. The latter must also be read from within the events of Christ's incarnation, death and resurrection, which in Illich's metaphorology are key to the narrative of daily living.

Watersheds

It is by now clear that Illich's close attention to early and medieval thought moves away from a chronological slide rule, as its logic follows other than a pattern of causal historical sequencing. Apart from locating contingency in a very different perspective from that of his contemporaries, viewing history through Illich's eyes reveals a different complexion to what is meant by "history" and "the historical." By now it should be clear that this belongs to a wider methodological approach, in that, as Illich frequently argued, his objective was always motivated by a broader sense of possibilities that operate on the same preterideological horizon travelled by Ladner's discussion of reform. As in the case for reform, this sense of boundlessness is expressed in constant reiterations of form and re-form.

Synchronically Possible

To view contingency through Illich's gaze is to find a way that is neither tied to the assumption of a substantive break that Heller and others have reasonably identified between the modern and pre-modern, and less so invested in trying to travel a route that Rorty carefully threads between determinism and relativism in his liberal argument for solidarity. Heller is historically right in stating that "[i]t is in the process of deconstructing the pre-modern social arrangement that men and women have become contingent." (1993, p. 18) Likewise, one is not inclined to dismiss Rorty's pragmatic hope in opening the possibilities of contingency by reminding us that we should reconcile ourselves "to the idea that most reality is indifferent to our descriptions of it." (Rorty 1989, p. 7) While there is more to Heller's and Rorty's discussion of contingency and it would do them no justice to condense their position in some kind of artificial dualism, it is safe to argue that in Illich's mapping of contingency one finds different (inasmuch as there are *other*) routes, some of which will invariably converge, while others would take off into innumerable directions.

But apart from *where* Illich places contingency in history, another insight that emerges from his exploration of this central concept is found in *how* he characterizes what is in store after contingency's sunset. This is presented as a set of reflections over what we could do in response to (but also in anticipation of) our own approach to contingency's equivocal "place" that we *inhabit*. Two key concepts always come up in Illich's work: (a) the tools with which we *make* the world, and (b) the manner of conviviality by which we *live in* the world, and by implication, *towards which* we direct our intentionality. However, this comes with a caveat, as at some point in his later work, Illich begins to question his approach to tools, keeping us wondering whether it would leave us with any hope for a convivial form of living.

> If it is true that "tool" is an age or epoch-specific concept which is characteristic of a certain period, a period during which the concept of tool, or technology, as one more often says, becomes perhaps the most unquestionable of everyday certainties, then the possibility is opened of doing what I have been trying to do during the last fifteen or twenty years: to claim, or, at least, establish the hypothesis that *sometime during the 1980s the technological society which began in the fourteenth century came to an end.* (RNF, p. 77, emphasis added)

For us to make sense of what would conviviality mean beyond the watershed that marked (what Illich regards as) the end of technological society, we cannot but resort to what he means by a contingent state of affairs. This keeps returning to the Franciscan perspective of a necessary God whose creation is extended as a contingent universe; a freedom whose possibilities hand over creation to us humans.

These days some would be tempted to remark that this is nothing but another way of engaging with "the Anthropocene." However, I hasten to add that beyond the merits or otherwise of this widespread discussion, to go off at such tangents would distract us from what, many centuries before the dreaded term was coined, John Duns Scotus was already developing his concepts of synchronic contingency and contingent causality (see Duns Scotus 1994; Sylwanowicz 1996 and Muller 2017, pp. 147–162). Even more to the point, though attempts to co-opt Illich into "the Anthropocene" crowd are there, Illich's point of departure is radically different from what some in this crowd would like it to be.

Discussing Duns Scotus, Voz Jaczn et al. explain that as we ask (if not wonder) where to find the origins of Scotus's concept of synchronic contingency, an unambiguous answer is clearly evident in his works. It comes "from a radical reflection on the experience of God's love, which is man's—and reality's—free source, and on the specifically Christian faith of God's trinitarian character." (Voz Jaczn et al., in Duns Scotus 1994, pp. 27–28) As much as the temptation to take this further into a detailed philosophical discussion is strong (though this time not on the Anthropocene, but on medieval philosophy), I suggest that we stay within the terms of Illich's work as the aim should be focused on his take on systems, as this is crucial for an understanding of contingency's relationship with reform and disestablishment.

Illich argues that it would appear to him "that the age of tools *has now given way to the age of systems*, exemplified in the conception of the earth as an ecosystem, and the human being as an immune system." (RNF, p. 77, emphasis added) He regards this as a watershed which he openly argues to have omitted in his earlier work. "I am at fault," he remarks, "for having persuaded some very good people who read me seriously that it makes sense to talk about a school system as a social tool, or about the medical establishment as a device." (RNF, p. 77) Though the terms *eco* and *immune* systems appear to resonate with the current discourses of technological and human-made shifts in the Earth's own physical existence, it would be mistaken to read Illich outside the dynamic relationship between reform and contingency as they have evolved in his unique conceptualization of disestablished practices. This is because to remain with tools is not what Illich can accept anymore.

Franciscan Hope?

The instrumental era of technology has been with us for centuries. Tools remained core to most of our lived experience—at least for those born before the late 1980s and early 1990s. But, as Illich explains in conversation with Cayley, "we now consider the human being as a system, that is, as an extraordinarily complex arrangement of feedback loops" whose fundamental characteristic "is to seek its own survival by maintaining an informational balance which keeps it viable." (RNF, p. 204)

Moving from tools to systems is not to be taken lightly with Illich. That this is expressed in his discussion of contingency and its sunset, is equally fundamental to our understanding of how his thought evolved from the time that he wrote *Tools for Conviviality* where he presented his readers with two other watersheds, this time marked by medical history. As one revisits these other watersheds, one cannot ignore how this puts in marked relief a short, albeit highly significant, reference that Illich makes when he tells Cayley that, "[t]he system analytic doctor imputes ever more complex feedback loops, most of which, if not all of which, he recognizes only *on the basis of probabilities.*" (RNF, p. 204, emphasis added) Illich is by no means yearning for or signaling towards a return to those Galenic medical practices where the doctor played an interpretative role which came close to "an exegesis of what the patient reveals about himself." (TCC, p. 35) Rather, Illich is saying that unlike the Galenic doctor and beyond the two thresholds which he comprehensively discussed many years before, the new doctor (and I dare add, the new educator) is now a systems analyst who sees the body in the same way a computer sustains an ecology of informational balance.

As the idea of instrumentality comes to an end, thereby signaling a new watershed, we are left wondering what is to be made of the two watersheds that Illich discussed in *Tools for Conviviality*. Then, Illich regarded the first watershed as coinciding with 1913, where "a patient began to have more than a fifty-fifty chance that a graduate of a medical school would provide him with a specifically effective treatment." (TFC, p. 1) Yet this was surpassed by a second watershed when in the mid-1950s, medicine "had itself created new kinds of disease." (TFC, p. 2) There, the "preservation of the sick life of medically dependent people in an unhealthy environment became the principal business of the medical profession." (TFC, p. 3)

Instrumentality surpassed any other possible understanding of medicine (just as it did with schooling); which also meant that access became a matter of commerce and treatment as it "became increasingly the privilege of those individuals who through previous consumption of medical services had established a claim to more of it." (TFC, p. 3) This did not simply appear as an imposition. As with all forms of hegemony, the institutionalization of care emerged from (and was nurtured by) a consensus informed by how tools have gained even more legitimacy through measured verification and results that reinforced the first watershed with forms of reassurance to which everyone was willing to pay a price set by the benefits of medical progress.

> People began to understand the relationship between health and a balanced diet, fresh air, calisthenics, pure water and soap. New devices ranging from toothbrushes to Band-Aids and condoms became widely available. The positive contribution of modern medicine to individual health during the early part of the twentieth century can hardly be questioned. (TFC, p. 6)

As this precipitated the second watershed with its breakthroughs in the cure of new diseases, it also meant that the instrumentality by which everyone welcomed progress also strengthened the institutionalization of such medical practices. Illich regards this as a turn where "[t]rust in miracle cures obliterated good sense and traditional wisdom on healing and health care." (TFC, p. 6)

> The second watershed was superseded when the marginal disutility increased as further monopoly by the medical establishment became an indicator of more suffering for larger numbers of people. After the passage of this second watershed, medicine still claimed continued progress, as measured by the new landmarks doctors set for them-selves and then reached: *both predictable discoveries and costs*. (TFC, pp. 6–7, emphasis added)

With Illich's attention shifting from tools to systems, we begin to understand why, ceding to the tacit tyranny which somehow expects us all to bring our reading of anything into the latest trends in theory and practice, is not an option. Recalling from where he begins to articulate his view of the watersheds by which he presents us with the manipulation of need and care, Illich's method and analysis cannot be understood outside its metaphorological pragmatic. As Illich's narrative of watersheds goes deeper into the understanding of the truths that emerge from the narratives of history, we begin to appreciate how, when speaking of systems, Illich is also emphasizing the juncture of contingency. By openly claiming such a juncture from the Franciscan take on creation, in whose being one cannot miss a radicalism embedded in the narrative of freedom as bequeathed by the Christ-event, he remains in keeping with the parameters of this narrative.

In taking his approach beyond what he presumed to remain unchallenged through a long era of instrumentality which only seems to have ended in the last couple of decades of the 20th century, Illich willfully leads his readers into a territory that would make no sense unless read from outside the established world of everything that includes charity, care and rights. Consistently and to the end, Illich probes into what this disestablished world would look like, even when to the majority such a possibility remains elusive. If anything, Illich remains Franciscan in his outlook on the mutuality of creation in its synchronic possibilities.

> Since I live in this world, I couldn't find a better world to live with those whom I love. And those are exactly people who overwhelmingly are aware of the fact that we are beyond a threshold, who are not any more so deeply imbued by the spirit of utility or instrumentality that they wouldn't be able to understand what I mean by gratuity. I do believe that there is a way of being understood today when you speak about gratuity and gratuity, in its most beautiful, flowering is praise, mutual enjoyment. (TCC, p. 48)

Abbreviations: Works by Illich

IC   *Ivan Illich In Conversation.*
MN   *Limits to Medicine. Medical Nemesis*
RNF   *The Rivers North of the Future.*
TCC   *The Corruption of Christianity*
TFC   *Tools for Conviviality.*
VT   *In the Vineyard of the Text*

References

Alter, R. (2019) (trans. & commentary). *The Hebrew Bible.* Vol. 2. Prophets Nevi'im. New York; London: Norton & Co.
Aquinas, T. (1991). *Summa Theologiae. A Concise Translation.* McDermott (ed.). London: Methuen.
Aquinas, T. (1993). *Selected Philosophical Writings.* McDermott (ed. & trans.). Oxford: Oxford University Press.
Aristotle. (1984a). *Metaphysics. The Complete Works of Aristotle Vol. II.* Princeton, NJ: Princeton University Press.
Aristotle. (1984b). *Rhetoric. The Complete Works of Aristotle Vol. II.* Princeton, NJ: Princeton University Press.
Avicenna. (2005). *The Metaphysics of The Healing.* Provo, Utah: Brigham Young University Press.
Baldacchino, J. (2017). Art's Ped(ago)gies. *What Is Art Education? After Deleuze and Guattaria.* Jagodzinski, J. (ed.). London: Palgrave Macmillan.
BBC (2014). Pope Francis warns on 'piecemeal World War III'. 13 September. http://www.bbc.co.uk/news/world-europe-29190890

Blumenberg, H. (2010). *Paradigms for a Metaphorology*. Ithaca, NY: Cornell University Press.
Dewey, J. (1893). The superstition of necessity. *The Monist*, 3(3), 362–379.
Duns Scotus, J. (1987). *Philosophical Writings*. Walter, A. (trans.). Indianapolis, IN: Hackett.
Duns Scotus, J. (1994). *Contingency and Freedom. Lectura I 39*. Dordrecht; Boston, MA: Kluwer Academic Publishers.
Goethe, J. W. (1994). *Theory of Colours*. Cambridge, MA: MIT Press.
Hegel, G. W. F. (1975 [1830]). *Hegel's Logic: Being Part One of the Encyclopaedia of the Philosophical Sciences*. Oxford: Clarendon Press.
Heller, A. (1993). *A Philosophy of History in Fragments*. Oxford; Cambridge, MA: Blackwell.
Hoinacki, L. (2003). The Trajectory of Ivan Illich. *Bulletin of Science, Technology & Society*, 23(5), October, 382–389.
Hugh, of Saint-Victor. (1991). *The Didascalicon of Hugh of St. Victor: A Medieval Guide to the Arts*. New York: Columbia University Press.
Illich, I. (1993). *In the Vineyard of the Text: A Commentary to Hugh's Didascalicon*. Chicago, IL: University of Chicago Press. (VT)
Illich, I. (2001). *Tools for Conviviality*. New York: Marion Boyars. (TFC)
Illich, I. (2010). *Limits to Medicine. Medical Nemesis: The Expropriation of Health*. New York: Marion Boyars. (MN)
Illich, I. & Cayley, D. (1992). *Ivan Illich in Conversation*. Toronto: House of Anansi Press. (IC)
Illich, I. & Cayley, D. (2000). *The Corruption of Christianity*. CBC Ideas transcript. Toronto: Canadian Broadcasting Corporation. Accessed: May 4, 2019, http://www.davidcayley.com/transcripts (TCC)
Illich, I. & Cayley, D. (2005). *The Rivers North of the Future: The Testament of Ivan Illich*. Toronto: House of Anansi Press. (RNF)
Ladner, G. B. (1959). *The Idea of Reform Its Impact on Christian Thought and Action in the Age of the Fathers*. Cambridge: Harvard University Press.
Muller, R. A. (2017). *Divine Will and Human Choice. Freedom, Contingency, and Necessity in Early Modern Reformed Thought*. Grand Rapids, MI: Baker Academic.
Nietzsche, F. (1968). *The Will to Power*. W. Kaufmann & R. J. Hollingdale (trans.). New York: Vintage Books.
Nietzsche, F. (1982). *Twilight of the Idols and The Anti-Christ*. R. J. Hollingdale (trans.). Harmondsworth: Penguin Books.
Pareyson, L. (2000). *Ontologia della libertà. Il male e la sofferenza*. Torino: Einaudi.
Rorty, R. (1989). *Contingency, Irony, and Solidarity*. Cambridge; New York: Cambridge University Press.
Sylwanowicz, M. (1996). *Contingent Causality and the Foundations of Duns Scotus' Metaphysics*. Leiden; New York: E.J. Brill.
Wittgenstein, L. (1990). *Remarks on Colour*. G.E.M. Anscombe (ed.) L.L. McAlister & M. Schättle (trans.). Oxford: Blackwell.

· 8 ·
DISESTABLISHMENT

Bookending, as it were, Illich's entire body of work are two major *critiques* by which one could somehow understand the width and depth of what he stood for. The first is marked by a need for the overall disestablishment of the historic institutionalization of daily living. The other end finds itself preoccupied with the demise of the tool and the emergence of a world of systems.

A Journey's Ends

Tools of Possibility

Illich's call for disestablishment is pretty well known, though it is often seen in isolation from his approach to reform and contingency, not to mention how tradition and immanence are central to his work yet often missed. Those who have read Illich for one reason or another, would know that disestablishment is best known from, if not emblematized by his books *Deschooling Society* and *Medical Nemesis*. There he articulates the disestablishment of knowledge and care as the transformation of institutionalized tools from professionalized means of a hierarchy of needs to the restoration of conviviality. The latter would emerge from a profound understanding of tools, which, when moved away from their instrumentalization, would realize a correlation between freedom and equality, thereby embracing the possibility of disentangling society from an economy of scarcity.

As discussed earlier in the chapters on tradition and learning, in Illich's critique, deschooling operates on a model that is shaped on the disestablishment of religion. This is informed by an anthropological assessment of how institutions work, which in Illich's case, is strongly influenced by Luckmann's work within that field. This model of disestablishment is recurring throughout Illich's work, whether it deals with teaching or medicine, care, the environment, gender, or anything that we would identify with our acts of living.

> Lay control over an expanding medical technocracy is not unlike the professionalization of the patient: both enhance medical power and increase its *nocebo* effect. As long as the public bows to the professional monopoly in assigning the sick-role, it cannot control hidden health hierarchies that multiply patients. *The medical clergy can be controlled only if the law is used to restrict and disestablish its monopoly on deciding what constitutes disease, who is sick, and what ought to be done to him or her.* (MN, p. 249, emphasis added)

One cannot but note that in what he proposes as possible solutions to the professionalization of daily living, Illich is by no means extra-legal. His approach is to stay within and change the Law, which in itself presents us with a degree of paradox in that disestablishment must also begin with the Law itself as it is the product of a legal system that is built and operated on institutions. However, one could read this from another direction, in that it was also the legal system that disestablished the church: "Two centuries ago the United States led the world in a movement to disestablish the monopoly of a single church. Now we need the *constitutional disestablishment* of the monopoly of the school." (DS, p. 11, emphasis added)

Illich further argues that "[t]o make this disestablishment effective, *we need a law forbidding discrimination* in hiring, voting, or admission to centers of learning based on previous attendance at some curriculum." (DS, p. 11, emphasis added) He entertains no illusion as to how being within this legal and structural milieu, means that reforming implies a synchronic set of states of affairs by which necessary structures must also become a space for contingent possibilities. Just as disestablishment through the Law implies an intrinsic change, it also means that the Law must be taken out of its instrumental function. Once disestablished, knowledge and learning forfeit groundedness to become horizons of possible solutions that could potentially act as agents of convivial opportunities. Basically, Illich is saying that what is immanent to knowledge is not the school, but the relationship between person and society, freedom and conviviality. A society that remains schooled cannot liberate its own schools from discrimination because it becomes a ground for an institutionalized form of living. The same goes for knowledge as we often trap it by the coupling of competence with what is defined by the institution's curriculum.

> To detach competence from curriculum, inquiries into a man's learning history must be made taboo, like inquiries into his political affiliation, church attendance, lineage, sex habits, or racial background. *Laws forbidding discrimination on the basis of prior schooling must be enacted.* Laws, of course, cannot stop prejudice against the unschooled—nor are they meant to force anyone to intermarry with an autodidact—but they can discourage unjustified discrimination. (DS, p. 12, emphasis added)

This already provides a deeper understanding of what one could identify with the idea of a system, especially if we read this through a discussion of reform and contingency. However, at that stage, Illich's approach to the concept of the whole (in terms of how change is launched from within) was different from what he would then identify with the dawn of a society of systems. At the stage of his theory of disestablishment Illich was not engaging with how contingency's sunset takes unexpected forms, though his approach to disestablishment has always been firmly articulated by his understanding of reform (qua *re*-form), as discussed earlier in this volume.

A Changed Nemesis

This brings us to the other end of Illich's theoretical horizon which, as discussed in the previous chapter, comes much later in his work. Illich begins to dispute his argument that a school system is a social tool and that the medical establishment is a device (RNF, p. 77). Challenging what Illich so strongly held as being central to his project cannot be taken lightly. It would invariably impact on how tools, and with them the possibility of convivial societies in their diversity, are put into a very different light, at least in terms of how we could create and sustain them.

The backdrop to this scenario comes with his argument that systems have now overtaken tools. Society, and with it the lived world, will have to be approached in a very different way. This raises several questions over what the role of the technological era would look and feel like in such an historical context. One cannot but wonder if Illich's claimed radical change in history does give way to a very different outlook and function of living, and if so, what would inhabit the spaces that it leaves behind. By this I mean that while humans would still inhabit such spaces, another fundamental question has to do with the manner by which our ways of *living* changes.

> Let me make it simpler. You have children, and you told me once you have great difficulty imagining why they are so fond of branded clothes. Why wear a T-shirt decorated with an icon? To me this is a poetical way of speaking about a person *swallowed by the system*, someone who needs an icon, which I can touch when I want to obtain something, be it only attention from the other. (RNF, p. 163, emphasis added)

As lifestyles always evolve and change, and as we continue to agree and disagree over different forms of being, knowing, doing and seeing within new forms of institutional organisms that simply swallow us, the idea of disestablishment comes up in terms of how or whether it retains the same significance by which Illich originally held it. How would disestablishment stop us from being *swallowed* by the system? What stops the *scopic* disembodiment of the self through our being laid bare by the icons which we embrace as being part of us, and where everything is laid bare to be viewed by everything and everyone as we find ourselves desiring this intrusion? Reading Illich's early works with this in mind, one begins to wonder if this has to do with how myth is played within the relationship between reform, contingency and disestablishment which, in a society of systems may well take different and unexpected forms.

Recalling how Nemesis "inflicted on [Prometheus] a kind of pain meant for demigods, not for men," Illich reminds his readers how Prometheus's "hopeless and unending suffering turned the hero into an immortal reminder of inescapable cosmic retaliation." (MN, p. 263) Given the way Illich's metaphorological practice operates, we need to cast our minds on how myth begins to describe our own daily living from such a narrative. In this case, the argument for Promethean action—which Illich always contrasts *a posteriori* with that of Epimethean hope—is put into question.

Invariably, those whose faith in industry remains unshaken—whether coming from social-democratic optimism or neoliberal managerialism—would get jittery and suspicious by statements like Illich's. In their perspective, Illich appears to be calling for a reversal of their political and economic solutions. But this would only be true if Illich were speaking on the basis of the same paradigms which progressive, liberal, and conservative pundits tend to operate. Illich's *modus operandi* is different. He tells us that the promethean is rendered irrelevant by the fact that its nemesis has changed tact, pulling the rug from under any form of political and economic consolation. The nemesis which afflicted the promethean dream of progress and liberty is not the same. In fact, "[t]he social nature of nemesis has now changed."

> With the industrialization of desire and the engineering of corresponding ritual responses, hubris has spread. Unbounded material progress has become Everyman's goal. Industrial hubris has destroyed the mythical framework of limits to irrational fantasies, has made technical answers to mad dreams seem rational, and has turned the pursuit of destructive values into a conspiracy between purveyor and client. Nemesis for the masses is now the inescapable backlash of industrial progress. Modern nemesis is the material monster born from the overarching industrial dream. It has spread as far and as wide as universal schooling, mass transportation, industrial wage labor, and the medicalization of health. (MN, p. 263)

One does wonder how this would hold in an era where tools have given way to systems. Or perhaps, one might be ready to suggest that even when Illich was entirely focused on tools, his ideas were prescient enough to anticipate a world of systems, mostly because his metaphorological practice is, in retrospect, still powerful and capable of sustaining the discourse and critique that he would never had time to fully articulate. I see the latter as being possible mostly because, as I will show in this concluding chapter, Illich does not only build his work on the fluid yet strong understanding of reform and contingency, but also because his work never ignored the aporetic nature by which myth continues to work in our versatile ways of doing, making and seeing this world of ours.

Myth and Transparency

Gianni Vattimo opens the third chapter of his book *The Transparent Society* with these words:

> One of the most urgent problems faced by contemporary consciousness as it becomes aware of how the world is 'fabled' by the media and the social sciences is that of redefining its own position with regard to myth. This is above all to avoid the (common) conclusion that the appropriate response to the question 'What does thinking mean?' in late modernity lies precisely in a rediscovery of myth. (Vattimo 1992, p. 21)

Vattimo's work holds ample relevance to how we can now read Illich, especially when Vattimo increasingly makes of society an object of his inquiry that is upheld and transformed into a system which is not that different from the manner that Illich suggests. *The Transparent Society* was published in 1989, eighteen years after *Deschooling Society* appeared in bookstores. While travelling different routes, which somehow run in a degree of parallelism with Vattimo's, Illich already offers several anticipations in how he positions himself right at the coalface of the massive problem by which education was then (and remains now) challenged. In more than one sense, schooling has evolved into a fabrication of what Vattimo and others before him, like Saussure and Barthes, recognize in the order of myth. Here, myth plays a dual role which, not unlike that of a synchronous contingency, reflects an aporetic state of affairs. By taking this position, one could explain why Vattimo and Illich have drawn a degree of criticism from both sides of the ideological equation, being deemed as reactionary and radical in equal measure by those who would prefer to see contradictions resolved and done away with.

Now that both *Deschooling Society* and *The Transparent Society* are distant enough to be regarded with a degree of objectivity and hindsight—especially when Vattimo and Illich subsequently wrote other texts which either extended or clarified their respective books—we can safely say that what these works stand for has been amply vindicated by how history has turned out to be(come). It is reasonable to argue that these books' *vindication* does not come about in the form of *factualized* scenarios. Beyond the empirie of measurement, other terms of reference afford us effective ways by which we approach the watershed of systems that were rightly signaled by Vattimo and Illich. By first understanding the aporetic character of myth and institutions, we come to understand with Vattimo that there is no such thing as a ground on which to sustain our hermeneutic ordering of the world, even when we cannot do without such a hermeneutic (see Vattimo 1995). This resonates with the prospect of a contingent world that is no longer scary, and which, as argued in the previous chapter, is clearly present in Illich's Scotian understanding of a universe of possibilities.

Constructed Equity

In seeking to make sense of Illich's *Deschooling Society*—and with it, his overall notion of disestablishment—one must get as close and as conversant as possible with the contingent reality of myth itself, especially in what it has come to represent in modernity as a form of self-articulation that warrants the need to what Vattimo (1992, p. 17) calls "self-transparency" [*autotrasparenza*] (see also Vattimo 2011).

To attempt to dismiss *Deschooling Society* by simplistic arguments for education is to miss what Illich aims to achieve when he talks about a schooled society. Not unlike schooling, the politics that emerge from the language of myth is aimed at a universal assumption of transparency by which we all thought everyone would gain the right to partake of everything else. Just like universal transparency the universality of schooling becomes an effective means that represents the very opposite. Those acts of emancipation conceived from the idea of universal schooling were always intended to bring everyone into the flow of knowledge. Nothing is spared to achieve this. Instrumentally or otherwise, everyone must partake of a common-held duty: to go to school. Those who refuse or play truant will be heavily fined. Schooling became a responsibility by which one shares a universalized assumption of knowing. The claim is that this gives individuals a degree of freedom, which in turn will also equip the same individual to respond to the demands that the industry of knowledge represents.

In schooling, one already finds a deeply set *fabular* assumption of truth. This is presented as a form of knowledge that is scaffolded and centered around the perceived growth and ability of pupils. In turn, pupils respond by integrating themselves into this world of knowing and become assimilated within the demands that society expects of them. The representational character of this fabular assumption of knowledge is mythical, in that it represents (and is articulated) in a way that it could in turn become *lexical*, as it finds itself recounted—*told*, as in *raccontato*—into the grammars of the Law. Inasmuch as it is directly a form of representation that begins to claim a universal metalanguage, myth remains a schooled affair. It makes the school possible because of its unique capacity to transcend the first level of signification (that of literal meaning) by which it would then become a referential armature for further levels to be constructed. This is the epicenter of the constructivist approach to education, and by which most liberal and progressive educators have vouched to put the child at the *center* of learning, only to reduce the child into an *object* of learning.

Through the lexical reassertion of myth, the schooled constructs of learning become themselves participants and fundamental to the dogmatic system of myth. This seems to be a paradox in that critical and liberal pedagogies claim that a learner-centered scenario empowers the student. However, Illich shows that the very opposite of empowerment happens. It is important to add that the origin of the dogma of schooling did not come from some force of evil or oppression, as some would argue in their digressive assumptions.

The origins were well-meant, and they resulted from those utopian desires of a society that in becoming self-transparent would ultimately show itself for what it is and be owned by everyone. But, Vattimo reminds us, just as we seek transparency as a form of deconstruction of the dogma of myth, we find ourselves trapped in the aporia of the Enlightenment, where "as the self-transparency of society becomes possible from a purely technical point of view, this self-transparency is shown to be an ideal of domination not emancipation." (Vattimo 1992, p. 23)

The impossibility of self-transparency comes from the fact that methodologically, for it to work, it would need a space that in and of itself is entirely analytical and never normative. This also warrants a common grounding on which everything must have an equal footing before we could even claim that self-transparency could happen on a universal scale where nothing is left concealed. The counter-point comes from the realization that self-transparency needs to be schooled on the common grounds by which the school, planned on a common-core curriculum that is in turn constructively scaffolded on presumed child-centered approaches, is planned to fulfil needed outcomes. This is proposed by the projections that those who school learning also seek (and demand) optimum results from it. As the common-core assumption of a transparent and therefore equitable schooling begins to make commerce of its supposedly emancipatory processes, one finds that for the latter to happen, the system must immediately differentiate the assumption of a common ground for self-transparency by means of measured discriminatory mechanisms. This raises the question of rights. Is there a right to reject schooling yet claim an equal right to self-transparent participation?

Some might read the call for differentiation as confirmation of the intrinsic democratic approach taken by a schooled common-core edifice. On a closer look, this call for differentiation is never benign. For it to function it would need to undermine the equitable levelling by which communication was supposed to be launched. The equitable levelling of communication always happens at the level of a meta-language, indeed at the language of myth, where meaning in itself is referential and operated by a multiplicity of empty signifiers whose meanings are premised on this free-flow.

Fabled Worlds

Vattimo argues that "instead of moving towards self-transparency, the society of the human sciences and generalized communication has moved towards what could, in general, be called 'the fabling of the world.'" [*fabulazione del mondo*] (Vattimo 1992, p. 25; see also Vattimo 2011, p. 38) He adds that these images are not simply representations of a given reality—as we find in the schooled common-core languages of constructivist education—but "they constitute the very objectivity of the world." (Vattimo 1992, p. 26) This objectivity is begotten by the fact that hermeneutically speaking, what constitutes reality is fed by the mechanism of interpretation. Citing Nietzsche, Vattimo reiterates that there are no facts but only interpretations, to which he attaches a further meaning by citing the title of a chapter in Nietzsche's *Twilight of the Idols*, which in Masini's Italian translation is rendered to "How the world becomes a fable" [*è diventato favola*] (Vattimo 2011, p. 38, emphasis added), while Hollingdale's English translation renders it as "How the 'Real world' has finally become a myth." (Nietzsche 1982, p. 40)

In *Deschooling Society* Illich argues that the school system sustains myth on three functions which he likens to (or rather links with) the power of the church in history. The school is "simultaneously the repository of society's myth, the institutionalization of that myth's contradictions, and the locus of the ritual which reproduces and veils the disparities between myth and reality." (DS, p. 37) This echoes Luckmann's hermeneutic approach to social organizations and religion. Intriguingly Illich confirms how myth is scaffolded by the school (in this case, the university system) *critically*, in that the university "provides ample opportunity for criticism of the myth and for rebellion against its institutional perversions." However, this myth takes the form of a suitable, almost natural ritual that "demands tolerance of the fundamental contradictions between myth and institution." As expected, this remains "largely unchallenged, for neither ideological criticism nor social action can bring about a new society." (DS, p. 38)

It becomes evident how this ritualization of critique emerges as a fabular reaction from the attempt to assume a self-transparency—an openness—which is often celebrated in the critical and progressive assumptions of one's ownership of education within the boundaries of a schooled critique, as respectably brought forth within a liberal arts program for which absolute democratic communication is the only address and direction. However, as we all know, this supposedly liberal affair turns on itself and begins to erode any freedom of thought or opinion. As evidenced by the neo-liberal turns in education, the freedom to learn is being increasingly framed by the demands of a parasitic system which expediently morphs every attempt for emancipation into its opposite (see Baldacchino 2019). Such a knowledge industry is now readied for the needs of an Establishment that distinctly sees the role, utility, and ultimate legitimation of schooling from a corporate assumption of truth.

What Habermas (1975) sees as a mechanism of legitimation, Illich reads through the rituals of initiation.

> The contemporary world civilization is also the first one which has found it necessary to rationalize its fundamental initiation ritual in the name of education. We cannot begin a reform of education unless we first understand that neither individual learning nor social equality can be enhanced by the ritual of schooling. *We cannot go beyond the consumer society unless we first understand that obligatory public schools inevitably reproduce such a society, no matter what is taught in them.* (DS, p. 38, emphasis added)

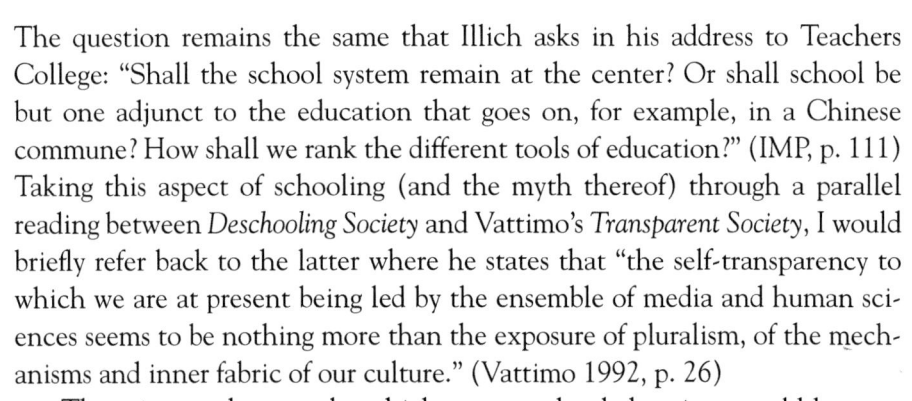

The question remains the same that Illich asks in his address to Teachers College: "Shall the school system remain at the center? Or shall school be but one adjunct to the education that goes on, for example, in a Chinese commune? How shall we rank the different tools of education?" (IMP, p. 111) Taking this aspect of schooling (and the myth thereof) through a parallel reading between *Deschooling Society* and Vattimo's *Transparent Society*, I would briefly refer back to the latter where he states that "the self-transparency to which we are at present being led by the ensemble of media and human sciences seems to be nothing more than the exposure of pluralism, of the mechanisms and inner fabric of our culture." (Vattimo 1992, p. 26)

There is no other way by which even a schooled society would have to articulate the reality that intrinsically we present to each other through our ability and need to fable a world out of the standardized assumptions by of which knowledge has been ordered. As I have argued elsewhere, the only viable way is always out of walled systems, which would include schooling as it has institutionalized education (see Baldacchino 2012). This form of exiting is prompted by the very same walled (and schooled) assumptions by which self-transparency is somehow expected to become emancipatory. The latter is claimed on those cues provided by the affectionate constructivist whose centering of the child's presumed learning is at the heart of those expected certainties by which education becomes a matter of faith and even zeal. Reflecting on Luckmann's sociology of religion, Illich strongly challenges such expectations and their claimed certainties. He argues that such manifestations of faith are nothing but a ritual and reinforcement of myth which is bereft of its inherent aporetic possibilities.

A Tomorrow Without a Future

In one of his conversations with David Cayley, Illich recalls how when he began to write *Tools for Conviviality* in 1971 and came to deal with "the multidimensional thresholds beyond which human endeavor becomes destructive of a human mode of existence," he "broke down." Describing this as the only deep depression that he ever experienced in his life, he intimates that if he had a son of his own, he would have probably stopped writing. "I would have had to join the rain dance." (IC, pp. 281–282)

Apart from being an intimate account of the intensity with which his writing in particular and his work in general were tied to his own personality, this episode in Illich's life is particularly significant in terms of how he would later regard *Tools for Conviviality* as being superseded by a turn in history where the very idea of a future from which we could articulate a world appears oblique:

> I think it is a necessary condition for thinking and reflecting, both with meaningful and sensual words and clear and distinct ideas, to know that *we have no future*. There might be a tomorrow, but *we have no future about which we can say anything, or about which we have any power*. We are radically powerless and engage in conversation because we want to find out ways of extending our budding friendships to others who, with us, can enjoy the experience of their own powerlessness and our joint powerlessness. The people who speak about Gaia and global responsibility, and suppose that some fantasy we should *do* something about it, *dance a crazy dance, which makes them mad*. (IC, pp. 281–282, emphasis added)

Before arguing that Illich has finally taken an existentialist turn where Sisyphus replaces Epimetheus, one must revisit his *silent* approach to the notion of a future. By the eloquence and dignity of silence, which he perceives as belonging to the commons, (see CoA, pp. 41ff; IMP, pp. 27ff and pp. 47ff) he begins to question the idea of *responsibility*, beyond which one finds how Illich ultimately aims at disestablishing myth and its rain dance.

Responsibility

Foregoing myth and how in its hermeneutic it impacts on the way we interpret and act upon the world, we continue to find Illich perplexing, especially when he deconstructs words like "responsibility" in whose amoebic character they inhabit a hegemonic space where the malleability of situations and meanings plays in the hands of the powerful. This power is not sustained by its ways of turning transparency into a medium of opaqueness, but where the tools by which we have hitherto succeeded to effectively play the pragmatics of plasticity—which Dewey, after James, rightly regarded as a powerful disposition (see Dewey 1966, pp. 44ff; James 1987, pp. 513ff; Baldacchino 2014, pp. 50ff)—find themselves absorbed by a society of systems in whose immediacy, the truths of mediation are exposed to further peril.

Without bearing this evolutionary process in mind, it is easy to fail to understand how the myth of singular truth as a *ground* is being played on a horizon which, instead of becoming a form of empowerment against its tyranny—as any progressive and liberal expectancy would assume—it is turned into a relationality whose qualities are played on relativism. This is why Illich cannot be dubbed a postmodernist. His sharp observation is that postmodernism is "incredibly disembodying" (RNF, p. 224) as even when it appears to reject fixed ideological spheres, it is ultimately legitimized into a social scientific language which continues to preserve the current state of affairs, just as, I would add, relativism fails to disestablish the relationality by which the plastic loses its plasticity.

Failing to recognize such distinctions, it would be difficult to understand why Illich argues that the word and notion of responsibility have shifted meaning. Many were scandalized when he described responsibility as "the soft underbelly of fantasies about power." He explains how, "it was impossible to question that those children whom they saw in the ads of the Children's Fund with hunger-blown-up bellies were their responsibility." The responsibility which many have felt (and still feel) when confronted with war, famine and other terrible man-made tragedies presented the opportunity for "a way of justifying their sense that because they were from a rich country, they had some power to plan, to organize, to change the rest of the world." (TCC, p. 43; see also RNF, pp. 220ff).

When Illich contests widespread concepts like "life" and "responsibility" he does not indulge in a hermeneutic exercise. Neither does he dispute the interpretation of these words. Instead, he directs his attention to how words, in becoming plastic, have become devoid of the very plasticity whose value was central to pragmatists like James and Dewey. In the distortion of their plasticity (with plasticity itself, as a word, being perverted) words and concepts are stripped off the dynamic range that their meaning originally gave them. Illich could make such an argument because his approach to myth allows him to move beyond a scaffolded ordering between a language-object and a meta-language (See Barthes 1973, pp. 124ff). While not denying the dynamic of this semiotic ordering, Illich moves away from constructivist scaffolds. Instead, he engages in an ongoing discussion with Poerksen, which takes them to what they identify with the mathematization of language.

Algorithms

Illich and Poerksen speak of an algorithmic state where what used to transform tool-based instrumentalism into a form of realization (in which liberal and social pragmatists invested their conviction), comes to lose any social coordinates that it might have had. This happens just as the possibilities of conviviality are offset by a disembodiment (and relativization) of human relations. "We are in a situation in which the disembodiment of the I-Thou relationship has led into a mathematization, an algorithmization, which supposedly is experienced." (RNF, p. 222; see also TCC, p. 42)

In *Plastic Words* Poerksen develops the idea of the "mathematization of the vernacular" which he sees as being "predisposed to accept the computer;" the computer being "the consequence and the expression of this process and its complement." (1995, p. 91) There he identifies six characteristics where the use of plastic words articulates and structures a mathematized vernacular. To start with, plastic words "are characterized by a high degree of abstraction." As it moves away from individual differences between terms, it is a language that "delivers the world into the hands of planners, levels the terrain, and places everyone at the mercy of the drawing board." (1995, p. 93)

Secondly, as words could be taken out of their historical or social dimension, they become "shallow and they taste of nothing." In their isolation from context they tend to lose their form. This moves away from the vernacular-dialectal context, where as we have seen earlier in Illich's discussion in *Shadow Work*, words are tied intimately to what makes them (See SW, pp. 46ff; IC, pp. 234–237; and Chapter 2, above). Poerksen adds that in being amorphous, "plastic words release language from such ties. They evoke no particular setting; they are universal. They recast life histories as natural processes and say that everything is basically the same—another module." With words being modules, mathematization uses them like Lego blocks that one could configure in any way, keeping them devoid of time or place (Poerksen 1995, p. 93).

Thirdly, "key words are used in the manner of boldly outlined building blocks, as though one were dealing with numeric quantities" suggesting a "quantifiable amount." (Poerksen 1995, pp. 93–94) This takes us to the fourth characteristic where, Poerksen argues that "plastic words have a tendency to create sentences when placed in almost any order. The words are alarmingly interchangeable, they can be equated with one another or strung together in a chain of equations." This gives them motility, where "their capacity to combine with other terms, seems almost unlimited; the possibilities of using them seem infinite." While this appears to have a positive sense in terms of how plasticity becomes an instrument of realization (as I suggested earlier in terms of James's and Dewey's approach to plasticity and disposition), Poerksen argues that this presents an opposite form of instrumentality. "Where power or material interests are at stake, for example in corporations with a turnover of tens or hundreds of billions, any kind of nonsense will serve." (Poerksen 1995, p. 94)

Already at this stage one begins to understand how the concept of the plastic and plasticity are perverted into their own opposite—almost in the same fashion by which Kant presents us with antinomies where the same concept or state of affairs represents both a thesis and its own antithesis. As with myth and its semiotic scaffold, plastic words come to represent the mathematization of a vernacular that becomes devoid of its own meaning in that its arbitrariness becomes "arbitrarily precise." Poerksen sums the distinction by stating that, "[i]n science, words are made arbitrarily precise; in the vernacular the same words are merely arbitrary." (Poerksen 1995, p. 94)

The fifth characteristic which Poerksen identifies has to do with "the building blocks of countless models of reality." Immaterial of topic or theme, ranging from politics, foreign affairs to the domestic economy, social services or urbanization, "in the mill of the plastic words models are manufactured and projects developed in an instant." In this immediacy we identify the method by which "[e]xperts inflect each word according to the sector to which it is assigned." This gives a substantial degree of power to those who want to exploit, in serial manner, the malleability of a world that is "continually refashioned into new structures." Poerksen notes that, "producing a variety of models by combining and multiplying a limited set of symbols has something arbitrary and something economical about it" to which he likens to simple mathematics (Poerksen 1995, p. 94).

In its final, sixth characteristic, one finds how in this state of affairs "mats of words creep across the surfaces of our living spaces and grip them fast. They are comprised of the advice of experts, catalogs of criteria, examination papers, marks, points, tests, test results, and percentages. Enumeration and geometrization reach into every crack." Citing Barthes, Poerksen notes that "any hierarchy of substances is destroyed, a single one replaces all the others: the entire world can be plasticized." (Poerksen 1995, p. 94)

If in Illich's work we only get glimpses of what he means by an era that gives way to systems, in Poerksen's we find a comprehensive picture of how this algorithmic order presents profound challenges that leave us with more than the odd question over the manipulation of meaning. Long before the awful term "post-truth" came to be bandied about in the algorithmic ocean of social media, Poerksen and Illich were busy elaborating a comprehensive understanding of what we are just waking up to. This sheds light on what Illich means by us not having a future, but also what he implies when he reflects on his own work, which in many ways, renders him prescient by how he tasks us with what our tomorrows might mean.

Holding onto the comprehensive significance of Illich's entire oeuvre, I would argue that waking up to our tomorrows would not leave us bereft of the possibility of an Epimethean disposition, even when one begins to wonder if the word "hope" has ever been immune to the perversion of its plasticity, especially when it struggles to retain its place in what Illich identifies with the unique *hic et nunc* in which we find ourselves. "[D]on't try to humanize the hospital or the school," he says, "but always ask, What can I do, at this very moment, in the unique *hic et nunc*, here and now, in which I am? What can I do to get out of this world of needs-satisfaction?" (RNF, pp. 222–223)

Neighbors and Foreigners

As hope begins to adopt a wider meaning, how would one avoid it from being transformed into another plastic word? And wouldn't hope have to struggle with the likelihood of becoming devoid of realization, especially when its previously enjoyed arbitrariness is now "made arbitrarily precise"?

Let us not forget that in 2009, barely seven years after Illich's death, hope became the shibboleth by which Barack Obama was the first African American admitted into the Oval Office as President of the United States. By what history had in store in the post-Obama era, could we entertain any doubts that the algorithmic fate of our vernacular has not only come true but has gained consent and become commonplace? Perhaps more than ever, Illich's words have turned out to be very prescient:

> I think that many people have very reasonably withdrawn from trying to improve the social agencies and organizations for which only twenty years ago they felt responsible. They know that all they can do is to try, by negative criteria, to diminish the impact and the hold of this idea on their milieu, in order to be *increasingly free to behave anarchically as human beings* who do not act for the sake of the city, but because

they have received the ability to respond as a gift from the other. (RNF, pp. 223, emphasis added)

In the wider scale of events and especially in how liberal and social democratic hope—as so often attributed to the early iterations of Obama's Presidency—have now totally vanished and replaced by an onslaught of reactionary misery, Illich's description has come to represent a Golgotha moment. By this I mean a felt need to exit into a world found beyond an intolerant and uncertain polis; out of which one seeks to move in what, in the previous chapter, I describe as Golgotha's *khôra*. It is a *khôra* because, bereft of *logos* and *mythos*, word and representation, it denotes a space, or indeed a time, where, to cite Arendt, "the world become so dubious that people have ceased to ask any more of politics than that it show due consideration for their vital interests and personal liberty." (Arendt 1995, p. 11) While some might raise eyebrows at Illich's idea of "being free to behave anarchically," this must be read through the distinct philosophical and historical lineage by which he contextualizes reform within the tradition and where the concept of contingency finds its Franciscan expression in a creation enhanced by the idea of synchronic possibilities. Far from a sense of Promethean persistence or Sisyphean absurdity, Illich's choice remains incessantly Epimethean; a choice which he frames in the story of the Samaritan, which, in the contemporary imaginary becomes the modern Palestinian whose life outside the walls cannot be missed out, let alone forgotten.

Being of equally strong Jewish and Catholic descent, with him and his family having fled from Nazi deportation and murder, Illich often brings up the image of the Samaritan to our immediate imagination by replacing it with that of a modern Palestinian (RNF, p. 206). Just like Jesus's Samaritan, Illich's Palestinian exercises his freedom and choice to rescue a dying Jew and save him, thereby moving outside the prejudices and legalities of the polis's expected "norms" of citizenship and belonging. This becomes a matter of a foreigner rescuing the citizen who was abandoned by his fellow citizens outside the walls of the city. Illich persists in reminding us that the Samaritan never rescues the abandoned Jew out of a sense of charity (as understood today). He also points out in some detail how the institutionalization of Samaritan "charity" has peddled the myth of welfare without choice. This distortion of Jesus's message of choice emerged from the Byzantine institutionalization of care by an established Christian Church whose sense of statehood remains unbroken to this day (RNF, pp. 33ff; TCC, pp. 7ff).

Early Christians believed love to be a personal free choice until it became an institutionalized form of charity, run by the establishment of duty where free choice was lost to a bargaining assumption of goodness. Established charity instituted a form of responsibility that deferred one's choice to the institution of care, of teaching, of welfare, etc., while the social sphere was newly established as we still know it today. In contrast, the Samaritan's choice was radical and to revisit it today is to disestablish the social spheres of the state's and church's social contract. The Samaritan's choice of neighbor is found outside the Law and expectations of the city. This might jar with what I argued above, where I said that Illich still resides within the Law when he makes the case for disestablishment. However, one should add that Illich's engagement with the Law also implied a disestablishment that would take it outside the walls that enclose it. This is how I would qualify his reference to the Law, and more so how one should read his "anarchic" references to one's freedom of choice beyond the walls of the city.

Keeping the centrality of the Golgotha in mind, in Illich's conceptualization of the Christ-event the parable of the Samaritan also means that we have the freedom to act outside the walls of habit and willfully decide whom we choose as our neighbor. The Jew is chosen by the Samaritan outside the city, just as the Palestinian is free to do the same in the Occupied Territories. Seen from the lens of contemporary history, this gains a degree of raw significance once we are reminded that the choice could be otherwise where these figures of foreignness would normally do the opposite.

Upon insisting on the freedom to choose whom to love and rescue, Illich insists that it is always possible that, "at any moment we still might recognize, that even when we are Palestinians, that there is a Jew lying in the ditch whom I can take in my arms and embrace." (IC, p. 242) On the back of this understanding of choice, Illich insists on how we have the Palestinian's freedom to choose and embrace the Jew who has been robbed, beaten and left for dead by the wayside. In line with the tradition in which Illich weaves his discourse, this is a freedom that we gain from contingency and the *grace*—that is the *gift*—by which the freedom we gain from contingency turns history into a reality where humanity also has the choice to meet (but also equally reject) its relationship with divinity. More importantly, this situation reveals a very concrete way of understanding what synchronic contingency means, where the possibility of love and friendship acts simultaneously with the reality of hatred prejudice and war. This is what one means by contingency as that by which we gain the freedom in whose gift we have the freedom to buck the trend, act against all odds and conventions, and assert that it is possible to move against established necessities.

Never failing to surprise and to put his audience in a picture that is as raw as it could get, Illich tells Cayley that, "having become very suspicious of care, which is the banner of the caring professions, considering caring professions as intrinsically disabling, when somebody says 'Don't you care for the people, for the bloated belly children on their sticky legs in the Sahel?' my immediate reaction is I will do everything I can to eliminate from my heart any sense of care for them." (PMTS, p. 12)

The will to experience horror comes from freedom but it is also a reaction that is reminiscent of a scripted duty to care for or to pity the other. In this scripted act the political dynamic is altered and we have to ask ourselves whether the sense of the other is in effect a passive receipt of a duty of care prompted by some moral imperative.

> I do not want to escape my sense of helplessness into a pretense that I care (...) I want to live with the inescapable horror of these children, these persons in my heart. I know that I cannot actively really love them, because to love them at least the way I am built, after having read the story of the Samaritan, means to leave aside everything which I am doing at this moment, at least for ten minutes, pick up that person (...) bring the guy, as that Palestinian did to the Jew who had fallen under the robbers, put him into an inn, which meant then a brothel, and say, "Please take care of that guy. When I come back, I hope I'll have made a little bit more money, and I'll bring it back to you for extra expenditures." (...) Why pretend that I care? (PMTS, p. 12)

This is how Illich insists on deconstructing the misplaced argument for *responsibility*. Care and responsibility cease to have any currency in a world where even the ownership of tools as one's own existential extension from the once hailed virtues of *homo faber* is seriously contested.

Maritain's Beautiful Face

In this conclusive chapter, I tried to bring together several strands in Illich's work, particularly those which converge in the three main threads of reform, contingency and disestablishment. The last, that of disestablishment, raises the notion of a radical promise by which Illich's project is often presented. Yet, as I have argued throughout this book, to assume that Illich was some latter-day radical who would qualify as a humanist sort of anarchist would miss the width and depth of his entire work. Coming to Illich with ready-made assumptions of what radical philosophy should be, is like claiming to have classified him within a species by which one could frame him by manner of an identifiable taxonomy. Both attempts go against the thrust by which this remarkable man dedicated his life and energy to break out of the ideological spheres that have trapped our cosmic imaginary over centuries.

One could cite many instances where Illich's storylines carry a good deal of inspiration. But one episode which I find particularly compelling is when he seeks advice from his old teacher and friend, Jacques Maritain, who at the time was in Princeton. This was in 1957, when Illich felt challenged by tasks given him over issues to do with educational administration in Puerto Rico, more specifically with the challenge of planning. As he puts it, "I had become deeply involved in the newly established manpower qualification planning board of the island's Government." His difficulty was in how several "philosophical ambiguities" were upsetting him. As he explains, he was not upset by the ambiguities of the church—with which he was more than familiar—but by how his direct involvement with planning was leading him into "something called *qualified manpower*." (IMP, p. 221).

> I went to see Professor Maritain, who had earlier guided my studies on the history of the practice and theory of virtue in the Christian West. How could I fit 'planning' into the traditional system of responsible habits within which I had learned to think? I had great difficulty in explaining to the old man the meaning of the term that I was using: planning was not accounting, nor was it legislation, nor a kind of scheduling of trains. We took tea on his veranda. It was to be my last visit with him. I was delighted to look at his beautiful face, close to death, transparent, like one of the patriarchs in a Gothic stained glass window. The cup in his hand was shaking. Then, finally, he put it down, looking disturbed, and said: 'Is not planning, which you talk about, a sin, a new species within the vices which grow out of presumption?' (IMP, pp. 221–222)

Illich's reflection on Maritain's advice is as inspiring as his teacher's words: "He made me understand that in thinking about humans as resources that can be managed, *a new certitude about human nature* would be brought into existence surreptitiously." (IMP, pp. 222, emphasis added) I would argue that this conversation between Illich and Maritain is key to understand what Illich's approach to disestablishment stands for. Maritain's comment about the sin of planning as a sin of certitude in whose engendering there is a "new species within the vices which grow out of presumption" already captures the essence of Illich's critique of the age of systems; an idea which then had not yet germinated in his work.

Recounting, thirty-two years later, the very last time he met Maritain, Illich was making a point about the "paralysis of language in a managed world." (IMP, p. 220) He was addressing the same Lutheran conference where he expressed his qualms over the amoebic use and idolatrous status of the word "life." As already mentioned earlier in Chapter 6, addressing the American Evangelical Lutheran Church, Illich presented the bishops with the scenario of human life becoming a new fetish of institutional construction (See IMP, pp. 218ff). Once objectified, human life has no choice but to fall into the managerial constructs by which an ecological, medical, legal, educational, political and ethical discourse turn it into an "essential referent" (IMP, p. 219), and thereby another mathematized narrative. Brought down to this condition, life becomes a social construct that is institutionally managed like any other resource.

Elsewhere Illich states that "[t]hinking about the body as a system, or a subsystem, is a way of hiding sin" (RNF, p. 168). There he was talking about the age of systems as an era that confronts us with a decision—what to do with our contingent being, and how as a *causa contingente* one could engage with the realty of being disembodied, visually violated, swallowed and linguistically mathematized; how, by dint of this condition we could make any sense of a world (which is the case we make for our being) that has taken away our tools from us, and made us indistinguishable from them (RNF, pp. 157–163). Even when tools were both means of instrumental realization and coercion, we still maintained a distinction by which we could decide one way or another. This also meant that we retained the awareness that contingency was both what causes our existence but also the cause by which we retained a claim on making our reality. However, in assuming that we would become one with our tools and partake of a monist system (*qua* totality) legitimized by its organic presumptions, we insist on bequeathing ourselves by acts of being in turn bequeathed to it.

As we bequeath ourselves to a scopic order to which, consciously or unconsciously, we have also surrendered our hermeneutic prerogative—as we cease to interpret the world by seeking an affirmation that is seen to be true—the rain dance in which we chose to participate becomes one with the fallacy of our organizational desires. Duden (1993, p. 15) and Illich (1998, pp. 6ff) use a term which is most apt in how we have succumbed to this scopic order: *libido vivendi*. While Illich goes into the historical context of this term, Duden defines it as "the ravenous urge to extend one's sight, to see more, to see things larger or smaller than the eye can grasp—to see things which have previously been off limits." In this case she was discussing *Life* magazine's vivid images of the Earth from outer space and the fetus in the womb, which back in the 1960s had an astounding effect on how we have bequeathed our ways of knowing, speaking and seeing. And that was still not what the age of systems, especially in the last few decades, has come to mean in terms of who and how we *own* our vision.

> When I contrast the *Life* of 1965 with the *Life* of 1990 on this deeper level, I recognize that the first is still strongly on the side of the representation of the visible, the second mainly concerned with the depiction of things that lie beyond the eye's horizon, which, to be "seen," *must be explained by some authority*. (Duden 1993, p. 16, emphasis added)

Just as the linguistic plasticization of words like "life" and "responsibility" become Lego blocks in an impersonal planning organizational order, what we see has evolved into what must be seen by the authority to which we have consented in the scopic order of things. We know how the processing and construction of the images of an embryo and fetus in *Life* in 1965 were still technically and conceptually constructed out of parts that were still discernible to those who chose to see them. That changes in the way photography, in its digitalization, came to probe further into a space that moves beyond the eye, and where, by implication, the visual intentionality is extended further, systematizing even the order of representation. "Now, we see what we are shown," explains Duden, "[w]e have gotten used to being shown no matter what, within or beyond the limited range of human sight. This habituation to the monopoly of visualization-on-command strongly suggests that only those things that can in some way be visualized, recorded, and replayed at will are part of reality." (1993, p. 17)

Pedagogically and culturally, we became habituated to ways of seeing on whose construct, a different disposition to the visual has emerged. Contrary to what arts educationalists continue to campaign for, this new visual disposition stands for the exact opposite of a visual empowerment, let alone a literacy that contests the logocentric prevalence by which we have been schooled. Considering the prevalence of the use of tablets and smartphones in schools, citing Duden already feels dated, though this makes the matter of authority in the pedagogical use of visual and other media no less disconcerting.

> Starting with children's TV and prekindergarten videos, new generations are being socialized to see whatever appears on the screen. We have all been trained to live by the recognition of flash cards, news bites, spots, ads, digests, catalogues, schedules, or

class hours. Each of these packages is a bundle of lures that inveigles a side of reality which beguiles us as something we must be told about because we cannot see it on our own. The result is a strange mistrust of our own eyes, a disposition to take as real only that which is mechanically displayed in a photograph, a statistical curve, or a table. (Duden 1993, p. 17)

This ties into what Illich says about an iconography which "no matter whether it represents the population curve or some other administrative reality, is in a frame, which I haven't chosen but somebody else has chosen for me" (RNF, p. 159).

Beyond Sinful Planning

Here we return to Maritain's admonition over the sin of planning and the assumption of certitude bestowed and imposed on others; that by which we become human resources. One could see how the freedom to choose one's neighbor, the revolutionary choice of the Samaritan who comes to the aid of the Jew outside the walls of the polis, comes at a juncture by which we could begin to understand what disestablishment might mean in this age of systems.

By way of directing my own understanding of Illich's work into a viable convergence, which in this book I am presenting as a triangulation between reform, contingency and disestablishment, I want to briefly recall five points that Illich offered to his Lutheran audience as "five historical observations." By these observations he was not simply making his point against the institutionalization of life. He offered them as pedagogical nodes (IMP, p. 219). Beyond the specificity of Illich's lecture, I find in these five observations an effective way of capturing the wider reach of his linguistic and historical critique of planned certitude, always bearing in mind his conversation with Jacques Maritain.

Illich's five "observations on the history of life" are the following: (1) As "a substantive notion," life appears at a specific point in history. (IMP, pp. 227–228); (2) "The loss of contingency, the death of nature and the appearance of life" as "distinct aspects of the same consciousness." (IMP, p. 228); (3) "Possessive individualism" as an ideology that "has shaped the way life could be talked about as property." (IMP, p. 229); (4) "The factitious nature of life" as it "appears with special poignancy in ecological discussion." (IMP, pp. 229–230); and (5) The "pop-science fetish" of "'a' life" as it "tends to void the legal notion of person." (IMP, pp. 230–231).

In the chapter on reform I have already discussed the imputation of how life has been idolized. Here I want to latch Illich's five observations to how, further contextualized by contingency (discussed in Chapter 6), this gains stronger and tangible value with disestablishment. Apart from how Illich's work with Duden and Poerksen shaped his analysis of the age of systems, these five observations come at a juncture with Maritain's comment on sinful planning. This is not because one could reduce Illich's critique to some kind of original sin, but because his attention to Maritain's comment does not make sense without understanding how matters to do with education, healthcare, social provision, welfare and every institutionalized aspect of life, remain a major cause for meaningful change as they warrant their disestablishment, even (if not especially) in this age of systems.

Whether welfare is set in a social democratic organism or is left to the non-existent mercy of the savage markets of private interests, the tyranny of plastic words remains a matter of utmost urgency that cannot stay unchallenged. The nomenclature of managerialism, whose lexicon of a system's mathematized vernacular has become a referent of an ecology that has swallowed us in ways that impede the freedom of contingency, marks the "end" of this freedom. This is boldly marked by the emergence of "life" as a "substantive notion" to which we are meant to prostrate as a latter-day idol of organizational planning where property has moved from being a form of "theft" (as Pierre-Joseph Proudhon famously put it) to an idolatry which in the name of "life" comes to legitimize the individual's prerogative to possess others.

Following these five observations, we realize how we have failed to recognize how our understanding of the world is an accumulation of dictated constructs of language and visuality in whose presumption of freedom and choice we find the very opposite. This is because, as Illich states in his first observation, such constructs know a specific point in history where their hegemonic structure was planned and inaugurated. In addition, we have deluded ourselves by an ecological frame of mind which, far from a green and benign image of belonging and care, has come to signify our modes of thinking in terms of what Illich identified with "a cybernetic system which, in real time, is both model and reality: a process which observes and defines, regulates and sustains itself." (IMP, pp. 229–230). This is where, Illich explains, "life is equated with *the* system: it is the abstract fetish that both overshadows and simultaneously constitutes it." (IMP, p. 230)

One must read Illich's five observations as an argument for finding a manner by which the loss of myth gives way to a reconsideration of reform. This is an approach to reform that is framed by the reassured freedom of contingency on one hand and disestablishment on the other. To understand reform in its relationship with contingency and disestablishment, one must look back at what Ladner (1959, p. 171) describes as Augustine's connection between "the *creatio-formatio* of the beginning and the *reformatio* of man to the image of God." With what one takes from Illich's Ladnerian influence, I would read this in a wider though no less preterideological sense. As the idea of origin, in terms of a *creatio-formatio*, gives us a milieu which deconstructs the stricture of an origin understood as a *hold*, Augustine's creative-formative approach affords us with a referent to concurrent origins where myth is recouped in all its potentials (while rejected in its forms of institutional immediacy). When I say myth is restored I also mean that its potentials for change and radical critique come in to their full realization. This allows and opens up the capacity and resolve of a continuous *reformatio*, understood as a human endeavor whose image we have traditionally attributed to God, but which, in the choice of both a theistic and non-theistic attestation of reality, extends to a dialectical dynamic where the necessary is matched with the synchronic contingency of infinite possibilities.

In view of what has been discussed above, the loss of myth stands for what has become monochromatically identified with the fetishism of systemic planning. This loss of myth came into its very own by how, in the last couple of decades, all manner of governments and political nomenclatures have nurtured the managerial politics of an extreme centrism. Rather than despair one could argue that while centrism continues to reap the dire consequences of managerial dogma, especially in the sense of helplessness ushered by the rise of reactionary entrenchment, one could likewise argue that this could well facilitate that moment where, to cite Illich one last time, we become "increasingly free to behave anarchically as human beings." (RNF, pp. 223)

Abbreviations: Works by Illich

CoA   *Celebration of Awareness*
DS   *Deschooling Society.*
IC   *Ivan Illich In Conversation.*
IMP   *In the Mirror of the Past*
MN   *Limits to Medicine. Medical Nemesis*
PMTS *Part Moon Part Travelling Salesman.*

RNF *The Rivers North of the Future.*
SW   *Shadow Work*
TCC *The Corruption of Christianity*
TFC *Tools for Conviviality.*

References

Arendt, H. (1995). *Men in Dark Times*. San Diego, CA: Harcourt, Brace & Company.
Baldacchino, J. (2012). *Art's Way Out. Exit Pedagogy and the Cultural Condition*. Rotterdam: Sense.
Baldacchino, J. (2014). *John Dewey. Liberty and the Pedagogy of disposition*. Dordrecht; New York: Springer.
Baldacchino, J. (2019). A brief critical historical analysis of neoliberalism in education. In Stephanie Chitpin & John P. Portelli (eds.), *Confronting Educational Policy in Neoliberal Times: International Perspectives*. Oxford: Routledge, pp. 11–24.
Barthes, R. (1973). Myth Today. In *Mythologies*, A. Lavers (trans.). Paladin: London
Dewey, J. (1966). *Democracy and Education*. New York: The Free Press.
Duden, B. (1993). *Disembodying Women. Perspectives on Pregnancy and the Unborn*. Hoinacki, L. (trans.). Cambridge, MA: Harvard University Press.
Habermas, J. (1975). *Legitimation Crisis*. Boston: Beacon Press.
Illich, I. (1998). The scopic past and the ethics of the gaze. Ivan Illich, Kleftingstr. 16, D-28203 Bremen. Accessed online: April 4, 2019, http://www.davidtinapple.com/illich/1998_scopic_past.PDF
Illich, I. (1981). *Shadow Work*. New York: M. Boyars. (SW)
Illich, I. (1992). *In the Mirror of the Past: Lectures and Addresses, 1978–1990*. New York: M. Boyars. (IMP)
Illich, I. (2001). *Tools for Conviviality*. New York: Marion Boyars. (TFC)
Illich, I. (2010). *Limits to Medicine. Medical Nemesis: The Expropriation of Health*. New York: Marion Boyars. (MN)
Illich, I. (2012). *Celebration of Awareness: A Call for Institutional Revolution*. New York: Marion Boyars. (CoA)
Illich, I. (2012). *Deschooling Society*. New York: Marion Boyars. (DS)
Illich, I. & Cayley, D. (1989). *Part Moon Part Travelling Salesman: Conversations with Ivan Illich*. Broadcasting Corporation. Accessed: May 30, 2019, http://www.davidcayley.com/transcripts (PMTS)
Illich, I. & Cayley, D. (1992). *Ivan Illich in Conversation*. Toronto: House of Anansi Press. (IC)
Illich, I. & Cayley, D. (2000). *The Corruption of Christianity*. CBC Ideas transcript. Toronto: Canadian Broadcasting Corporation. Accessed: May 4, 2019, http://www.davidcayley.com/transcripts (TCC)
Illich, I. & Cayley, D. (2005). *The Rivers North of the Future: The Testament of Ivan Illich*. Toronto: House of Anansi Press. (RNF)
James, W. (1987). Pragmatism. In *Writings 1902–1910*. New York: The Library of America.

Ladner, G. B. (1959). *The Idea of Reform Its Impact on Christian Thought and Action in the Age of the Fathers*. Cambridge, MA: Harvard University Press.
Nietzsche, F. (1982). *Twilight of the Idols and The Anti-Christ*. R. J. Hollingdale (trans.). Harmondsworth: Penguin Books.
Poerksen, U. (1995). *Plastic Words. The Tyranny of Modular Language*. Mason, J. & Cayley, D. (trans.). University Park: Penn State University Press.
Vattimo, G. (1992). *The Transparent Society*. D. Webb (trans.). Cambridge: Polity Press.
Vattimo, G. (1995). *Oltre l'Interpretazione*. [Beyond Interpretation]. Bari: Laterza.
Vattimo, G. (2011). *La società trasparente*. Milano: Garzanti.

BIBLIOGRAPHY

Major Works by Ivan Illich

When referring to Illich's major books the following abbreviations have been used:

ABC   Illich, I. & Sanders, B. (1988). *ABC. The Alphabetization of the Popular Mind*. San Francisco: North Point Press.
ADW   Illich, I. (1974). *After Deschooling, What?* London: Writers' and Readers' Publishing Cooperative.
CDD   Illich, I. (1970). *The Church, Change and Development*. F. Eychaner (ed.). Chicago: Urban Training Center Press.
CoA   Illich, I. (2012). *Celebration of Awareness: A Call for Institutional Revolution*. New York: Marion Boyars.
DS   Illich, I. (2012). *Deschooling Society*. New York: Marion Boyars.
G   Illich, I. (1983). *Gender*. London; New York: M. Boyars.
IC   Illich, I. & Cayley, D. (1992). *Ivan Illich In Conversation*. Toronto: House of Anansi Press.
IMP   Illich, I. (1992). *In the Mirror of the Past: Lectures and Addresses, 1978–1990*. New York: M. Boyars.
MN   Illich, I. (2010). *Limits to Medicine. Medical Nemesis: The Expropriation of Health*. New York: Marion Boyars.
PMTS Illich, I. & Cayley, D. (1989). *Part Moon Part Travelling Salesman: Conversations with Ivan Illich*. Broadcasting Corporation. Accessed: May 30, 2019, http://www.davidcayley.com/transcripts

RNF	Illich, I. & Cayley, D. (2005). *The Rivers North of the Future: The Testament of Ivan Illich*. Toronto: House of Anansi Press.
RUU	Illich, I. (2009). *The Right to Useful Unemployment and Its Professional Enemies*. New York: Marion Boyars.
SW	Illich, I. (1981). *Shadow Work*. New York: M. Boyars.
TCC	Illich, I. & Cayley, D. (2000). *The Corruption of Christianity*. CBC Ideas transcript. Toronto: Canadian Broadcasting Corporation. Accessed: May 4, 2019, http://www.davidcayley.com/transcripts
TFC	Illich, I. (2001). *Tools for Conviviality*. New York: Marion Boyars.
VT	Illich, I. (1993). *In the Vineyard of the Text: A Commentary to Hugh's Didascalicon*. Chicago: University of Chicago Press.

Other Works by Illich

Illich, I. (1998). The scopic past and the ethics of the gaze. Ivan Illich, Kleftingstr. 16, D-28203 Bremen. Accessed: April 4, 2019, http://www.davidtinapple.com/illich/1998_scopic_past.PDF

Illich, I. & Cayley, D. (2014a). *The Corruption of Christianity: Ivan Illich on Gospel, Church and Society*. Cayley, D., Podcasts. Accessed: May 4, 2019, http://www.davidcayley.com/podcasts/category/Ivan+Illich

Illich, I. & Cayley, D. (2014b). *Part Moon, Part Travelling Salesman: Conversations with Ivan Illich*. Cayley, D., Podcasts. Accessed: May 30, 2019, http://www.davidcayley.com/podcasts/category/Ivan+Illich

Illich, I. & Cayley, D. (2015). *Life as Idol*. Cayley, D., Podcasts. Accessed: May 3, 2019, http://www.davidcayley.com/podcasts/category/Ivan+Illich

Illich, I. & Domenach, J. M. (1972). Video interview. *Un certain regard* series. Institut National de l'Ausiovisuel. Accessed: May 5, 2019, https://www.ina.fr/video/CPF86658011/ivan-illich-video.html

General Bibliography

Adorno, T. W. (1990). *Negative Dialectics*. London: Routledge.
Adorno, T. W. (1993). *Hegel: Three Studies*. Cambridge, MA: The MIT Press.
Adorno, T. W. & Horkheimer, M. (1990). *Dialectic of Enlightenment*. New York: Continuum.
Alter, R. (2019) (trans. & commentary). *The Hebrew Bible*. Vol. 2. Prophets Nevi'im. New York; London: Norton & Co.
Aquinas, T. (1991). *Summa Theologiae. A Concise Translation*. McDermott (ed.). London: Methuen.
Aquinas, T. (1993). *Selected Philosophical Writings*. McDermott (ed. & trans.). Oxford: Oxford University Press.
Arendt, H. (1978). *The Life of the Mind*. New York: Harcourt Brace Jovanovich.

BIBLIOGRAPHY

Arendt, H. (1995). *Men in Dark Times*. San Diego, CA: Harcourt, Brace & Company.
Arendt, H. (1998). *The Human Condition*. Chicago, IL: The University of Chicago Press.
Aristotle. (1984a). *Metaphysics. The Complete Works of Aristotle Vol. II*. Princeton, NJ: Princeton University Press.
Aristotle. (1984b). *Rhetoric. The Complete Works of Aristotle Vol. II*. Princeton, NJ: Princeton University Press.
Armstrong, K. (2006). *The Great Transformation. The World in the Time of Buddha, Socrates, Confucius and Jeremiah*. London: Atlantic Books.
Avicenna. (2005). *The Metaphysics of The Healing*. Provo, Utah: Brigham Young University Press.
Baldacchino, J. (2009). *Education beyond Education: Self and the Imaginary in Maxine Greene's Philosophy*. New York: Peter Lang.
Baldacchino, J. (2012). *Art's Way Out. Exit Pedagogy and the Cultural Condition*. Dordrecht: Sense.
Baldacchino, J. (2014). *John Dewey. Liberty and the Pedagogy of Disposition*. Dordrecht; New York: Springer.
Baldacchino, J. (2017). Art's ped(ago)gies. *What Is Art Education? After Deleuze and Guattari*. jagodzinski, j (ed.). London: Palgrave Macmillan.
Baldacchino, J. (2018). *Art as Unlearning: Towards a Mannerist Pedagogy*. London: Routledge.
Baldacchino, J. (2019). A brief critical historical analysis of neoliberalism in education. In Stephanie Chitpin & John P. Portelli (eds.), *Confronting Educational Policy in Neoliberal Times: International Perspectives*. Oxford: Routledge, pp. 11–24.
Balibar, E. (1994). *Masses, Classes, Ideas. Studies on Politics and Philosophy Before and After Marx*. London; New York: Routledge.
Barthes, R. (1973). Myth today. In *Mythologies*, A. Lavers (trans.). Paladin: London.
BBC (2014). Pope Francis warns on 'piecemeal World War III'. 13 September. http://www.bbc.co.uk/news/world-europe-29190890
BBC (2015). School term-time holiday fines 'unworkable', says LGA. Accessed: 2 November 2015, http://www.bbc.co.uk/news/education-34591050
Berlin, I. (1998). "Two Concepts of Liberty." In *The Proper Study of Mankind: An Anthology of Essays*, H. Hardy & R. Hausheer (eds), pp. 191–242. London, UK: Pimlico.
Biesta, G. (2006). *Beyond Learning: Democratic Education for a Human Future*. Boulder, CO: Paradigm Publishers.
Blumenberg, H. (2010). *Paradigms for a Metaphorology*. Ithaca, NY: Cornell University Press.
Buber, M. (1948). *Tales of the Hasidim*. New York: Schocken Books.
Buber, M. (1970). *I and Thou*. New York: Scribner.
Copleston, F. (2003). *A History of Philosophy. Volume 1. Greece and Rome*. London: Bloomsbury.
Dewey, J. (1893). The superstition of necessity. *The Monist*, 3(3), 362–379.
Dewey, J. (1966). *Democracy and Education*. New York: The Free Press.
Dewey, J. (2000). *Liberalism and Social Action*. Amherst: Prometheus Books.
Du Plessix Gray, F. (1970). *Divine Disobedience. Profiles in Catholic Radicalism*. New York: Alfred A Knopf.
Duden, B. (1993). *Disembodying Women. Perspectives on Pregnancy and the Unborn*. Hoinacki, L. (trans.). Cambridge, MA: Harvard University Press.
Duns Scotus, J. (1987). *Philosophical Writings*. Walter, A. (trans.). Indianapolis, IN: Hackett.

Duns Scotus, J. (1994). *Contingency and Freedom. Lectura I 39.* Dordrecht; Boston: Kluwer Academic Publishers.
Emerson, R. W. (ND). *The Works of Ralph Waldo Emerson. Four Volumes in One.* New York: Tudor Publishing Company.
Engels, F. (1977a). Letter to Bebel. Marx, K. & Engels, F., *Selected Works.* Vol. 3, pp. 31–37. Moscow: Progress Publishers.
Engels, F. (1977b). Socialism: Utopian and scientific. Marx, K. & Engels, F., *Selected Works.* Vol. 3, pp. 95–151. Moscow: Progress Publishers.
Fukuyama, F. (2006). *The End of History and the Last Man.* New York: Free Press.
Gadamer, H. G. (1976). *Philosophical Hermeneutics.* S.E. Linge (ed. & trans.). Berkeley: University of California Press.
Goethe, J. W. (1994). *Theory of Colours.* Cambridge, MA: MIT Press.
Goldstein, R. (2006). *Betraying Spinoza. The Renegade Jew Who Gave Us Modernity.* New York: Nextbook, Schocken.
Gramsci, A. (1967). *La formazione dell'uomo. Scritti di pedagogia.* G. Urbani (ed.). Roma: Riuniti Editori.
Greene, M. (1978). *Landscapes of Learning.* New York: Teachers College Press.
Gutierrez, G. (1988). *A Theology of Liberation: History, Politics, and Salvation.* Maryknoll, NY: Orbis Books.
Habermas, J. (1975). *Legitimation Crisis.* Boston, MA: Beacon Press.
Hartch, T. (2015). *The Prophet of Cuernavaca: Ivan Illich and the Crisis of the West.* New York, NY: Oxford University Press.
Hegel, G. W. F. (1975 [1830]). *Hegel's Logic: Being Part One of the Encyclopaedia of the Philosophical Sciences.* Oxford: Clarendon Press.
Heller, A. (1993). *A Philosophy of History in Fragments.* Oxford; Cambridge, MA: Blackwell.
Hoinacki, L. (2003) The trajectory of Ivan Illich. *Bulletin of Science, Technology & Society,* 23(5), October, 382–389.
Hoinacki, L. & Mitcham, C. (2002). *The Challenges of Ivan Illich: A Collective Reflection.* Albany: State University of New York Press.
Hugh, of Saint-Victor. (1991). *The Didascalicon of Hugh of St. Victor: A Medieval Guide to the Arts.* New York: Columbia University Press.
Husserl, E. (2014). *Ideas for a Pure Phenomenology and Phenomenological Philosophy. First Book: General Introduction to Pure Phenomenology.* Indianapolis, IN: Hackett.
James, W. (1987). Pragmatism. In *Writings 1902–1910.* New York: The Library of America.
Kant, I. (1974). *Critique of Judgement.* J.H. Bernard (trans.). New York: Hafner Press.
Kant, I. (1900). *Kant On Education (Ueber pädagogik).* A. Churton (trans.). Boston, MA: Heath & Co.
Kristeva, J. (2001). *Hannah Arendt.* New York: Columbia University Press.
Laclau, E. (1996). *Emancipation(s).* London: Verso.
Ladner, G. B. (1959). *The Idea of Reform Its Impact on Christian Thought and Action in the Age of the Fathers.* Cambridge, MA: Harvard University Press.
Lévinas, E. (1990). *Nine Talmudic Readings.* Bloomington, IN: Indiana University Press.

Lévinas, E. (1998). *Otherwise than Being, or, Beyond Essence*. Pittsburgh, PA: Duquesne University Press.
Lewis, C. S. (1947). *The Abolition of Man. Or Reflections on Education With Special Reference to the Teaching of English in the Upper Forms of Schools*. New York: Macmillan.
Luckmann, T. (1967). *The Invisible Religion. The Problem of Religion in Modern Society*. New York: Macmillan.
Lyotard, J. F. (1989). *The Postmodern Condition: A Report on Knowledge*. Manchester: Manchester University Press.
Marcuse, H. (1986). *One-Dimensional Man. Studies in the Ideology of Advanced Industrial Society*. London: Ark Paperbacks.
Marcuse, H. (1988). *Negations. Essays in Critical Theory*. London: Free Association Books.
Marx, K. (1977). *Critique of the Gotha Programme* (Marginal notes to the programme of the German Workers' Party). Marx, K., Engels, F., *Selected Works*. Vol. 3, pp. 13–30. Moscow: Progress Publishers.
Marx, K. (1990). *Capital: A Critique of Political Economy*. London; New York, NY: Penguin Books.
Muller, R. A. (2017). *Divine Will and Human Choice. Freedom, Contingency, and Necessity in Early Modern Reformed Thought*. Grand Rapids, MI: Baker Academic.
Nietzsche, F. (1968). *The Will to Power*. W. Kaufmann & R. J. Hollingdale (trans.). New York: Vintage Books.
Nietzsche, F. (1982). *Twilight of the Idols and The Anti-Christ*. R. J. Hollingdale (trans.). Harmondsworth: Penguin Books.
Pareyson, L. (2000). *Ontologia della libertà. Il male e la sofferenza*. Torino: Einaudi.
Petri, E. et al. (2002). *La classe operaia va in paradiso*. DVD. Roma: Minerva Pictures Group.
Pistola, R. (2017). *DwA: Draw with(out) Authority*. Unpublished doctoral dissertation. Faculty of Fine Arts, University of Porto.
Poerksen, U. (1995). *Plastic Words. The Tyranny of Modular Language*. Mason, J. & Cayley, D. (trans.). University Park: Penn State University Press.
Rancière, J. (2007). *On the Shores of Politics*. L. Heron (trans.). New York: Verso.
Rocha, S. D. (2017). *Tell Them Something Beautiful*. Eugene, OR: Cascade Books.
Rorty, R. (1989). *Contingency, Irony, and Solidarity*. Cambridge; New York: Cambridge University Press.
Rose, G. (1978). *The Melancholy Science: An Introduction to the Thought of Theodor W. Adorno*. New York: Columbia University Press.
Rose, G. (1992). *The Broken Middle: Out of Our Ancient Society*. Oxford, UK; Cambridge, MA, USA: Blackwell.
Rose, G. (1995). *Love's Work: A Reckoning with Life*. New York: Schocken Books.
Rose, G. (1996). *Mourning Becomes the Law: Philosophy and Representation*. Cambridge; New York: Cambridge University Press.
Rose, G. (1999). *Paradiso*. London: Menard Press.
Rubinoff, L. (ed.) (1971). *Tradition and Revolution*. Toronto: Macmillan of Canada; New York: St. Martin's Press.
Spinoza, B. (1951). *Political Treatise. The Chief Works of Benedict de Spinoza*. New York: Dover Publications.

Sylwanowicz, M. (1996). *Contingent Causality and the Foundations of Duns Scotus' Metaphysics*. Leiden; New York: E.J. Brill.
Tijmes, P. (2002). Ivan Illich's break with the past. In Hoinacki, L. & Mitcham, C. (eds.), *The Challenges of Ivan Illich: A Collective Reflection*. Albany: State University of New York Press.
Tillich, P. (1965). *Ultimate Concern: Tillich in Dialogue*. London: SCM Press.
Varoufakis, Y. (2017). *And the Weak Suffer What They Must?: Europe, Austerity and the Threat to Global Stability*. London: Vintage Books.
Vattimo, G. (1988). Dialettica, differenza, pensiero debole. [Dialectics, difference and weak thought]. *Il Pensiero Debole* [Weak Thought]. G. Vattimo & P. A. Rovatti (eds.). Milano: Feltrinelli, pp. 12–28.
Vattimo, G. (1992). *The Transparent Society*. D. Webb (trans.). Cambridge: Polity Press.
Vattimo, G. (1995). *Oltre l'Interpretazione*. [Beyond Interpretation]. Bari: Laterza.
Vattimo, G. (2011). *La società trasparente*. Milano: Garzanti.
Williams, R. (1967). *Modern Tragedy*. Stanford, CA: Stanford University Press.
Williams, R. (2015). Pope of the masses: Is Francis really the people's champion? *New Statesman*. 10 September. Accessed: 10 October 2015, http://www.newstatesman.com/politics/religion/2015/09/pope-masses-francis-really-people-s-champion
Wittgenstein, L. (1990). *Remarks on Colour*. G.E.M. Anscombe (ed.) L.L. McAlister & M. Schättle (trans.). Oxford: Blackwell.

INDEX

A

academia 16, 44–45
academic
  character 100
  hospitality 18
  management 44
  production 44
  promise 44;
accidental 126
  accidentality 127
Adorno, Theodor, W. 11–12, 26, 73
aletheia 132–133
algorithm 33, 155, 157
alma ubera 32, 34
Alter, Robert 129
alterity, historical 123
amoeba words 14, 105, 109, 153, 162
Amos, prophet 76, 128–130
apophatic
  method 28, 128
  theology 62–63, 122, 124
  thinking 28

Aquinas, Thomas, St. 72, 97, 117, 132
Arendt, Hannah 24, 26, 28, 29, 31, 74, 158
Aristotle 125, 132, 141, 171
armas y letras 31
Armstrong, Karen 76
Armstrong, Neil 51
assembly, as *ecclesia* 25, 41, 63
Augustine, of Hippo, St. 30, 106, 126, 166
authorship 12
autonomy
  academia 45
  as liberty (and freedom) 39–41, 43
  autonomous living 40, 43, 66
  church politics 62, 63
  education 95, 98, 66
  heteronomy 37, 38
  immanent 29
  institutional 41
  intelligence 40
  politics of 38, 44
  prism of 39
  vernacular 100
  will 27

autotrasparenza
See self-transparency
Avicenna, Ben Sina 132

B

Baldacchino, John 12, 13, 16, 59, 61, 132, 151, 152, 154
Balibar, Etienne 81–82
Barthes, Roland 148, 154, 156
BBC, British Broadcasting Corporation 86, 88, 130
Benedict XIV, Pope *See* Ratzinger
Berlin, Isaiah 37, 47
Biesta, Gert 61
Blair, Tony 47
  Blairism 47–49
Blumenberg, Hans 2, 15, 121–122, 126, 131–132, 134–135
British Labour Party 49
Bruno, Giordano 97–98
Buber, Martin 26
Butler, Judith 13

C

Camara, Helder 73
caminar, concept of 30
Caputo, John 34
Catholic
  Anglo-Catholicism 27, 28
  Christian narrative 122
  church politics 62, 70
  conservative-progressive 74
  culture 31
  faith 24
  formation 4, 23, 158
  Illich, as Catholic priest 3, 4, 34, 50
  immanence 25
  philosophy 53, 72
  radicalism 103
  Roman Catholicism 28, 70
  small "c" 73
  tradition 26
  Catholic International American Cooperation Program 18
Catholic University, Puerto Rico 17
Cayley, David 17, 19, 25, 67–69, 105, 108, 127, 138–139, 153, 160
CBC, Canadian Broadcasting Corporation 127
Centro Intercultural de Documentación (CIDOC) 18, 104
charity
  beyond 140
  institutionalization 159
  misunderstanding of 158
  seamy side of 18
  structure 19
  welfare and aid 5
  See also Samaritan
Charlie Hebdo, massacre 50
Chirac, Jacques 47
choice
  choice irony 71
  education 86–89
  fertility politics 70, 109
  free 5, 159, 165
  God and contingency 6, 20
  hopeful 158
  language of 65
  making choices 74
  perversion of 65
  plural 17
  radical 69
  Samaritan 5, 159, 164
  work politics 114
Christian pilgrim 20, 123
Christie, Agatha 27
CIDOC, *See Centro Intercultural de Documentación*
Cold War 38, 48, 51
common sense 21, 85–89, 94, 96
conservative
  as an insufficient category 70
  claims 17, 57, 146

educational thinking 1–2, 57, 60, 86
English Conservatives 66
fallacy 116
Illich, accusation of 103–104
Kant, education 90–91
myths 76
reluctance 25
tradition as conservative, fallacy of 54
tradition, conservative appropriation of 74
contingency 4, 5, 10, 14, 143, 146–148
   and reform 128
   and the incarnation 125
   as God's gift 20, 125, 127, 129
   causa contingente 162
   dialectical potentials 126
   Franciscan 158–166
   historical 20, 126, 130–131, 132–137
   Illich's metaphor of 132, 139–140
   kenosis 125
   marking one's existence 30
   possibility 128
   sunset 128, 131, 145
   synchronous 6, 159–166
conversos 23–26
conviviality 5, 74–80
   contingency 126–129, 137–138, 143, 145
   ecclesial 62, 72
   education 81–82
   freedom, multitude 68–69, 73, 82
   immanence and community 73–75, 77
   laic 63
   politics of 38, 68
   salvific 25
   tools 43, 125, 143–145, 153–155
   utopian possibilities 7
   vernacular potential of 112–113
   world outlook 5, 99, 116
Copernicus, Nicolaus 97–99
Copleston, Frederick 53, 72
Corbyn, Jeremy 49
critical pedagogy 3, 66
   Illich's distance from 3, 25, 56, 61
   Freire's burden 13
crucifixion 4
   Christ-event 73
   historical turn 70, 121, 126–127
   Illich's signifier 72, 75
   kenosis and contingency 76, 131–132
   radical event 5, 30, 70, 122–123, 126
Cuernavaca, See *Centro Intercultural de Documentación*
curriculum 59, 63, 85, 98, 144–145, 150

D

Day, Dorothy 131
Derrida, Jacques 13, 34
deschooling
   as disestablishment 114
   as secularization 61
   concept 13–15, 55–57
   Deschooling Society 1, 4, 32, 55, 57, 61, 67, 69, 83, 143, 148–152
   term 14, 56–57, 115
Dewey, John 12–13, 39–41, 92, 132, 154–156
Deweyan 13
disestablishment 6, 77, 143–164
   church 62
   contingency 144–146, 148, 160, 166
   daily living 143
   deschooling 61–62, 143, 165
   idols 122
   laïcité 74
   Law, the 144–145, 159
   planning (as sin) 164–166
   reform 15, 134, 138
disposition
   creative 113
   Epimethean 157
   formative 23
   intellectual 131
   moral 131
   plasticity 156
   reading, of 21
   visual 163–164
docentia 32

Domenach, Jean-Marie 67, 69
doubt 43, 75–77
de omnibus dubitandum 21
  Talmudic 26
drawing 32
  drawing out 32
Du Plessix Gray, Francine 103–104, 118
Duden, Barbara 15, 29, 104, 107–109, 162–165
Duns Scotus, John, St. 6, 128, 132–138

E

ecclesía 25, 41
  ecclesial 61–65
Eco, Umberto 13
Edna, Sister 27–28, 34
education
  beyond 3, 12, 35, 61
  commodification 59, 77
  conservative thinking 1
  constructivism 149–152
  critical 56–57
  educandus 97
  educat nutrix 32
  educational spheres 96–100
  educationalism 14, 59
  equality 63, 82, 95–96
  field 12, 13, 40
  higher 11, 17, 161
  institutionalization 44, 59–60, 63–67, 115
  Kant 89–92
  learning, schooling, and 15, 57, 85–89, 116
  Lewis 92–94
  mainstream critique 55
  Marx 94–96, 99–100
  objectification 2, 59
  politics 33, 42, 53, 163–165
  program for missionaries 18
  schooled 58
  stultification 16
  system 2, 30–31, 42

  theories 23
  universal 56, 87, 95
educe 32, 34
  educit obstetrix 32
Einstein, Albert 7
emancipation 59–60, 65–67, 75, 95, 115, 123, 149–152
Emerson, Ralph, Waldo 116–118
empirie 16, 132, 148
emptying, See *kenosis*
Engels, Friedrich 46–47, 50, 95–96
Epimetheus 32–33, 69, 153
  disposition 157–158
  hope 19, 32–35, 146
  man 68–69
Episcopal Church 76
epoché 53–54, 74
equaliberty 81–82
equality 82–84, 95–96, 144, 152
Erasmus, Desiderius 27
European Union 48
Evangelical Lutherans of America 105, 162
exiting 16, 88, 100, 109–111, 114, 122–125, 128, 152, 158
  pentecostal 16
exousia 26

F

fable, fabular 116, 149, 150–153
femina domestica 112
formation 17, 23, 111, 126
  creatio-formatio 166
Fourier, Charles 46
Francis, Pope, Jorge Bergoglio 70, 130
Franciscan
  contingency, concept of 135–137
  hope 138–141
  theology 135–137, 140, 158
freedom 7, 37, 68
  autonomous 41–43
  choice 5, 88, 159, 164–165
  civil 48
  convivial 73, 82, 145

given by God, (as contingency) 6, 20, 128–131, 134–137, 140
heteronomous 29
individual 69, 72, 149
intelligence, and 39–40, 130–131
Kant 89–91
liberty 38–40
Marx 94–96
philosophy of 28
radical 71, 122–124
relative 53, 58
responsibility 6
Samaritan 158–160, 164–166
schools 66
to learn 151
will 27
Freire, Paulo 1, 12, 56–57, 61
friendship 5, 153
love (*philia*) 18–19, 159
tables of 17–21
Fromm, Eric 21, 61
Fukuyama, Francis 38
futuring
Kant 89–91
Sartre (and Greene) 92
Marx 95

G

Gadamer, Hans Georg 76
Gagarin, Yuri 51
Galilei, Galileo 97
Gandhi, Mohandas 131
German Workers Party 94
Gilson, Etienne 34
Goethe, Johann Wolfgang 131–132
Goldstein, Rebecca 23–24, 32
Golgotha
crucifixion 4–5
khôra, as 121–124, 158–159
outside, as 4–5, 123–124
theology of 122–123
Gramsci, Antonio 1, 61, 88
Greene, Maxine 1, 3, 12–13, 92

Gutierrez, Gustavo 73

H

Habermas, Jurgen 152
Hartch, Todd 26, 62, 71, 73
Hawking, Stephen 7
healthcare 2, 5, 16, 42, 57, 165
See also medicine
Hegel, Georg, Fredrich 11–12, 27, 38, 68, 132
Heller, Agnes 126, 132–137
hermeneutic 10, 42, 84, 88, 91, 115–116, 148–154, 162
heteronomy 27–29, 37–41, 43
hiddenness 28–31
Hoinacki, Lee 26, 67, 124
homo artifex 114
homo economicus 112–114
Horáková, Milada 131
Horkheimer, Max 73
hospitality, *See* friendship
Hugh of St Victor 125
Husserl, Edmund 54

I

identitarian thinking 44, 73, 110
see also non-identitarian
ideological spheres 7, 104, 108, 110, 154, 161
idolatry 104–106
life 29, 105–107, 122, 162, 165
immanence 14–15, 23–36, 44
autonomy 29
convivial 69
faith 25, 31, 68, 73–74, 126
hope 33
knowledge 42–43, 78, 145
lived 38–40
socialist 25
Incarnation 6, 20, 105, 121, 124, 127, 136

instrumentalism 40, 105, 144, 155, 162
  instrumentality 138, 139, 141, 156
intelligence 6, 39–41
invisibility 29–30

J

James, William 154, 156
Jesus, of Nazareth, rabbi, Christ 4, 32, 57–58, 68, 117, 158
  as life 105
  crucifixion 76, 121
  incarnation 121
Jewishness
  ancestry 20, 24, 70, 158
  faith 128, 132
  in Samaritan parable 159, 160, 164
  formation 23, 70
  history 123, 128
  tradition 26, 30, 34, 76
John of the Cross, St. 26
John XXIII, Pope, Roncalli, Angelo 25, 70

K

Kant, Immanuel 27–30, 89–96, 98–100, 116, 156
Kennedy, John F., President 62
kenosis 75–76
  Christian 70, 75, 76, 125
  Judaic 129
  kenotic tools 124–128
  love 33, 125
  modernity 76, 131
Kepler, Johannes 98–99
Khol, Helmut 47
khôra 25, 121–124, 158
Kristeva, Julia 24

L

labor, See shadow work
Laclau, Ernesto 13, 88

Ladner, Gerhart B. 2, 15, 62, 109–113, 126, 136, 166
laic 61–65
  laicism 25, 48, 50, 61–63, 73, 128
  laïcité 25, 49–50, 61–62, 74
  laikós 25, 62
Lassalle, Ferdinand 94, 98–99
learning 81–102
  child-centered 149, 152
  disestablished 30
  disestablished 61
  Kant 89–92
  positivistic method 40
  scarcity, and 66
  schooled 5, 64, 88, 115, 150
  schooling, education, and 15, 60–61, 85–87, 116
  secularization 63
  traditions of 58–59, 85, 144
Levinas, Emmanuel 26, 34, 12–122
Lewis, Clive Staples 92–96, 98–100
liberalism 39–41
  liberal educators 2, 57, 60–61, 86, 97–98, 149
  liberal reformists 110, 113, 136, 154–155
liberal arts 151
liberation 75, 111, 117, 124
liberation theology 25, 72–73, 121
liberty 38–43, 82–85, 95, 111, 147, 158
  positive and negative 37–38
  see also freedom
libido vivendi 162
Life Magazine 163
life
  contemplative and active 75
  fetish 65
  folkish view 113
  hidden 29–30
  idolatry 29, 104–109, 122, 154, 162–165
  Mind, of the 28–29
love 28
  choice (Samaritan) 159–161
  friendship 5
  God's 138
  kenotic 33, 125, 128–131
  personalization 76

philia 18–19
  stranger, of the 68
Luckmann, Thomas 2, 15, 62, 67, 82–85, 144, 151–152
Luther King Jr, Martin 58, 143

M

Machado, Antonio 30
Mannheim, Karl 61
Marcuse, Herbert 43, 114
Maritain, Jacques 15, 34, 161–162, 164–165
Marx, Karl 61, 65, 68, 77, 92, 94–100, 109
meaning 14, 40, 76–78, 82–85, 122, 150, 157
medicine
  medical establishment 106, 138, 140, 145
  medical practice 64, 139, 144
  medicalization of health 147, 162
  See also healthcare
Merkel, Angela 47
metaphor 132–136
  metaphorology 121–122, 124, 127, 140, 147
Miss Marple
  See Christie, Agatha
Mitterrand, François 47
modo, il, modern
Montini, Giovanni, Pope Paul VI 70
Morris, Gerry 18
Morton, James 62–63
Mouffe, Chantal 13
Muller, Richard, A. 138
myth 75, 117
  language of 65, 149–150, 153–156
  loss of 165–166
  mythos 158
  society of 116
  systems of 114, 115, 146–147, 151–153
  transparency, and 147–148

N

Nancy, Jean Luc 34
natality 24, 74
National Health Service, NHS 64–65
nativism 36
Nea Dimokratia 49
Nebrija, Antonio de 31–32
neoliberalism 48, 146
Nicolas Cusano 26
Nietzsche, Friedrich 27, 115–117, 132, 151
non-identitarian thinking 26–27, 43
nostalgia 56, 77, 113
  nostalgia, pre-modern 17, 20

O

Obama, Barack, President 48, 157–158
ontology
  contingency 135
  dissent, of 5
  question, in education 88
  utopian promise 45
organon, see tool
orthodoxy 20, 71
Ottaviani, Cardinal Alfredo 71
overcoming 113

P

pagus 123
Palestinian, as Samaritan 68, 158–160
Pandora
  box, jar 33, 69
Pareyson, Luigi 132
Parmenidean logic 146
Partido Popular 49
Partido Socialista Obrero Español 49
Petri, Elio 25
philia, See friendship
philosophia perennis 31, 71–74
Picasso, Pablo 11
Pistola, Ricardo 32

plasticity 154, 156
plastic vernacular 155–157
plastic words 14, 15, 105, 155–157, 163, 165
Plato 57
   philia 18, 19
Podemos 49
Poerksen, Uwe 14, 15, 105, 155–157, 165
poíesis 10
positivism 26, 40, 43, 76, 84, 132
possibility 6, 16, 75, 104, 128, 130
   aporetic 68, 152
   freedom 43
   multidimensional 57
   power of 42
   synchronic 135–138, 141
   see also contingency
   tools of 143–145
   utopian 37
   vernacular 115
pre-modern 17, 20, 43, 56, 113, 136
   See also, nostalgia
preterideological 109, 136, 166
progressive conservative 70–71
progressive
   education 56, 61, 85, 98, 149, 151
   myths 92
   politics 45, 50, 60, 97
   reformists 110, 113
   theology 70, 74
   thought 2, 45, 54, 103, 146, 154
Prometheus 69, 146
   powers of technology 34
   progress, dream of 147
Protestantism 25
   ethic 73
   modernity 27
   religious socialism 25
   small "p" 73
   tradition 72
Proudhon, Pierre Joseph 46, 165
Putin, Vladimir, President 37

R

Rancière, Jacques 13, 47–49
Ratzinger, Joseph, Cardinal, Pope Benedict XVI 105–106
reform 14, 103–120
   Christian thinking 62, 103
   contingency, disestablishment, and 4, 6, 14–15, 21, 128, 134, 138, 143, 145–147, 160, 164, 166
   education, in 115, 152
   formative 126, 166
   Law, and the 156
   political 2
   re-form, as 6, 10–11, 75, 110–112, 118, 136, 145
   reformatio 166
   See also *creatio-reformatio*
   Reformation, the 28
   reformism 97, 111–112
   return to form 109–112
   self-reform, ecclesiastical 25
   tradition, within the 158
renunciation 117
Rocha, Samuel 57–58
Roncalli, Angelo, Pope John XXIII 25, 70
Rorty, Richard 126, 132, 136–137
Rose, Gillian 26–31
Rubinoff, Lionel 62

S

sacrifice 75, 94, 107, 131
Saint Simon, Claude Henri de 46
salvation 54, 63, 134–135
Samaritan 5, 68, 124, 158–160, 164
   Palestinian, as 68, 158–160
   see also choice
Sanders, Barry 17
Sanders, Bernie 49
Sartre, Jean Paul 104
Saussure, Ferdinand de 160
Scholasticism 6, 97

school 50, 81, 84, 95–96
  free schools 66, 97–98
  schooling 2–3, 14–15, 20–21, 38–39, 42, 55–67, 82–83, 85–89, 106, 113, 115–116, 139, 147–152, 163
  the school 34, 82, 83, 85, 95, 99, 138, 144–145, 157
Schröder, Gerhard 48
scopic 29, 106, 122, 146, 162–163
Scotus, Duns, John, See Duns Scotus
Second Vatican Council 17–25, 70–71
secularism 32, 48–49, 74, 76
  centrism 47
  history 62
  life, notion of 105
  secular, the 24, 25, 31, 42, 48, 111, 130
  secularization of teaching 61–63
  state 48–50
  See also laic
self-transparency 150–152
shadow
  shadow-less 112–115
  shadow work 111–112, 114–115
  Shadow Work 16, 31, 99, 109, 114, 117, 155
spheres
  celestial 97–98
  social 96, 100, 159
  See ideological spheres
  See also educational spheres
Spinoza, Baruch 23–24, 32, 68–69
Stancioff, Feodora 18
Stein, Edith 26, 131
Steinberg, Shirley 3
Stoics 134
stranger 14–16, 68
  estrangement 83, 107
Suenens, Leo Jozef, Cardinal 71
suffering 33, 124, 140, 146
Sylwanowicz, Michael 138
synchronic contingency
  see contingency
synchronous possibilities
  see contingency

Syriza 49
systems 6, 62, 82–83, 138–140, 143, 145–148, 150, 154, 157, 162–166

T

table
  See friendship
Talmud 26, 121
Tao, the 93
Taylor, Charles 25, 34
Teresa of Avila, St. 24, 30
three-legged stool, analogy of 86–88
Tijmes, Pieter 17
Tillich, Paul 7, 25
tool 77, 81–83, 125, 137–140, 143–145, 147, 153–155, 160
  organon 125
  scarcity of 67
  Tools of Conviviality 16, 43, 57, 77, 81, 125, 139, 153
  See also conviviality
tradition 3, 4, 53–81
  Christian 121–122, 124–125, 159
  Franciscan 135–136
  humanist 28
  Jewish and Catholic 26, 34, 68–78
  philosophical 134
  teaching 57–58, 61, 92–93
  See also *philosophia perennis*
transparency 147–148, 150, 161
  See also self-transparency
Trump, Donald, President 37, 48

U

Übermensch 115
United Nations 41
unlearning 21, 30
utopia 37–53
  approach, utopian 3, 14, 30, 43–44, 150

condition of freedom 39, 43
politics 47–48
utopian socialists 46, 50

V

Varoufakis, Iannis 48
Vattimo, Gianni 76, 115, 147–148, 150–152
Velázquez, Diego 11
vernacular 107, 109, 112–114, 116, 123
  Emerson 116
  homolog 99
  mathematization (Poerksen) 155–157, 165
  pluralism 32, 100, 127
  values 31

via negativa 26, 43
vir laborans 112
volk 112–113
Voz Jaczn, Antoine 138

W

Williams, Raymond 77
Williams, Rowan, Archbishop 70–71, 74
Wittgenstein, Ludwig 132
work
  See shadow work

Z

Zeus 69
Zizek, Slavoj 13

TEACHING
❧CONTEMPORARY❧
SCHOLARS

Shirley R. Steinberg
General Editor

This innovative series addresses the pedagogies and thoughts of influential contemporary scholars in diverse fields. Focusing on scholars who have challenged the "normal science," the dominant frameworks of particular disciplines, Teaching Contemporary Scholars highlights the work of those who have profoundly influenced the direction of academic work. In an era of great change, this series focuses on the bold thinkers who provide not only insight into the nature of the change but where we should be going in light of the new conditions. Not a festschrift, not a re-interpretation of past work, these books allow the reader a deeper, yet accessible conceptual framework in which to negotiate and expand the work of important thinkers.

For additional information about this series or for the submission of manuscripts, please contact:
 Shirley R. Steinberg
 msgramsci@gmail.com

To order other books in this series, please contact our Customer Service Department:
 peterlang@presswarehouse.com (within the U.S.)
 order@peterlang.com (outside the U.S.)

Or browse online by series:
 WWW.PETERLANG.COM